COLLECTED
ARCHITECTURAL
DESIGNS

KARL FRIEDRICH
SCHINKEL

COLLECTED
ARCHITECTURAL
DESIGNS

ACADEMY EDITIONS · LONDON
ST. MARTIN'S PRESS · NEW YORK
MCMLXXXII

PUBLISHERS' NOTE

This edition of Karl Friedrich Schinkel's *Collected Architectural Designs* reproduces all 174 engravings from the *Sammlung architectonischer Entwürfe*, originally published in serial form between 1819 and 1840, but omits the accompanying commentary by the architect. The publication coincides with an exhibition of the engravings organised by *Architectural Design* magazine, and we are grateful to Professor Colin St John Wilson for the loan of material and for his help.

First published in Great Britain in 1982 by
Academy Editions 7/8 Holland Street London W8

Copyright © Academy Editions 1982 *All rights reserved*
No parts of this publication may be reproduced
in any manner whatsoever without permission
in writing from the copyright holders

Published in the United States of America in 1982 by
St. Martin's Press 175 Fifth Avenue New York NY10010

Library of Congress Catalog Card Number 81-21515
ISBN 0-312-44952-6 Cloth 0-312-44953-4 Paper

Printed in Great Britain by
BAS Printers Limited, Over Wallop, Hampshire

FOREWORD

The appearance of Karl Friedrich Schinkel's Collected Architectural Designs in a reasonably priced single volume is both timely and laudable. It gives us the opportunity to study Schinkel's own selection of what he considered to be the best of his architecture, represented in a medium which he considered ideal for communicating the essential qualities of this architecture. This chronologically ordered series of engravings, released originally in parts between 1819 and 1840 with the assistance of some twenty collaborators, is condensed from the 530 or so drawings of his total œuvre. The 174 plates depict fifty projects, most of which were realised.

When first published as a bound folio volume in 1873, long after Schinkel's death, the engravings and their commentary joined a select tradition of definitive architectural publications. Admirers of Schinkel have favourably compared their importance to architecture with the engraved works of Vitruvius, Alberti and Palladio and have further suggested that Schinkel, more than any other nineteenth-century architect, brought back to earth the visionary speculations of the previous century, while being a primary source of influence for some of the best twentieth-century practitioners.

Published both initially and today for their use to teaching, these architectural engravings are made accessible in this particular volume to the student and the practitioner, and not just to the historian and the élite. These engravings are thus published today as material not only for historical understanding, but also for creative interpretation. As such, the volume is another important indication of the recent popularity of Neoclassicism, a fact which raises weightier issues concerning historicism.

Schinkel identified 'Utility' and 'The Historic and the Poetic' as the principal preoccupations of his work. In his writings he searched for basic and human qualities as creative foundations for design, and an approach to each building task which dealt with it in its own terms. In this way, he linked himself to the tradition of great architectural intention which grounds itself on timeless human values as the only adequate basis for architecture. For Schinkel, it was extremely important that these philosophical intentions should not be divorced from realistic representation and construction; hence the concreteness and clarity of the engravings. Yet these engravings have been correctly viewed as portraying a dominance of technique, lacking a differentiation and a hierarchy which would properly accord with human considerations. They possess a mechanical quality which requires appraisal.

This perceptible dilemma—between intention and representation—in his work can perhaps best be understood when one considers the somewhat doctrinaire and dogmatic character of post 1815 Prussia. This relatively poor State, committed to a process of industrialisation based on the rigours of utility, sought to mould a society by using centralised power. As Architect-in-Chief to Prussia throughout much of his career, Schinkel was essential to the State's attempt to represent itself through architecture. The engravings before us are symbols of this attempt, which explains the predominance of public buildings and country estates. Their technique, so different to that adopted by Frick to illustrate some of the work of Schinkel's master Friedrich Gilly, is as much influenced by the exigencies of centralised political power and of the industrial, as it is by Schinkel's interest in the timelessness of human values. This is not of course to say that power and architecture necessarily create the dilemma apparent in Schinkel's work, but it is important to note that of his three stated primary intentions, the 'Poetic' foundation is most notably absent. Yet this is not only a problem with Schinkel, but with much of Neoclassical architecture in general.

Since Schinkel's time, political possibilities and structures have changed, while the breakthrough into a wider understanding of spatial possibilities in architecture has provided not only new conceptual frameworks, but uncertainty and rootlessness. The importance today of this book of engravings, and more generally of Schinkel's overall achievement is, for many people, a positive step towards stronger architectural roots and greater certainty. Undoubtedly his achievement is impressive. In the process of re-interpreting the Neoclassical era, however, it is perhaps worth bearing in mind not only that Schinkel was conditioned by his times and his chosen mode of practice, but also that his achievement acts as a symbol of how difficult, but how absolutely necessary, it is to place human considerations as essential and unmediated intentions above those of the expression of techniques. Karl Friedrich Schinkel's engravings touch on the fragile thread of understanding of what is great architecture.

Doug Clelland

LIST OF PLATES

Plate 1. Earlier Design for the New Guard House in Berlin
Plate 2. Perspective View of the New Guard House in Berlin
Plate 3. Bas Relief on the Pediment and Frieze Decoration of the New Guard House for Berlin
Plate 4. Elevation, Plan and Details of the New Guard House (*top*); Plan of the Modification of Berlin City Hall (*bottom*)
Plate 5. Perspective View of the Design for the Modification of the City Hall in Berlin
Plate 6. Design for an Open Fountain as a Memorial to the Events of the Years 1813, 1814, 1815
Plate 7. Perspective View of the New Theatre for Berlin
Plate 8. Geometrical Elevation of the Main Façade of the New Theatre
Plate 9. Plans A. of the Substructure, B. of the First Floor, C. of the Second Floor of the New Theatre in Berlin
Plate 10. Sections of the New Theatre in Berlin
Top Section through the line D.E. of the floor plans; *Bottom* Section through the line A.B.C.F. of the floor plans
Plate 11. Perspective View of the Side Elevation of the New Theatre
Plate 12. Main Pediment, Capital and Base of the Columns, Sculpture in and on the Pediment of the Peristyle for the New Theatre for Berlin
Plate 13. Perspective View of the Auditorium in the Royal Theatre for Berlin, from the Stage towards the Spectators
Plate 14. Perspective View from the Auditorium onto the Stage, with the Representation of the Decoration installed for the Inaugural Prologue, in the Royal Theatre for Berlin
Plate 15. Ceiling Decoration of the Auditorium in the Theatre for Berlin
Plate 16. Perspective Representation of the Concert Hall in the Royal Theatre for Berlin
Plate 17. Elevation of one of the Long Walls of the Concert Hall in the Royal Theatre for Berlin
Plate 18. Ceiling Decoration of the Concert Hall in the Royal Theatre for Berlin
Plate 19. Extension of the Wilhelms-Strasse
A Elevation of the gateway to the extended Wilhelms-Strasse at Unter den Linden; *B* Perspective view of the extended Wilhelms-Strasse; *C* Site plan
Plate 20. Design for a Building for the Academy of Music in Berlin
A Floor plan of the part of the building located below the grandstand; *B* Entire floor plan; *C* Cross section; *D* Front elevation; *E* Main entrance; *F* Detail of the sculpture on the centre of the pediment
Plate 21. Design for a Building for the Academy of Music in Berlin
Top Perspective; *Bottom* Longitudinal section
Plate 22. War Memorial in Wrought-Iron at Kreutzberg, near Berlin
Plate 23. The Combined Academy of Artillery and Engineering, Unter den Linden, Berlin
Top Elevation; *Bottom* Plan
Plate 24. New Schlossbrücke (Palace Bridge) in Berlin
Plate 25. Tegel Castle
Top View of the site and surroundings of Tegel Castle; *Bottom* Second floor, first floor and third floor plans
Plate 26. Tegel Castle
Top Side elevation of Tegel Castle; *Centre* Main façade of Tegel Castle; *Bottom* Vestibule in Tegel Castle
Plate 27. Perspective View of the Antonin Hunting Lodge in the Przygodzice Dominions Belonging to His Highness Prince Radziwill, Royal Governor
Plate 28. Perspective View of the Great Hall of the Antonin Hunting Lodge
Plate 29. Antonin Hunting Lodge
Top Elevation of the Hunting Lodge; Section of the Hunting Lodge; *Bottom* Column and gallery in the Hall; Floor plan of the Hunting Lodge with the arrangement of the ceiling (*left*) and of the floor (*right*); Principal moulding
Plate 30. Spa Drinking Fountain on Friedrich-Wilhelms-Platz, Aachen
Top Ceiling of the rotunda; Section; Column with entablature; *Centre* Plan; *Bottom* Elevation of the Drinking Fountain for Aachen
Plate 31. Plan and Sections of the Design for the New Building of St. Gertraud's Church
Top Cross section of the pulpit area; Longitudinal section; *Bottom* Site plan
Plate 32. Side View of the Projected St. Gertraud's Church for Berlin
Plate 33. Perspective View of the Interior of the Projected St. Gertraud's Church for Berlin
Plate 34. Perspective View of the Interior of the Altar Area of the Projected St. Gertraud's Church for Berlin
Plate 35. Design for a Monument to Frederick the Great in Berlin
Plate 36. Country House for the Banker Behrend in Charlottenburg
Top Front elevation; Side elevation; *Centre* Perspective view of the Country House; *Bottom* Plan of the first floor; Plan of the upper floor
Plate 37. Perspective View of the New Museum in Berlin, from a Viewpoint between the Arsenal and the New Schlossbrücke (Palace Bridge)
Plate 38. Plans A. of the Substructure, B. of the First Floor, C. of the Second Floor of the New Museum
Plate 39. Elevation of the Main Façade of the New Museum
Plate 40. Section of the New Museum and Proportions of the Columns in the Entrance Hall
Plate 41. Elevation of the Rear Façade of the New Museum, View of the Main Staircase and Details
Plate 42. Site Plan of the Changes to the Town brought about by the Construction of the New Museum, and Details of the Orders of the Columns
Left Column and ceiling decoration in stone of the gallery in the rotunda and view of half of one of the doors beneath the gallery; View from below of the ceiling decoration; *Centre* Site plan of the changes brought about in Berlin by the construction of the New Museum; *Right* Column and ceiling decoration in the long rooms on the first floor; View from below of the ceiling decoration
Plate 43. Perspective View from the Gallery of the Main Staircase of the Museum through the Portico onto the Pleasure Garden and its Surroundings
Plate 44. Perspective View of the Rotunda of the Museum
Plate 45. New Museum in Berlin
Left Capital of the pilasters in the Museum portico; Section of part of the stone ceiling above the Museum portico; Plan of part of the ceiling above the portico; *Centre* Front view of the column capitals; Half plan of the column capitals in the Museum portico; Base of the columns in the Museum portico; Wrought balustrade of the gallery in the rotunda of the Museum; *Right* Side view of the column capitals; Section of part of the ceiling above the main staircase behind the Museum portico; Plan of part of the ceiling above the main staircase
Plate 46. New Museum in Berlin
Left Figures on the corners of the Museum; *Centre* Eagle crowning the parapet above the columns; One of the group on the corners of the raised central part of the Museum; *Right* Figures on the corners of the Museum
Plate 47. New Museum in Berlin
Left Column capital from one of the sculpture rooms; Column capital from one of the sculpture rooms; Pilaster capital from one of the sculpture rooms; *Centre* Column capital from one of the sculpture rooms; Column capital from the Museum rotunda; Column capital from one of the sculpture rooms; *Right* Column capital from one of the sculpture rooms; Pilaster capital from one of the sculpture rooms; Pilaster capital from one of the sculpture rooms
Plate 48. View of the Arrangement of the Ceilings of the Museum's Sculpture Rooms
Plate 49. Perspective View of Krzescowice Castle

Plate 50. Krzescowice Castle
Fig. I Section through the line AB of the plan; *Fig. II* Section through the line CD of the plan
Plate 51. Krzescowice Castle
Fig. I Section through the line EF of the plan; *Fig. II* Elevation of the west side of the castle; *Fig. III* Elevation of the east side of the castle
Plate 52. Krzescowice Castle
Top Detail of the long gallery; Corridor joining the vestibule; *Centre* Library with bookcases; *Bottom* Part of the ceiling; Part of the floor
Plate 53. Krzescowice Castle
Top Section of the ballroom; Section of the dining room; *Bottom* Quarter plan of the ballroom ceiling; Quarter plan of the parquet floor in the ballroom; Quarter plan of the dining room ceiling; Quarter plan of the parquet floor in the dining room
Plate 54. Krzescowice Castle
Top Plan at main floor level; *Bottom* Plan of the substructure; Plan of the second floor
Plate 55. Design for a Church in the Werdersche Markt in Berlin
Fig. I Gable façade towards the market; *Fig. II* Altar recess; *Fig. III* Section looking towards the altar; *Fig. IV* Section looking towards the entrance
Plate 56. Design for a Church in the Werdersche Markt in Berlin
Fig. I Plan of the church; *Fig. II* Longitudinal section
Plate 57. Design for a Church in the Werdersche Markt in Berlin
Fig. I Side view of the church; *Fig. II* Front view of the pulpit and altar; *Fig. III* Side view of the pulpit and altar
Plate 58. Perspective View of the Interior of the Projected Church in the Werdersche Markt in Berlin
Plate 59. Perspective View of the Leipzig Gate from the Outside
Plate 60. Leipzig Gate
Top View of the Leipzig Gate from Leipzig Platz; *Bottom left* Plan of one of the gate houses; Section of the Doric entablature and corner pilaster; *Bottom centre* Site plan; *Bottom right* View of one of the gate houses; Doric order on the gate house
Plate 61. Perspective View of a Memorial to General von Scharnhorst
Top Front view; Side view; *Bottom* Perspective
Plate 62. Design for a City Residence
Top Street elevation of the residence; *Centre* Section through the line C.D.; Side elevation; *Bottom* Section through the line A.B.
Plate 63. Design for a City Residence
Top First floor; *Centre* Second floor; Third floor; *Bottom* Site plan
Plate 64. Design for a City Residence
Top Street elevation; *Bottom* Perspective view of the vestibule
Plate 65. Design for a City Residence
Top Section through the line A.B.; *Centre* Plan of the second floor; *Bottom* Plan of the first floor
Plate 66. Perspective View of a Pleasure Villa near Potsdam
Top Perspective view of a Pleasure Villa; *Bottom* Side view; Plan; Rear view
Plate 67. Design for a City Residence
Top Perspective view of the house from the street; *Bottom* Perspective view of the courtyard surrounded by a loggia
Plate 68. Design for a City Residence
Left First floor; Second floor; Third floor; *Right* Street elevation; Section through A.B.; Section through C.D.; Section through E.F.
Plate 69. Design for a City Residence
Top Elevation; *Centre* Perspective view of the vestibule and staircase; *Bottom* Elevation with different proportions
Plate 70. Design for a City Residence
Top Section through A.B.; *Bottom* Lower floor; Middle floor
Plate 71. Design for a City Residence (Plan for a Simple House)
Top Plan of the first floor; *Bottom* Plan of the second floor; Plan of the third floor
Plate 72. Design for a City Residence
Top Neighbouring site; Annex; Entrance; Elevation of the main building; Entrance; Annex; Neighbouring site; *Bottom* Section of the total design through the line ABCDEFG of the plan
Plate 73. Design for a Church for the Market Place of Potsdam
Top Side view; *Centre* Gable façade; Section through the line A.B.; *Bottom* Plan; Section through the line C.D.
Plate 74. Design for a Small Church with a Square Floor Plan
Top View of the church from the entrance façade; *Bottom* View of the altar; View of the pulpit; Side view of the altar
Plate 75. Design for a Small Church with a Square Floor Plan
Top Section through the line E.F.; *Bottom* Plan at level A.B.; Plan at level C.D.
Plate 76. Design for a Small Church for the District of Malmedy
Top View of the church from the entrance façade; *Bottom* Section through the line A.B.
Plate 77. Design for a Small Church for the District of Malmedy
Top Side view of the church; *Centre* Plan; *Bottom* Section through the line C.D.
Plate 78. Design for a Small Church with a Tower
Top View of the tower façade; Side view; View of the rear façade; *Centre* Part of the ceiling; *Bottom* Section through the line A.B.; Section through the line E.F.; Plan; Section through C.D.; Section through the line A.B. looking towards the entrance (note: The descriptions for top left and right are transposed on the plate)
Plate 79. Plans of the Theatre in Hamburg
Plate 80. Elevation of the Entrance Façade of the Theatre in Hamburg
Plate 81. Architectural Detail of the Elevation of the Theatre in Hamburg at a Larger Scale
Plate 82. Sections of the Theatre in Hamburg
Top Longitudinal elevation of the Theatre; *Centre* Structure of the roof above the art gallery; Section through the line A.B. of the plan; Section X of the vestibule at a larger scale; *Bottom* Section through the line C.D. of the plan
Plate 83. View of the Proscenium Arch and the Boxes Surrounding it with the Perspective View of the Theatre as a Backdrop
aa Width of the proscenium; *bb* Boxes beside the proscenium; *cc* Boxes around the auditorium
Plate 84. Casino in Potsdam
Top Elevation; *Bottom* Section through the line A.B.; Plan; Section through the line C.D.
Plate 85. Perspective View of the Exterior of the Church on the Werdersche Markt in Berlin
Plate 86. Church on the Werdersche Markt in Berlin
Top Elevation of the towers; *Bottom* Plan
Plate 87. Church on the Werdersche Markt in Berlin
Top Longitudinal section through the line A.B.; *Bottom* Section through the line C.D. with the view of a wall through which the building is divided into two churches; Section through the line C.D. looking towards the altar; Section through the line C.D. looking towards the entrance
Plate 88. Perspective View of the Interior of the Church on the Werdersche Markt in Berlin
Plate 89. Portal of the Church on the Werdersche Markt in Berlin
Plate 90. Windows of the Church on the Werdersche Markt in Berlin
Left Window between the towers; *Right* Window in the altar recess
Plate 91. Church for Straupitz in Lausitz
Top View of the grouping of the pulpit, the altar and the font; *Bottom* Section through the line D.C. looking towards the altar; Plan; Section through the line C.D. looking towards the entrance
Plate 92. Church for Straupitz in Lausitz
Left Longitudinal view; *Centre* Elevation of the towers; *Right* Longitudinal section through A.B.
Plate 93. Design for a Church in the Oranienburg Suburb of Berlin No. I
Top Gable façade with entrances; Section through the line A.B.; *Bottom* Plan
Plate 94. Design for a Church in the Oranienburg Suburb of Berlin No. I
Top Longitudinal elevation; *Bottom* Section through the line C.D.
Plate 95. Design for a Church in the Oranienburg Suburb of Berlin No. II
Top Gable façade with entrances; Section through the line A.B.; *Bottom* Plan
Plate 96. Design for a Church in the Oranienburg Suburb of Berlin No. II
Top Longitudinal elevation; *Bottom* Section through the line C.D.
Plate 97. Church in the Oranienburg Suburb of Berlin, after Design No. III
Top Perspective view; *Bottom* Plan
Plate 98. Church in the Oranienburg Suburb of Berlin, after Design No. III
Left Gable elevation; *Right* Section
Plate 99. Church in the Oranienburg Suburb of Berlin, after Design No. III
Left Longitudinal section; *Right* Part of the side elevation
Plate 100. View of the Church in the Oranienburg Suburb of Berlin, after Design No. IV
Plate 101. Section of the Church in the Oranienburg Suburb of Berlin, after Design No. IV
Plate 102. Church in the Oranienburg Suburb of Berlin, after Design No. IV
Top left Moulding and decoration for the organ; *Bottom left* Moulding for the church; *Centre* (Interior view) Pulpit, altar, pulpit; *Top right* Moulding for the portal; *Bottom right* Portal; *Bottom* Plan
Plate 103. Perspective View of Design No. V for a Church in the Oranienburg Suburb of Berlin
Plate 104. View of the Church in the Oranienburg Suburb of Berlin, after Design No. V
Plate 105. Section of the Church in the Oranienburg Suburb of Berlin, after Design No. V
Plate 106. Church in the Oranienburg Suburb of Berlin, after Design No. V
Left Window above the portal; *Centre top* Crown of the pediment; *Centre* Side view of the pulpit; Pulpit; *Centre bottom* Plan; *Right* Corner decoration beside the pediment; Portal of the church
Plate 107. Casino in the Friedrich Wilhelms-Garten, Magdeburg
Top Perspective view; *Bottom* Elevation
Plate 108. Plans and Section of the Casino in the Friedrich Wilhelms-Garten, Magdeburg
Plate 109. Site Plan of the Charlottenhof with the Plan of the Building
Plate 110. Charlottenhof near Potsdam
Top View from the portico; *Bottom* View of the chimney of the steam engine building; View of the semicircular banquette on the terrace of the Charlottenhof; Side view of the steam engine building
Plate 111. Charlottenhof near Potsdam
Top Perspective from northwest; *Centre* Perspective from southeast; *Bottom* Former condition of the residence
Plate 112. Charlottenhof near Potsdam
Top Elevation towards the terrace; *Centre* Elevation after the conservatory; *Bottom* Section through the vestibule and portico; Section through the vestibule

Plate 113. HOUSE FOR MR FEILNER IN BERLIN
Top Elevation of the house which the stove-maker Feilner had executed in baked clay in the Hasenheger-Gasse; *Centre* Projected floor plan of the house; *Bottom* Two window sills of the house executed in baked clay

Plate 114. HOUSE FOR MR FEILNER IN BERLIN
Left Half the inside of the door casement; Half the top of the door casement; *Centre* Part of the elevation of the house of the stove-maker Feilner in Berlin, for which all the architectural details were executed in baked clay; *Right* Section of the façade

Plate 115. PERSPECTIVE VIEW OF THE ACADEMY OF BUILDING IN BERLIN

Plate 116. ACADEMY OF BUILDING IN BERLIN
Top Site plan; *Centre* First main floor (containing the classrooms and library for the Academy of Building); Ground floor (containing vaulted stores to be hired out); *Bottom* Section through the line ABC

Plate 117. ELEVATION OF THE ACADEMY OF BUILDING

Plate 118. ILLUSTRATION FOR THE WINDOW SILLS IN BAKED CLAY

Plate 119. ACADEMY OF BUILDING IN BERLIN
Left Window and surrounding mouldings at a larger scale; *Centre* Section of a window; Ornament on the inside of the window casement; *Right* Main cornice; Decoration of the curved lintels of the windows; *Far right* Section of the main cornice

Plate 120. ONE OF THE TWO MAIN DOORS OF THE ACADEMY OF BUILDING

Plate 121. PERSPECTIVE VIEW OF THE BUILDING FOR THE NEW ACADEMY OF BUILDING IN BERLIN From a nearby viewpoint

Plate 122. VIEW OF THE SECOND PORTAL WITH ITS DECORATION FOR THE NEW ACADEMY OF BUILDING IN BERLIN

Plate 123. NEW GUARD HOUSE IN DRESDEN
Top Main façade of the new Guard House in Dresden; *Centre* First Floor — *A* Guardroom; *B* Officers' room; *C* Quarters of an official; *D* Passage; *E* Detention room; Second floor — *F* Quarters of an official; *G* Quarters of an official; *H* Corridor; *I* Storage rooms; *J* Staircase; *Bottom* Side view

Plate 124. TOWN HALL FOR ZITTAU
Top Front elevation; *Bottom* Side elevation; Rear elevation

Plate 125. TOWN HALL FOR ZITTAU
Top Section through AB; Section through CD; *Centre* Second floor; Third floor; *Bottom* Ground floor; First floor

Plate 126. PALACE OF COUNT REDERN IN BERLIN
Top Section of the main building; Perspective view of the Palace; Plan of the second floor; *Centre* Perspective view of the salon; Candelabra; Perspective view of the vestibule; *Bottom* Previous form of the building; Remodelled façade of the building

Plate 127. CASTLE KURNIK In the Grand Duchy of Posen, belonging to Count Dzialinksi

Plate 128. CASTLE KURNIK
Top Plan of the first floor; Plan of the second floor; *Centre* View of the roof from above; Sections of the roof through the lines A.B., C.D., E.F.; *Bottom* Former elevation of façade A. on the plan; Former elevation of façade B. on the plan

Plate 129. CASTLE KURNIK
Top Section through the line E.F.; Section through the line C.D.; *Bottom* Section through the line A.B.; Detail of the upper part of one of the windows in the centre section of façade A.; Detail of an ordinary window

Plate 130. CASTLE KURNIK
Top Elevation of façade A. on the plan; *Bottom* Elevation of façade E. on the plan

Plate 131. DESIGN FOR A PALACE FOR HIS ROYAL HIGHNESS PRINCE WILHELM ON THE PARISER-PLATZ
Top Plan; *Bottom* Section through the whole site along the line A'. B'.

Plate 132. DESIGN FOR A PALACE FOR HIS ROYAL HIGHNESS PRINCE WILHELM ON THE PARISER-PLATZ

Plate 133. DESIGN FOR A PALACE FOR HIS ROYAL HIGHNESS PRINCE WILHELM ON THE PARISER-PLATZ
Fig. I First floor plan; *Fig. II* Third (main) floor plan and lay-out of the gardens

Plate 134. DESIGN FOR A PALACE FOR HIS ROYAL HIGHNESS PRINCE WILHELM ON THE OPERNPLATZ

Plate 135. DESIGN FOR A PALACE FOR HIS ROYAL HIGHNESS PRINCE WILHELM ON THE OPERNPLATZ

Plate 136. DESIGN FOR THE COUNTRY HOUSE OF H.R.H. PRINCE WILHELM ON THE BABELSBERG NEAR POTSDAM

Plate 137. CASTLE AT GLIENICKE
Top View of the entire Castle of Glienicke after its remodelling and expansion; *Bottom left* Front façade of the building after remodelling; Side view of the building after remodelling; *Bottom centre* Plan of the castle and its surroundings; *Bottom right* Side view of the building before remodelling; Front façade before remodelling

Plate 138. CASTLE AT GLIENICKE
Top View of the house on the lake at Glienicke; *Bottom left* Decoration of the central salon; *Bottom centre* View of the house on the lake and its pergola; Plan of the house on the lake and its pergola; Former condition of the building; *Bottom right* Decoration of the side room

Plate 139. CASTLE AT GLIENICKE
Top View of the Country House for Glienicke from the side with the courtyard of the coach-house and the garden behind; *Bottom* Tower of the Country House; Pergola on the corner; Coach-House

Plate 140. PALACE FOR H.R.H. PRINCE KARL IN BERLIN
Top Elevation of the Palace after its restoration as a residence for His Royal Highness Prince Karl; *Centre* Detail of the balcony after the restoration; Former condition of the building; Plan of the Palace of His Royal Highness Prince Karl in Berlin, formerly the Palace of the Knights of the Johanniter Order; Detail of the central section of the front façade; *Bottom* Detail of the staircase; Vestibule in which the marble staircase is now located; Detail of the columns for the marble staircase

Plate 141. PLANS OF THE FIRST AND SECOND FLOORS, SITE PLAN AND PERSPECTIVE VIEW OF THE NEW OBSERVATORY IN BERLIN

Plate 142. NEW OBSERVATORY IN BERLIN
Top Pediment of the Observatory; *Centre* Side elevation of the Observatory; Section of the Observatory; *Bottom* View of the iron structure and machinery of the revolving dome; Plan of the iron structure and machinery of the revolving dome on the Observatory

Plate 143. RESTORATION OF THE CHURCH OF ZITTAU
Top Longitudinal section of the restored Church of Zittau; *Bottom* Plan of the restored Church of Zittau

Plate 144. RESTORATION OF THE CHURCH OF ZITTAU
Top Former elevation and section of the Church of Zittau before restoration; *Bottom* Elevation of the altar façade of the Church of Zittau; Section of the restored Church of Zittau

Plate 145. RESTORATION OF THE CHURCH OF ZITTAU
Left Former condition of the tower façade of the Church in Zittau; *Right* Section through the restored towers and the adjacent part of the church

Plate 146. ELEVATION OF THE TOWER FAÇADE OF THE RESTORED ST. JOHANNIS' CHURCH FOR ZITTAU

Plate 147. PERSPECTIVE VIEWS OF THE NEW GATE NEAR THE CHARITÉ BUILDING IN BERLIN

Plate 148. SITE PLAN, FLOOR PLAN AND ARCHITECTURAL DETAILS OF THE NEW GATE NEAR THE CHARITÉ BUILDING IN BERLIN

Plate 149. PERSPECTIVE VIEW OF THE NEW CUSTOMS STATION SEEN FROM THE SCHLOSSBRÜCKE (PALACE BRIDGE)

Plate 150. NEW CUSTOMS STATION IN BERLIN
Top Site plan; *Centre* View of the new Customs Station for Berlin; *Bottom* Elevation of building *e*; Elevation of building *h*

Plate 151. PERSPECTIVE VIEW OF THE NEW CUSTOMS STATION FROM THE BRIDGE TO THE FLOUR STORE

Plate 152. NEW CUSTOMS STATION IN BERLIN
Top Composition of the sculpture on the pediment; *Bottom* Section of the warehouse; Elevation of the warehouse

Plate 153. CHAPEL FOR THE IMPERIAL GARDENS OF THE PETERHOF NEAR ST. PETERSBURG

Plate 154. SECTION OF THE CHAPEL IN THE IMPERIAL GARDENS OF THE PETERHOF NEAR ST. PETERSBURG

Plate 155. FRONT VIEW OF ST. NICOLAI'S CHURCH IN POTSDAM

Plate 156. ST. NICOLAI'S CHURCH IN POTSDAM
Top Plan of the dome; *Bottom* Plan of the church

Plate 157. SECTION OF ST. NICOLAI'S CHURCH IN POTSDAM

Page 158. SIDE VIEW OF ST. NICOLAI'S CHURCH IN POTSDAM

Plate 159. CHURCH IN FRONT OF THE ROSENTHAL GATE IN BERLIN (*left*); CHURCH IN MOABIT NEAR BERLIN (*right*)

Plate 160. PERSPECTIVE VIEW OF THE INTERIOR OF THE CHURCH IN MOABIT NEAR BERLIN

Plate 161. PERSPECTIVE OF THE INTERIOR OF THE CHURCH IN FRONT OF THE ROSENTHAL GATE NEAR BERLIN

Plate 162. CHURCH AT WEDDING NEAR BERLIN (*left*); CHURCH AT GESUNDBRUNNEN NEAR BERLIN (*right*)

Plate 163. PLAN FOR THE ERECTION OF A MEMORIAL TO FREDERICK THE GREAT IN BERLIN AFTER VARIOUS DESIGNS

Plate 164. DESIGN FOR A MEMORIAL TO KING FREDERICK THE GREAT
Top Perspective; *Bottom* Side view of the memorial and section of the portico through AB; Plan of the memorial

Plate 165. DESIGN FOR A MEMORIAL TO KING FREDERICK THE GREAT

Plate 166. DESIGN FOR A MEMORIAL FOR KING FREDERICK THE GREAT

Plate 167. DESIGN FOR A MEMORIAL FOR FREDERICK THE GREAT ON THE PLATZ DER ALTEN HOFAPOTHEKE IN BERLIN

Plate 168. DESIGN FOR A MEMORIAL FOR KING FREDERICK THE GREAT
Top Perspective; *Centre* Plan of the third storey; View of the niche and the side wall of the entrance hall; Plan of the first storey; *Bottom* Section through AB; Section through CD

Plate 169. PERSPECTIVE OF THE GARDENER'S HOUSE IN CHARLOTTENHOF NEAR POTSDAM TAKEN FROM POINT B. ON THE PLAN (*top*); PLAN OF THE LAY-OUT OF THE GARDENER'S HOUSE IN CHARLOTTENHOF NEAR POTSDAM AND ITS SURROUNDINGS (*bottom*)

Plate 170. PERSPECTIVE OF THE GARDENER'S HOUSE IN CHARLOTTENHOF NEAR POTSDAM TAKEN FROM THE FLAT ROOF AT POINT A. ON THE PLAN

Plate 171. GARDENER'S HOUSE IN CHARLOTTENHOF NEAR POTSDAM
Top Baldachin E.E. of the Gardener's House in Charlottenhof; View of the small courtyard D. on the plan of the Gardener's House in Charlottenhof; *Bottom* Perspective of Charlottenhof near Potsdam taken from the point C. on the plan

Plate 172. PERSPECTIVE OF THE GARDENER'S HOUSE IN CHARLOTTENHOF NEAR POTSDAM, TAKEN FROM POINT E. ON THE PLAN

Plate 173. COUNTRY HOUSE NEAR CHARLOTTENHOF
From left to right and top to bottom View of the garden of the Country House near Charlottenhof; Side garden of the Country House; View of the garden of the Country House near Charlottenhof; Front elevation of the Country House near Charlottenhof; Side view of the Country House with its adjacent buildings near Charlottenhof; View of the hippodrome of the Country House near Charlottenhof

Plate 174. COUNTRY HOUSE NEAR CHARLOTTENHOF
Top Plan of the Country House with its garden lay-out; *Bottom* Section of the Country House

THE PLATES

FRÜHERER ENTWURF ZUM NEUEN WACHT=GEBÄUDE IN BERLIN.

Entworfen und gezeichnet von Schinkel.   Gestochen von J. L. Lgonicht in Darmstadt.

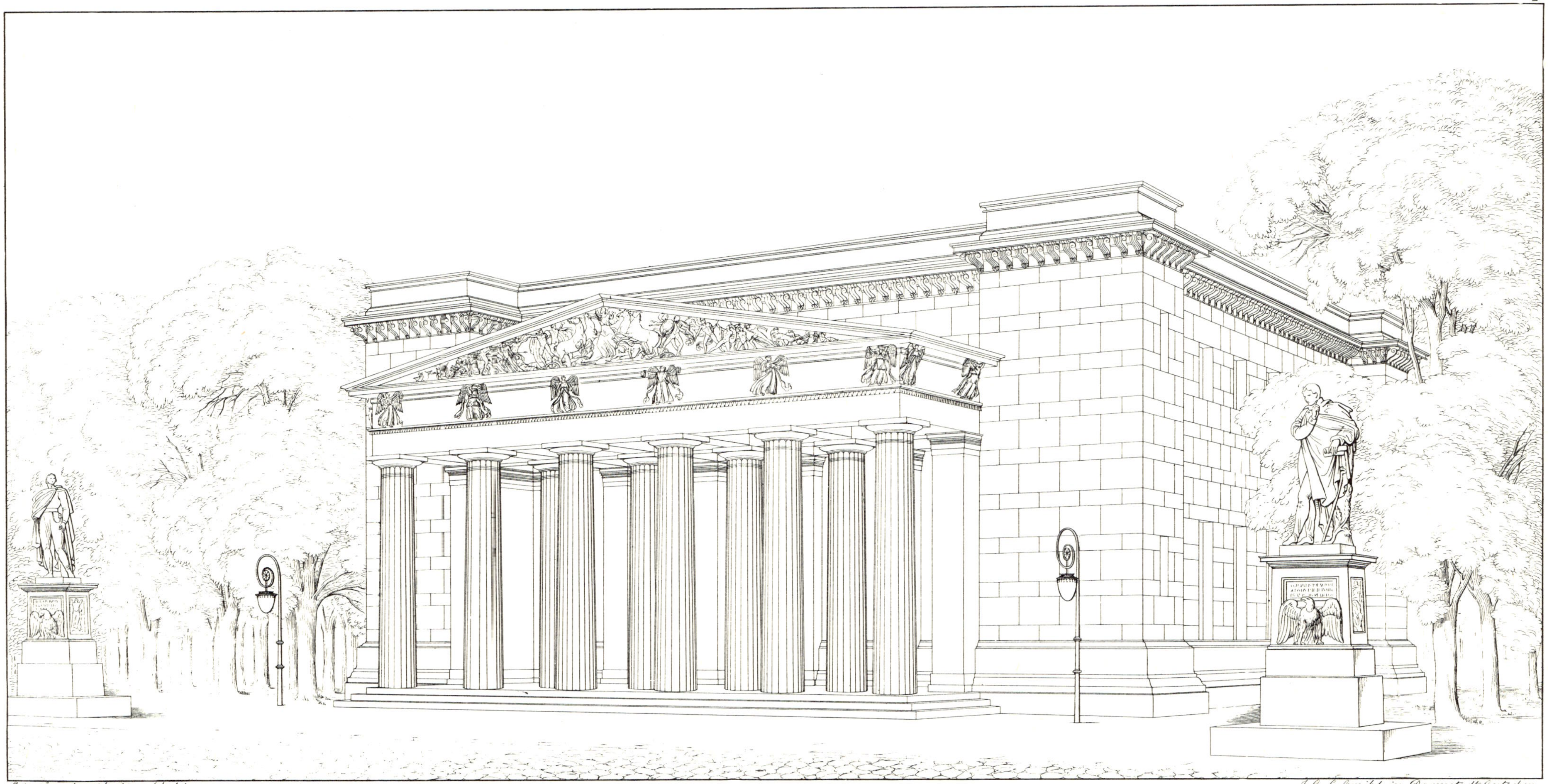

PERSPECTIVISCHE ANSICHT DES NEUEN WACHT-GEBÄUDES IN BERLIN.

BASRELIEF IM GIEBEL-FELDE UND FRIES-VERZIERUNG AM NEUEN WACHT-GEBÄUDE ZU BERLIN.

Entworfen und gezeichnet von Schinkel.
gestochen von Ferd Berger in Berlin.

Aufriß Grundriß und Theile des neuen Wachtgebäudes.

Grundriß zur Veränderung des Berliner Rathhauses.

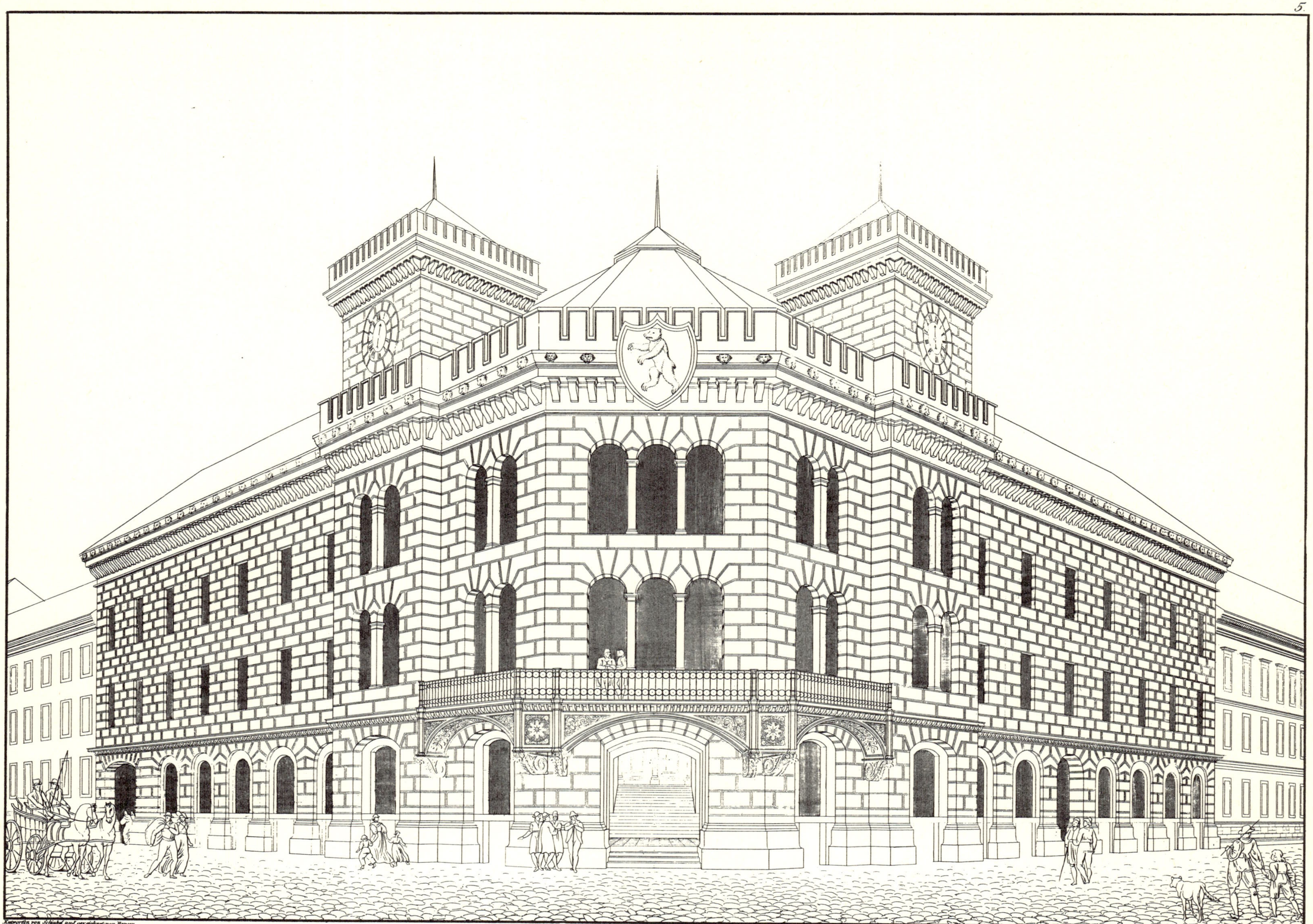

PERSPECTIVISCHE ANSICHT VON DEM ENTWURFE ZUR VERÆNDERUNG DES RATH=HAUSES IN BERLIN.

ENTWURF FÜR EINEN ÖFFENTLICHEN BRUNNEN ALS DENKMAL DER EREIGNISSE IN DEN JAHREN 1813. 1814. 1815.

PERSPECTIVISCHE ANSICHT DES NEUEN SCHAUSPIELHAUSES ZU BERLIN.

GEOMETRISCHER AUFRISS DER HAUPTFAÇADE DES NEUEN SCHAUSPIELHAUSES.

GRUNDRISS A. DES UNTERBAUES B. DES ERSTEN C. DES ZWEITEN GESCHOSSES VOM NEUEN SCHAUSPIELHAUSE IN BERLIN.

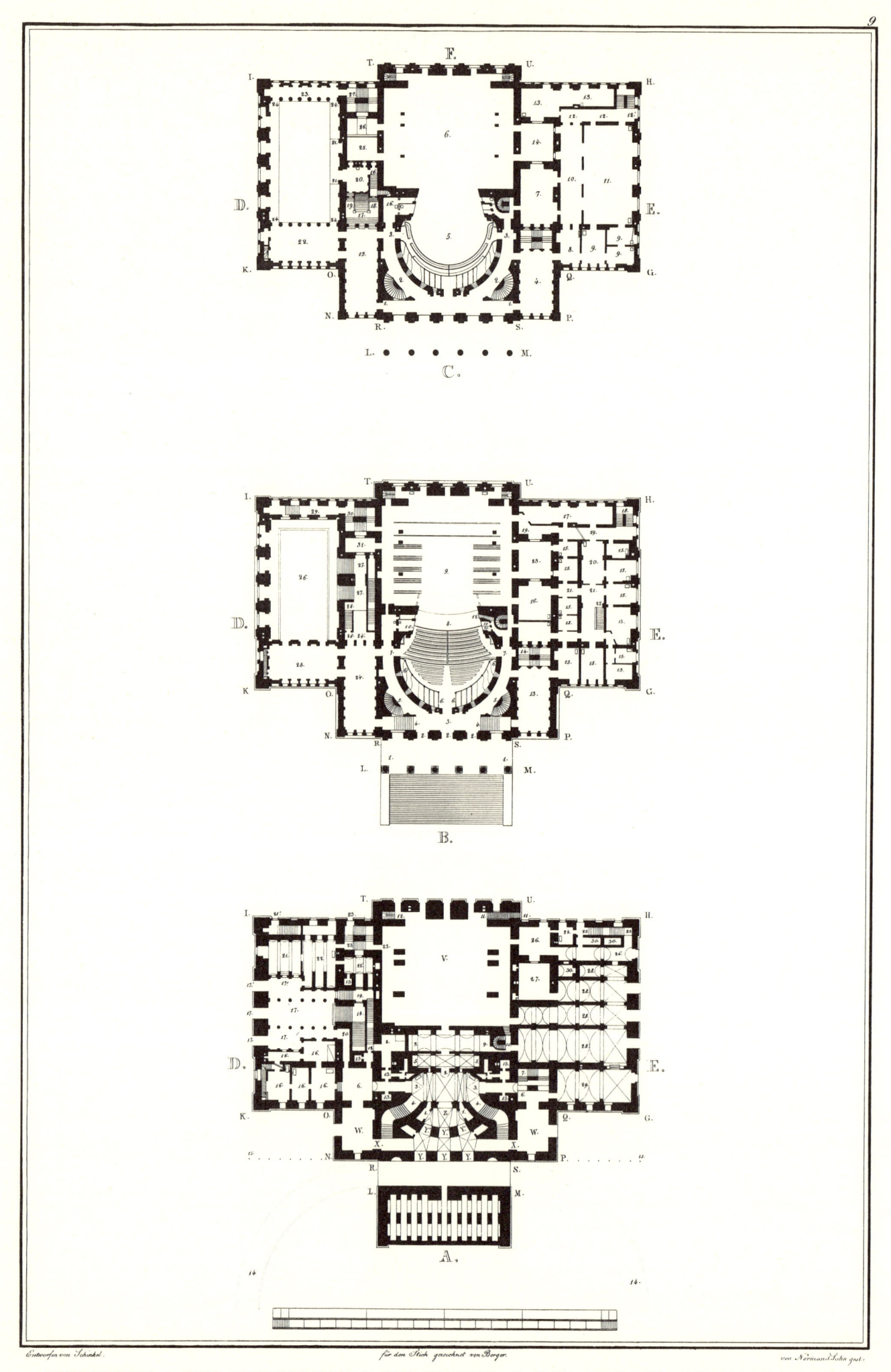

DURCHSCHNITT NACH DER RICHTUNG D.E. DER GRUNDRISSE.

DURCHSCHNITT NACH DER RICHTUNG A.B.C.F. DER GRUNDRISSE.

PROFILE VOM NEUEN SCHAUSPIELHAUSE IN BERLIN.

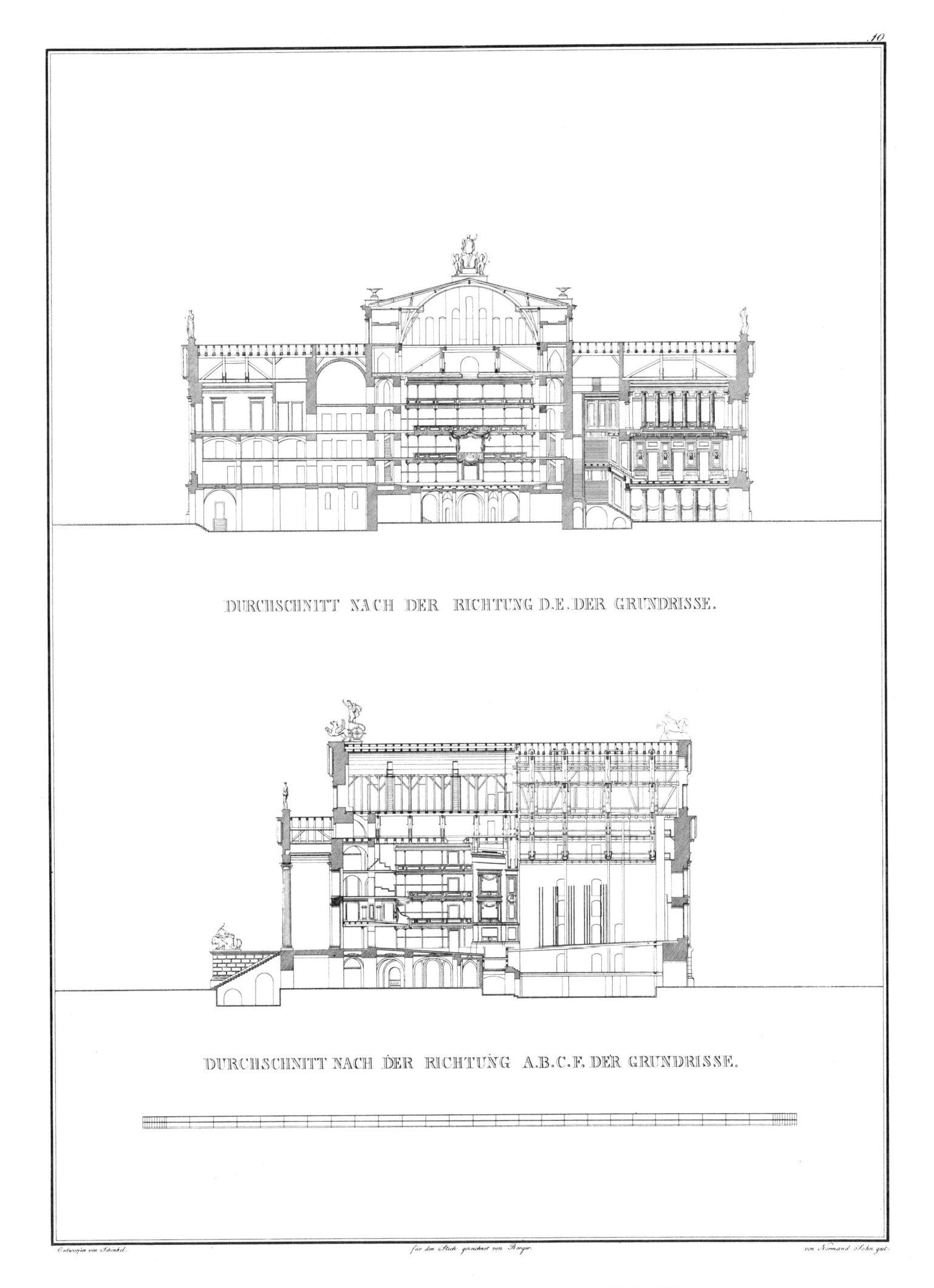

PERSPECTIVISCHE ANSICHT DER SEITENFAÇADE DES NEUEN SCHAUSPIELHAUSES.

HAUPTGESIMSS, CAPITÆL UND BASE DER SAEULE, SCULPTUREN IN UND AUF DEM GIEBEL DES PERISTYLS AM NEUEN SCHAUSPIELHAUSE ZU BERLIN.

PERSPECTIVISCHE ANSICHT DES ZUSCHAUERRAUMES IM KÖNIGL. SCHAUSPIELHAUSE ZU BERLIN, VON DER SCENE AUS GESEHEN.

PERSPECTIVISCHE ANSICHT AUS DEM ZUSCHAUERRAUM AUF DIE SCENE, MIT DER VORSTELLUNG DER BEIM EINWEIHUNGS-PROLOG
AUFGESTELLTEN DECORATION, IN DEM KÖNIGL. SCHAUSPIELHAUS ZU BERLIN.

PLATFOND-VERZIERUNG DES ZUSCHAUERRAUMES IN DEM SCHAUSPIELHAUSE ZU BERLIN.

PERSPECTIVISCHE DARSTELLUNG DES CONCERTSAALS IM KOENIGL. SCHAUSPIELHAUSE ZU BERLIN.

AUFRISS EINER LANGEN WAND DES CONCERTSAALS IM KOENIGL. SCHAUSPIELHAUSE ZU BERLIN.

PLAFOND-VERZIERUNG DES CONCERTSAALS IM KOENIGL. SCHAUSPIELHAUSE ZU BERLIN.

A

Façade des Durchgangs der verlängerten Wilhelms-Strasse
unter den Linden.

B

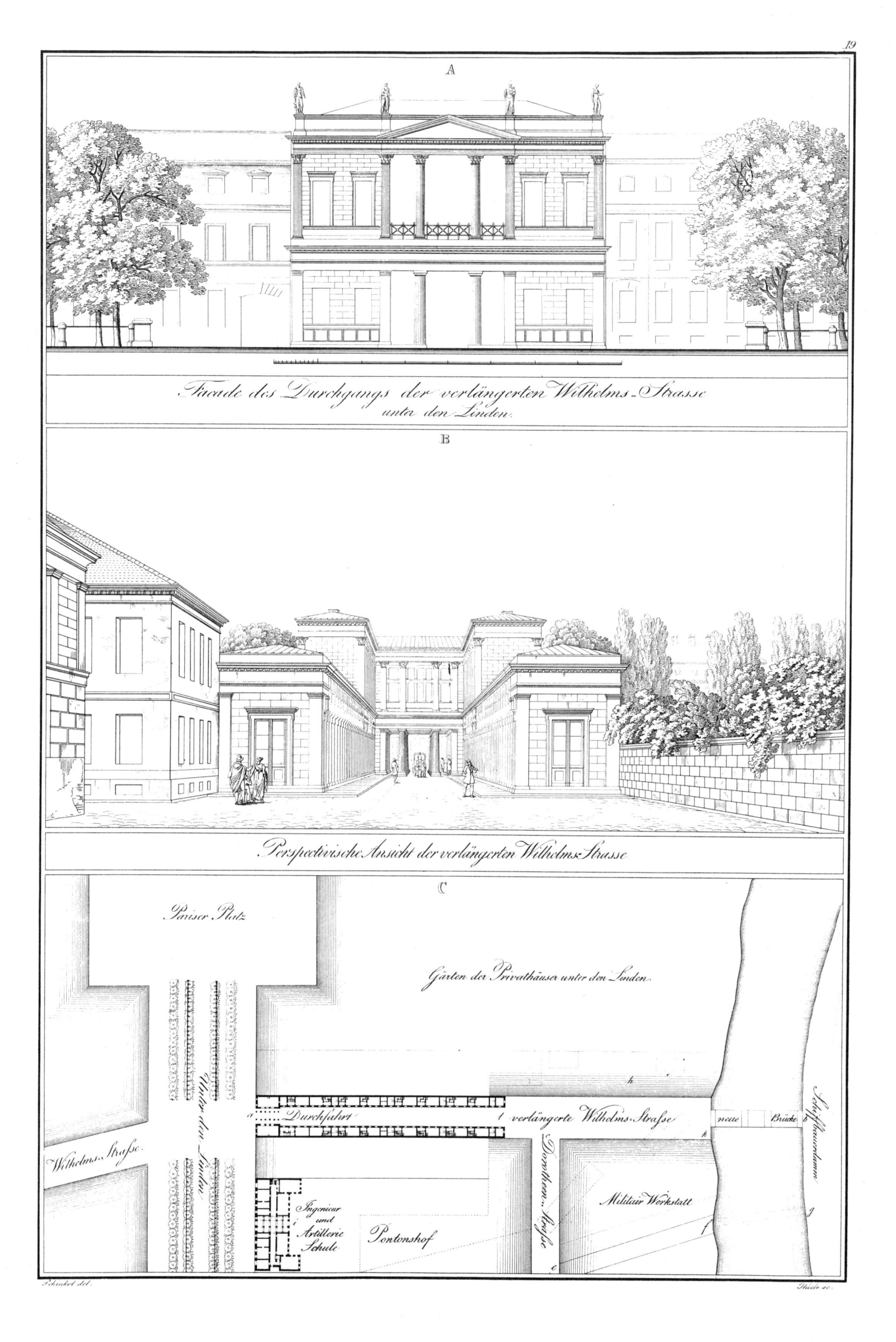

Perspectivische Ansicht der verlängerten Wilhelms-Strasse.

C

Pariser Platz

Gärten der Privathäuser unter den Linden.

Wilhelms-Strasse.

Unter den Linden

Durchfahrt

verlängerte Wilhelms-Strasse

neue Brücke

Schiffbauerdamm

Ingenieur und Artillerie Schule

Pontonshof

Dorotheen-Strasse

Militair Werkstatt

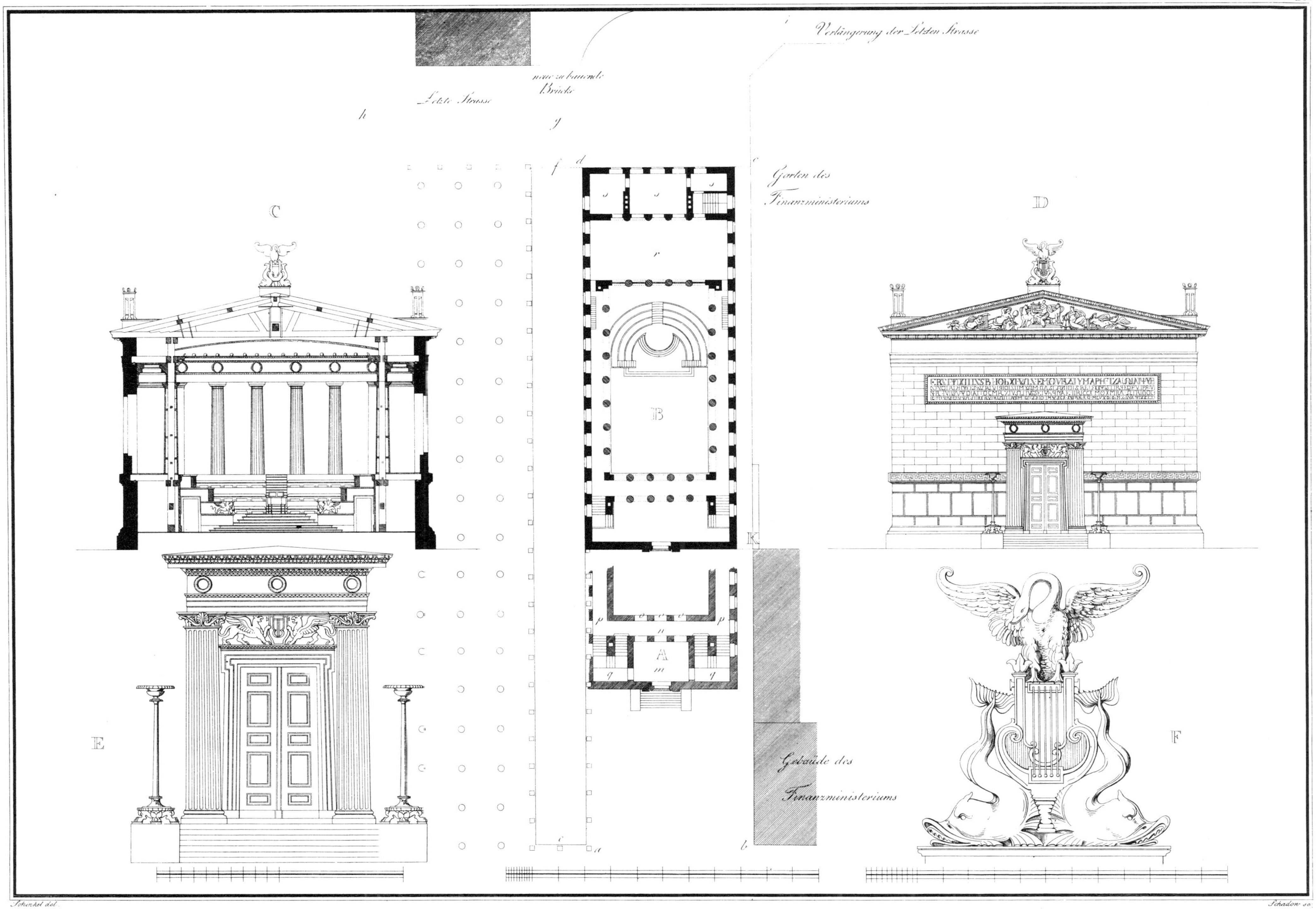

ENTWURF FÜR EIN GEBÄUDE DER SINGACADEMIE IN BERLIN.

ENTWURF FÜR EIN GEBÄUDE DER SINGACADEMIE IN BERLIN.

DAS KRIEGES-DENKMAL IN GEGOSSENEM EISEN AUF DEM KREUTZBERG BEI BERLIN.

DIE VEREINTE ARTILLERIE- UND INGENIEUR-SCHULE UNTER DEN LINDEN IN BERLIN.

NEUE SCHLOSSBRÜCKE IN BERLIN.

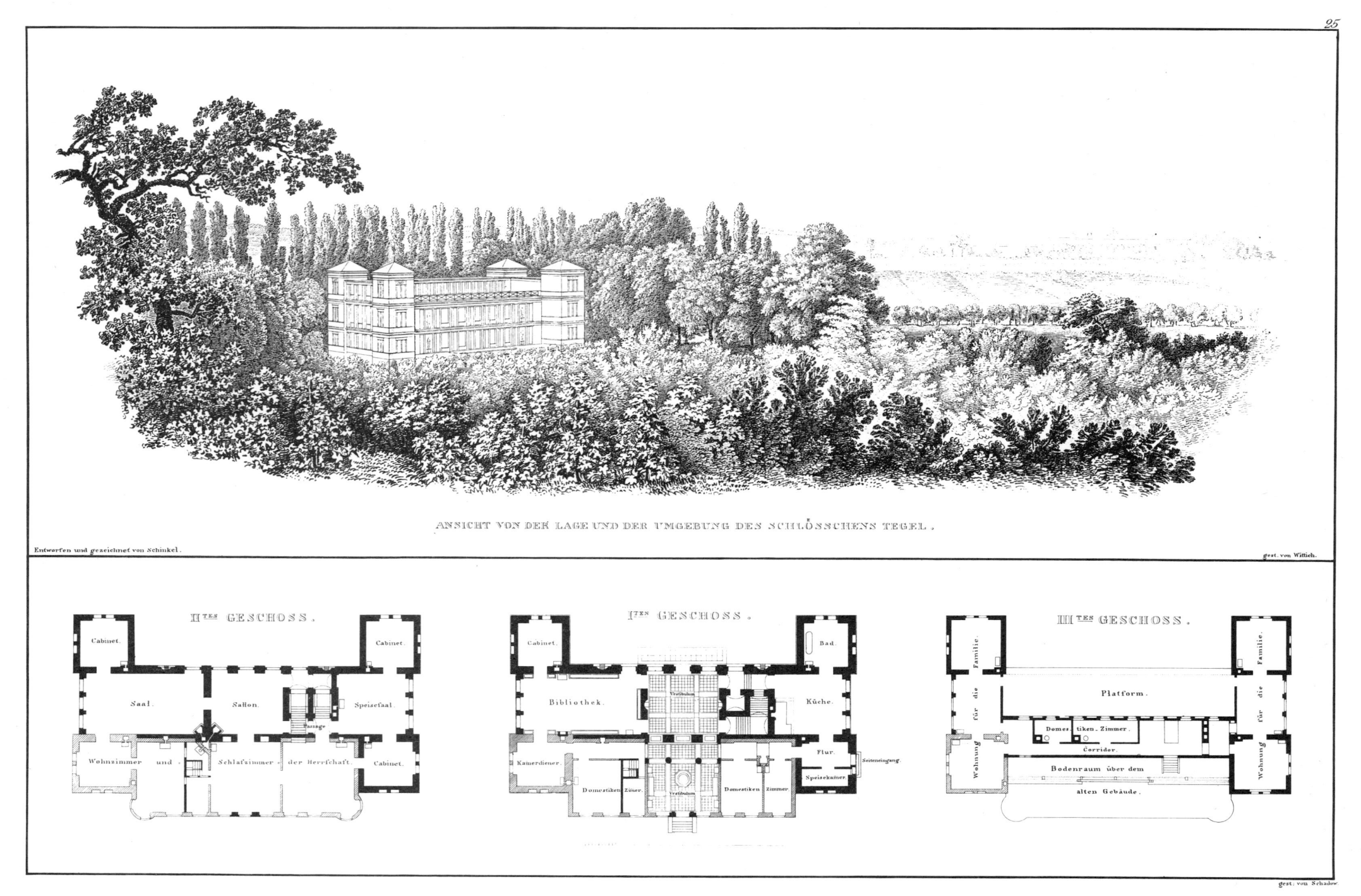

Entworfen und gezeichnet von Schinkel.   gest. von Wittich.

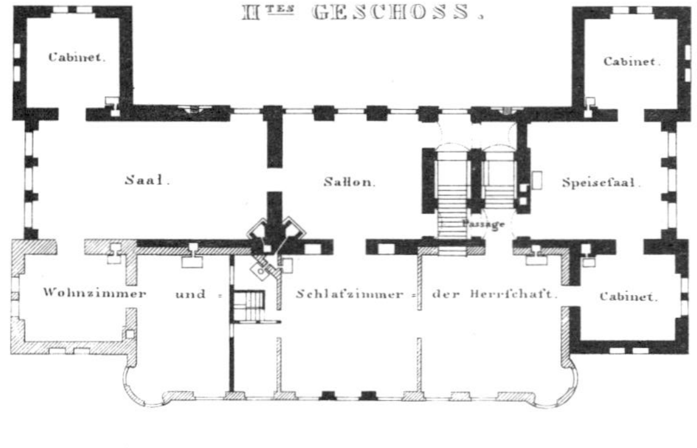

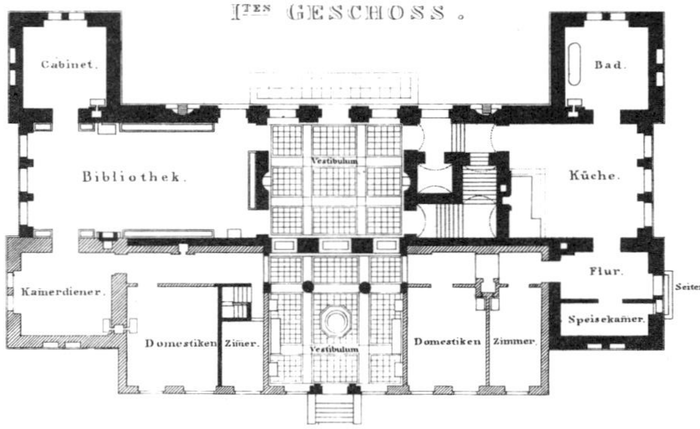

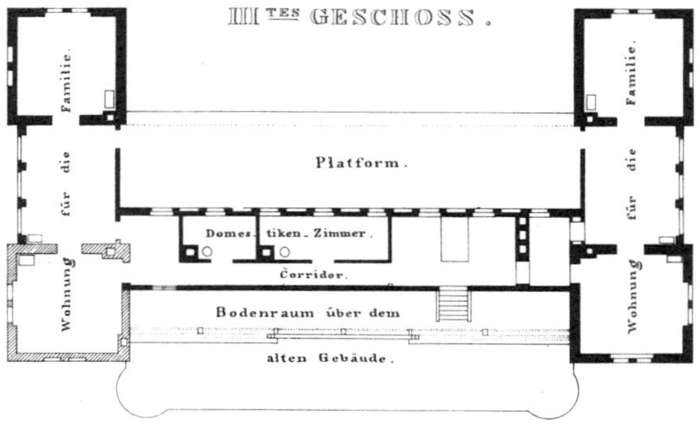

ANSICHT VON DER LAGE UND DER UMGEBUNG DES SCHLÖSSCHENS TEGEL.

gest. von Schadow.

II.tes GESCHOSS.

Cabinet. Saal. Cabinet. Speisesaal. Cabinet.
Wohnzimmer und Schlafzimmer der Herrschaft.

I.tes GESCHOSS.

Cabinet. Bibliothek. Kammerdiener. Domestiken Zimmer. Domestiken Zimmer.
Bad. Küche. Flur. Speisekammer. Seiteneingang.

III.tes GESCHOSS.

Wohnung für die Familie. Wohnung für die Familie.
Domestiken-Zimmer. Platform. Corridor. Bodenraum über dem alten Gebäude.

DAS SCHLOESSCHEN TEGEL.

SEITEN FAÇADE DES SCLOESSCHENS TEGEL.

HAUPTFAÇADE DES SCHLOESSCHENS TEGEL.

VESTIBULUM IM SCHLOESSCHEN TEGEL.

Entworfen u. gezeichnet von Schinkel. gest. v. Normand

DAS SCHLOESSCHEN TEGEL.

N° 2.

erfunden u. gezeichnet von Schinkel.
gest. von C.F. Thiele.

PERSPECTIVISCHE ANSICHT DES JAGDSCHLOSSES ANTONIN IN DER HERRSCHAFT PRZYGODZICE,

SEINER DURCHLAUCHT DEM FÜRSTEN RADZIWILL, KÖNIGL. STATTHALTER, ZUGEHÖRIG.

Nº 1.

Erfunden u. gezeichnet von Schinkel. gest. von C.F. Thiele.

PERSPECTIVISCHE ANSICHT DES GROSSEN SAALS IN DEM JAGDSCHLOSSE ANTONIN.

N.º 2.

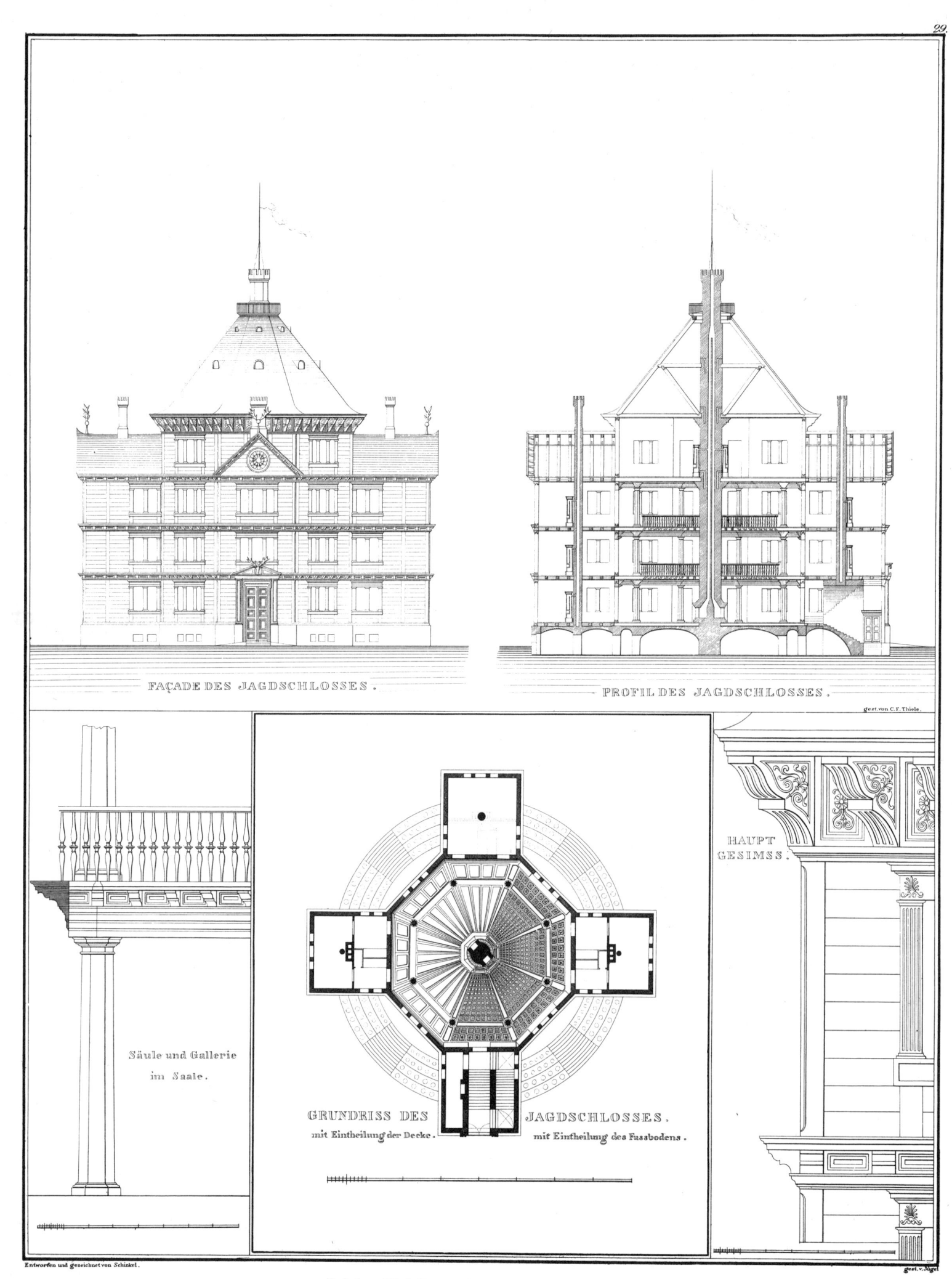

FAÇADE DES JAGDSCHLOSSES.   PROFIL DES JAGDSCHLOSSES.

Säule und Gallerie im Saale.

HAUPT GESIMSS.

GRUNDRISS DES JAGDSCHLOSSES.
mit Eintheilung der Decke.   mit Eintheilung des Fussbodens.

DAS JAGDSCHLOSS ANTONIN.
No 3.

Entworfen und gezeichnet von Schinkel.   gest. von C. F. Thiele.   gest. v. Jügel.

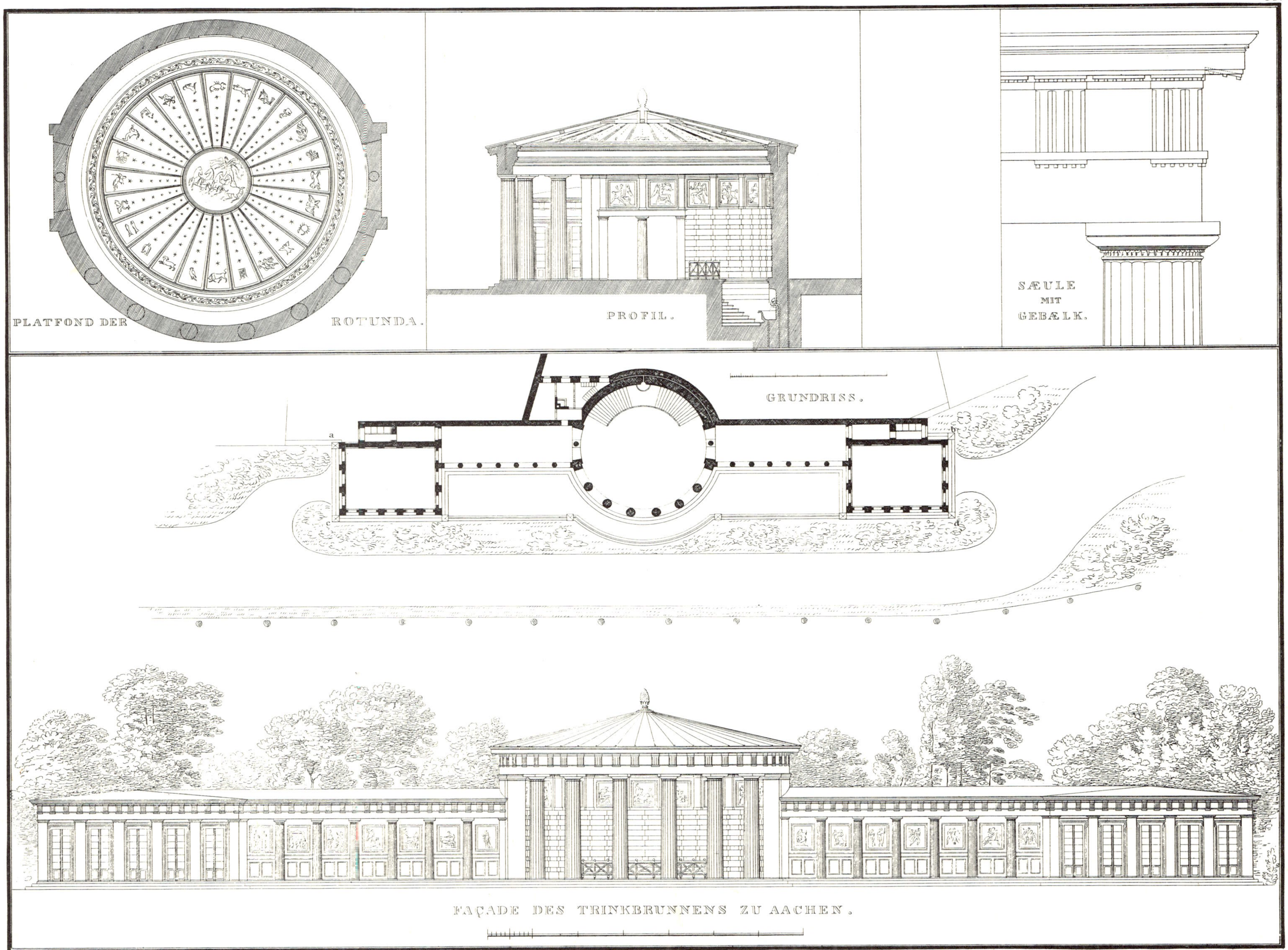

SÆULE MIT GEBÆLK.

PROFIL.

GRUNDRISS.

PLATFOND DER ROTUNDA.

FACADE DES TRINKBRUNNENS ZU AACHEN.

DER MINERAL-TRINKBRUNNEN AUF DEM FRIEDRICH-WILHELMS-PLATZ ZU AACHEN.

Entworfen und gezeichnet von Schinkel. gest. von Mauch jun.

PROFIL DER KIRCHE.

GRABEN

GRUNDSTÜCKE

GRUNDRISS DER KIRCHE.

GRUNDSTÜCKE

ALTE ST GERTRAUDS KIRCHE.

LEIPZIGER STRASSE

SPITTEL MARKT

GRUNDSTÜCKE

GRUNDRISS UND DURCHSCHNITTE DES ENTWURFS FÜR DEN NEUBAU DER ST GERTRAUDS-KIRCHE.

N° 1.

SEITENANSICHT DER ENTWORFENEN ST GERTRAUDS-KIRCHE ZU BERLIN.

Erfunden u. gezeichnet von Schinkel. gest. v. Mauch jun.

PERSPECTIVISCHE ANSICHT VOM INNEREN DER ENTWORFENEN St GERTRAUDS-KIRCHE ZU BERLIN.

Erfunden u. gezeichnet von Schinkel. gest. von C. Thiele.

PERSPECTIVISCHE ANSICHT VOM INNEREN DES ALTARRAUMES
DER ENTWORFENEN ST GERTRAUDS KIRCHE ZU BERLIN.

No 4.

ENTWURF FÜR EIN MONUMENT FRIEDRICHS DES GROSSEN IN BERLIN.

VORDERFAÇADE. SEITENFAÇADE.

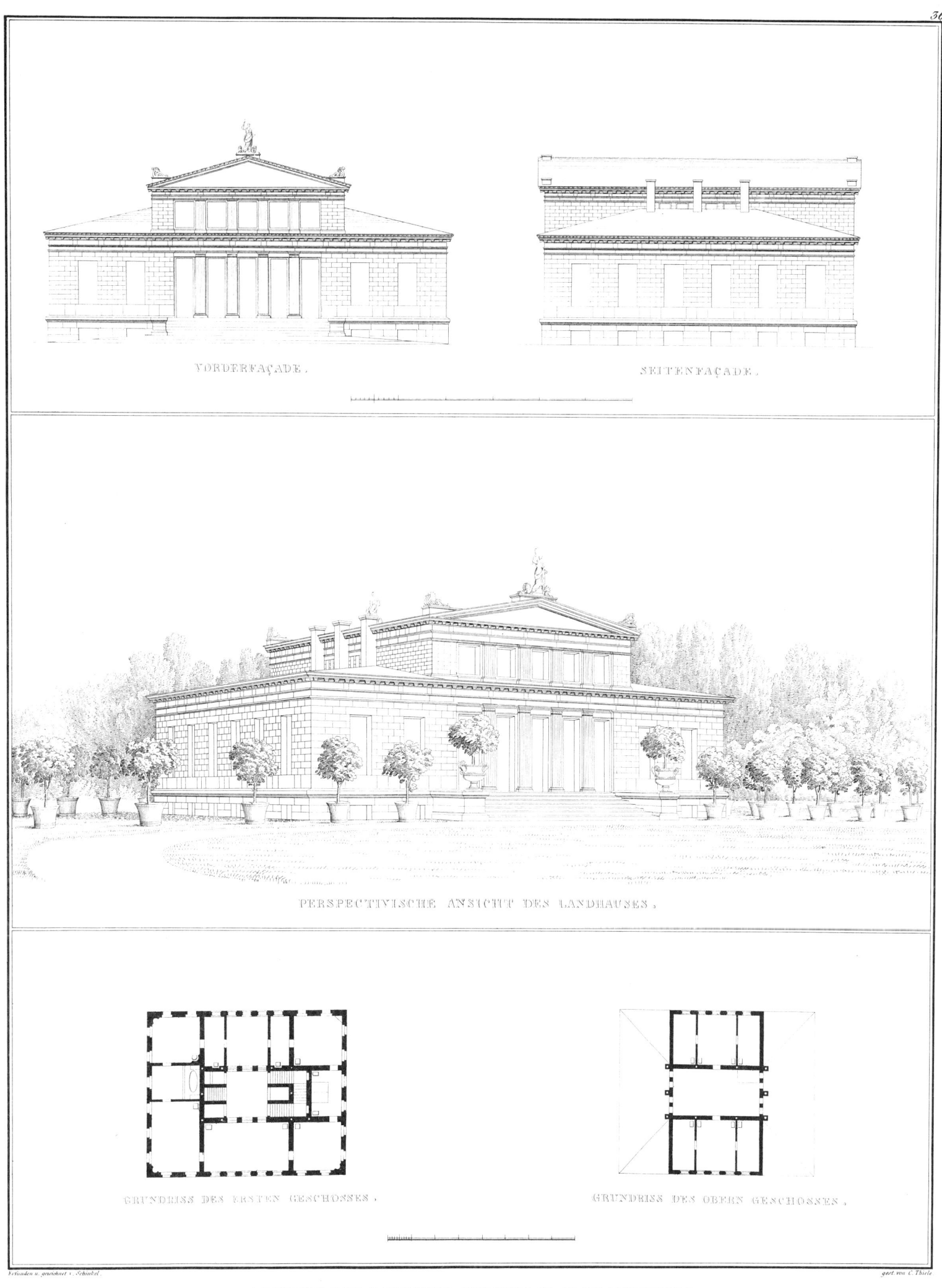

PERSPECTIVISCHE ANSICHT DES LANDHAUSES.

GRUNDRISS DES ERSTEN GESCHOSSES. GRUNDRISS DES OBERN GESCHOSSES.

LANDHAUS DES BANQUIERS BEHREND IN CHARLOTTENBURG.

PERSPECTIVISCHE ANSICHT DES NEUEN MUSEUMS IN BERLIN, VOM STANDPUNKTE ZWISCHEN DEM ZEUGHAUS UND DER NEUEN SCHLOSSBRÜCKE.

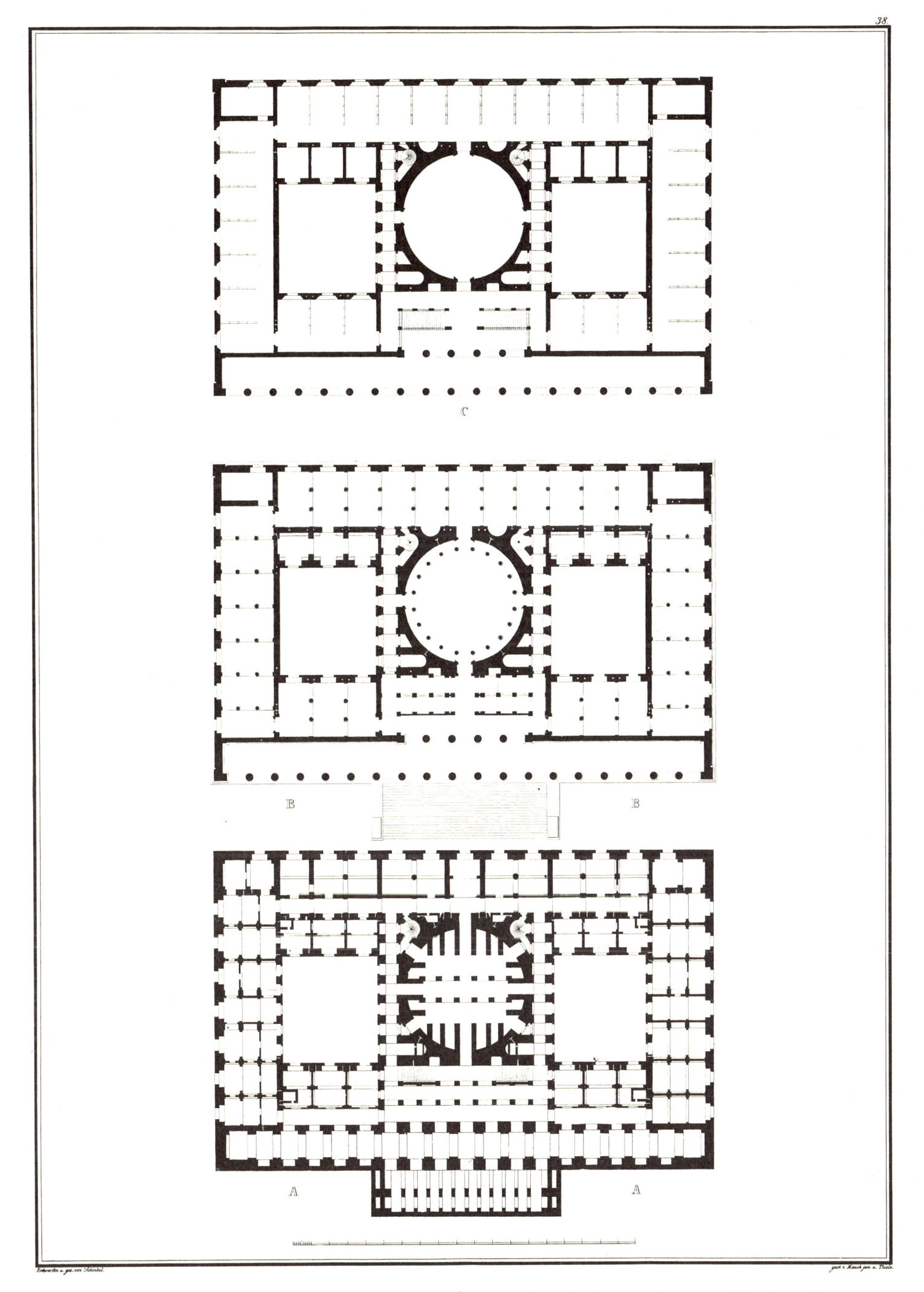

GRUNDRISS A VOM UNTERBAU B VOM ERSTEN C VOM ZWEITEN GESCHOSS DES NEUEN MUSEUMS.

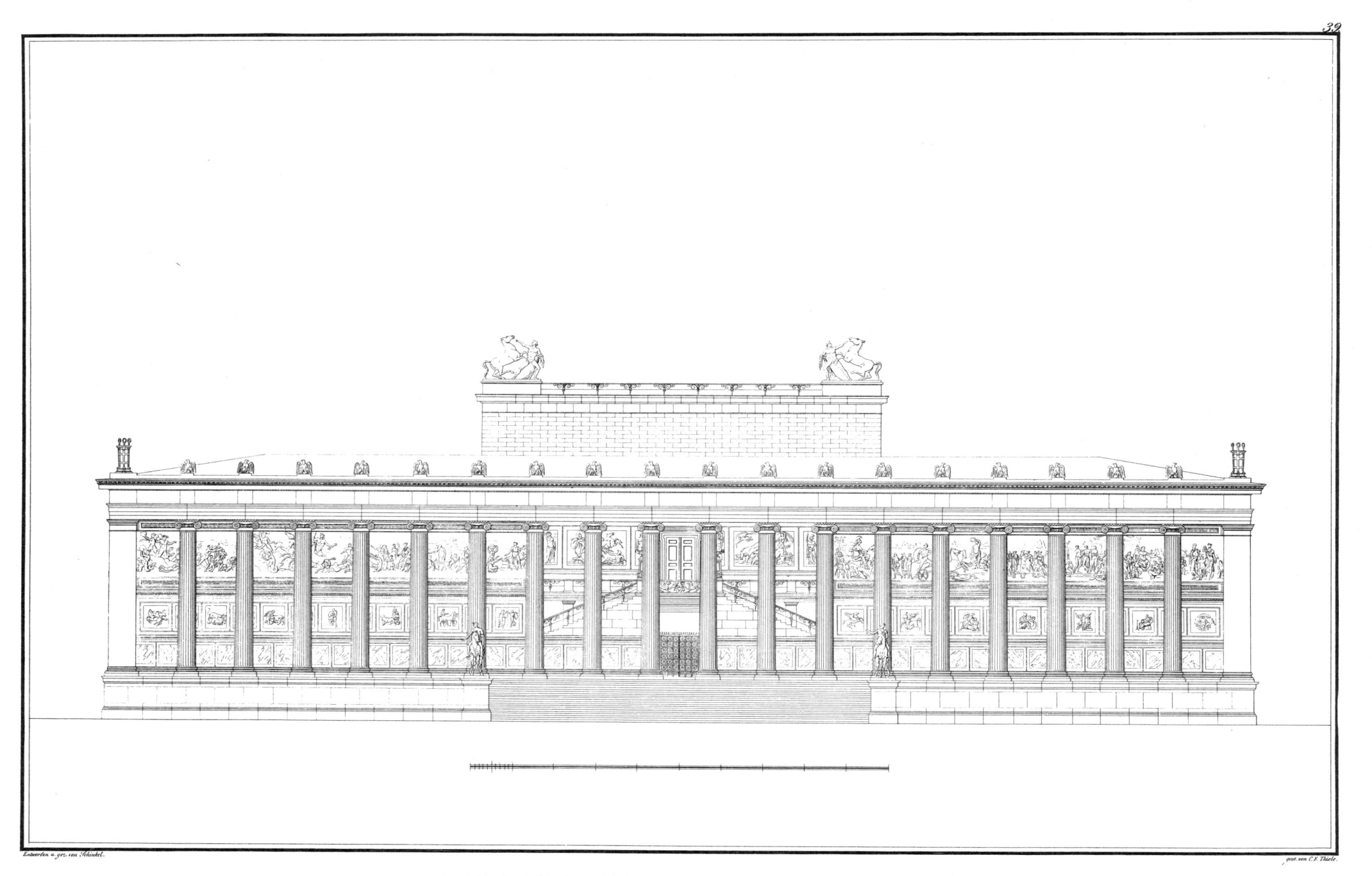

FAÇADE DER HAUPTFRONTE DES NEUEN MUSEUMS.

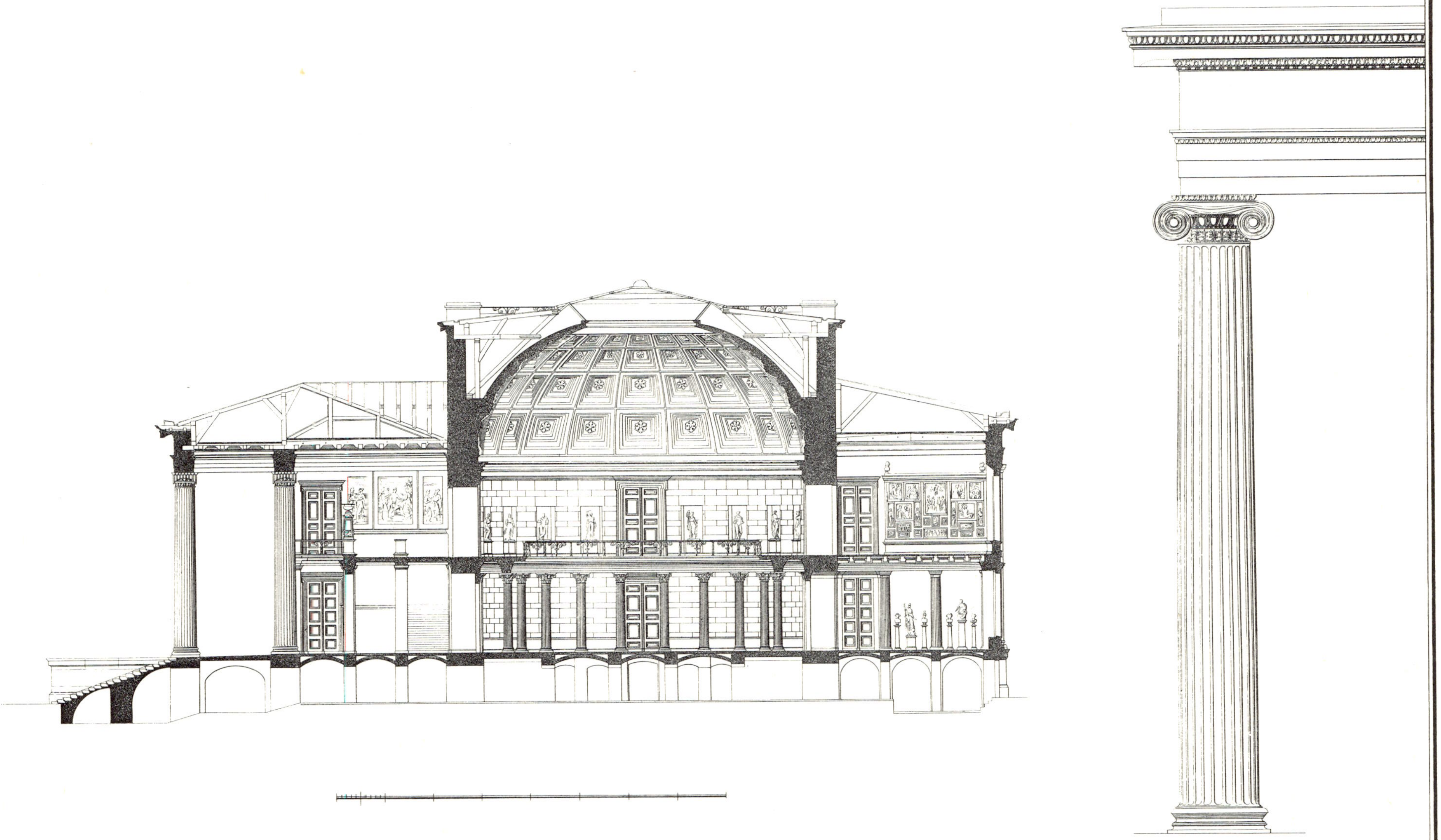

DURCHSCHNITT DES NEUEN MUSEUMS UND VERHÄLTNISS DER SÄULEN IN DER VORHALLE.

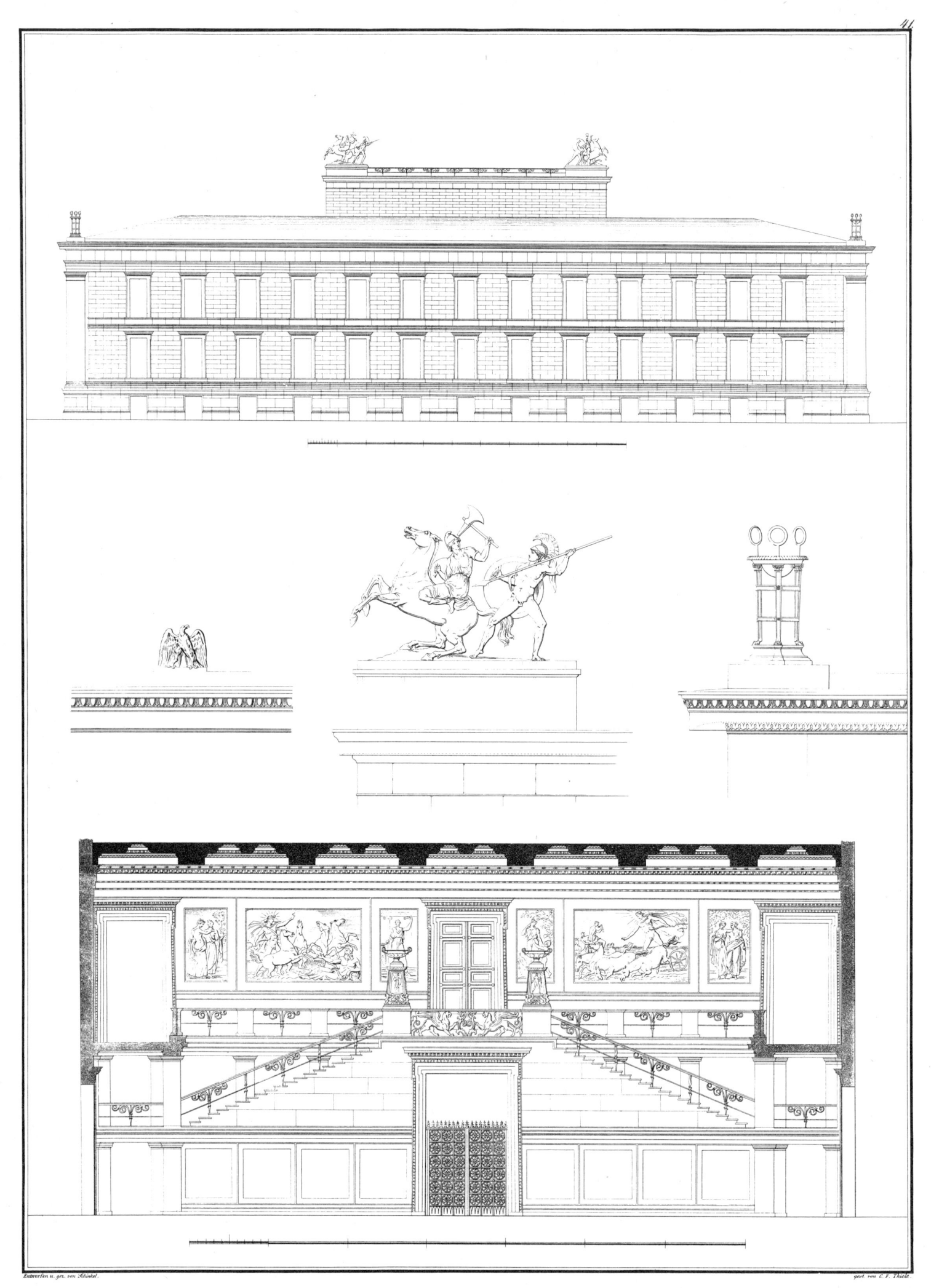

FAÇADE DER HINTERFRONTE DES NEUEN MUSEUMS, ANSICHT DER HAUPTTREPPE UND DETAILS.

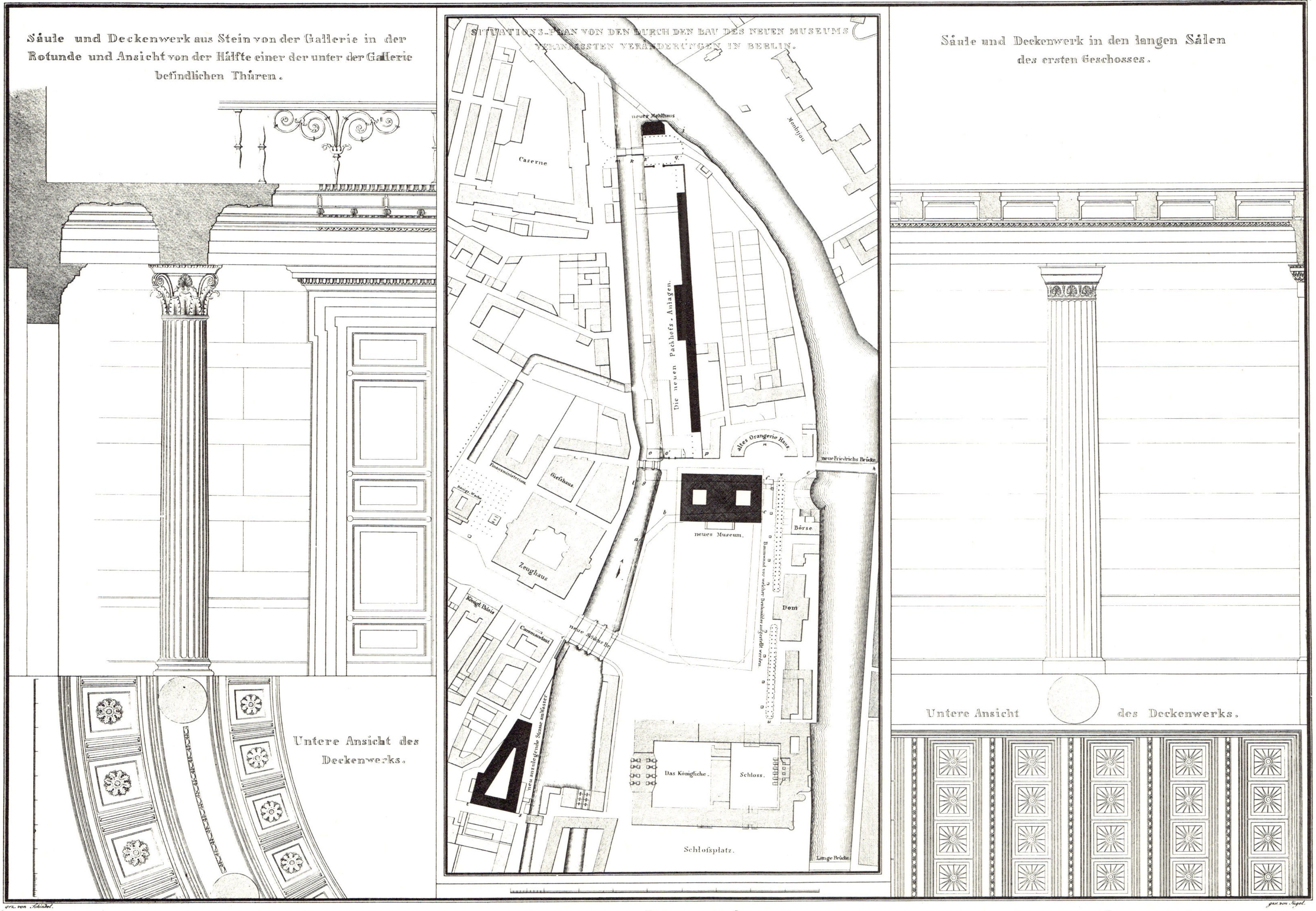

Säule und Deckenwerk in den langen Sälen des ersten Geschosses.

Untere Ansicht des Deckenwerks.

SITUATIONS-PLAN VON DEN DURCH DEN BAU DES NEUEN MUSEUMS HERBEIGEFÜHRTEN VERÄNDERUNGEN IN BERLIN.

Monbijou
Altes Orangerie Haus
Die neuen Packhofs-Anlagen
neues Packhaus
Baumwand vor welcher Denkmäler aufgestellt werden
neues Museum
Börse
Dom
Lange Brücke
Das Königliche
Schloss
Schlossplatz
neue Friedrichs Brücke
neu anzulegende Strasse am Wasser
Caserne
Giesshaus
Zeughaus
Commandant
Finanzministerium
Königl. Wache

Säule und Deckenwerk aus Stein von der Gallerie in der Rotunde und Ansicht von der Hälfte einer der unter der Gallerie befindlichen Thüren.

Untere Ansicht des Deckenwerks.

SITUATIONSPLAN ALLER DURCH DEN BAU DES NEUEN MUSEUMS HERBEIGEFÜHRTEN VERÄNDERUNGEN IN DER STADT, UND DETAILS DER INNEREN SÄULENORDNUNGEN.

PERSPECTIVISCHE ANSICHT VON DER GALERIE DER HAUPT-TREPPE DES MUSEUMS DURCH DEN PORTICUS AUF DEN LUSTGARTEN UND SEINE UMGEBUNGEN.

PERSPECTIVISCHE ANSICHT DER ROTUNDE DES MUSEUMS.

45

SEITEN-ANSICHT DES SÄULEN-KAPITELS.

DURCHSCHNITT EINES THEILS DER DECKE ÜBER DER HAUPT-TREPPE HINTER DEM PORTICUS DES MUSEUMS.

GRUNDRISS EINES THEILS DER DECKE ÜBER DER HAUPT-TREPPE.

VORDER-ANSICHT DES SÄULEN KAPITELS.

HÄLFTE DES GRUNDRISSES VOM KAPITÄL DER SÄULE AM PORTICUS DES MUSEUMS.

BASIS DER SÄULE AM PORTICUS DES MUSEUMS.

GEGOSSENES GELÄNDER DER OBEREN GALLERIE IN DER ROTUNDE DES MUSEUMS.

KAPITÄL DES PILASTERS AM PORTICUS DES MUSEUMS.

DURCHSCHNITT EINES THEILS DER STEINERNEN DECKE ÜBER DEM PORTICUS DES MUSEUMS.

GRUNDRISS EINES THEILS DER DECKE ÜBER DEM PORTICUS.

Gezeichnet von Schinkel.

FIGUREN AUF DEN ECKEN DES MUSEUMS.

ADLER ALS KRÖNUNG AUF DEM GESIMSSE ÜBER DEN SÄULEN.

EINE DER GRUPPEN AUF DEN ECKEN DER HÖHER GEFÜHRTEN MITTELPARTIE DES MUSEUMS.

FIGUREN AUF DEN ECKEN DES MUSEUMS.

Entworfen von Schinkel.

SÆULEN-KAPITÆL IN EINEM DER SCULPTUR-SÆLE.

SÆULEN-KAPITÆL IN EINEM DER SCULPTUR-SÆLE.

SÆULEN-KAPITÆL IN EINEM DER SCULPTUR-SÆLE.

SÆULEN-KAPITÆL IN EINEM DER SCULPTUR-SÆLE.

SÆULEN-KAPITÆL IN DER ROTUNDE DES MUSEUMS.

PILASTER-KAPITÆL IN EINEM DER SCULPTUR-SÆLE.

PILASTER-KAPITÆL IN EINEM DER SCULPTUR-SÆLE.

SÆULEN-KAPITÆL IN EINEM DER SCULPTUR-SÆLE.

PILASTER-KAPITÆL IN EINEM DER SCULPTUR-SÆLE.

Entworfen von Schinkel. Gest. von Finke.

ANSICHT DER ANORDNUNG FÜR DIE BALKENDECKEN IN DEN SCULPTUR SAELEN DES MUSEUMS.

PERSPECTIVISCHE ANSICHT DES SCHLOSSES KRZESCOWICE.

Verlag von Ernst & Korn in Berlin.

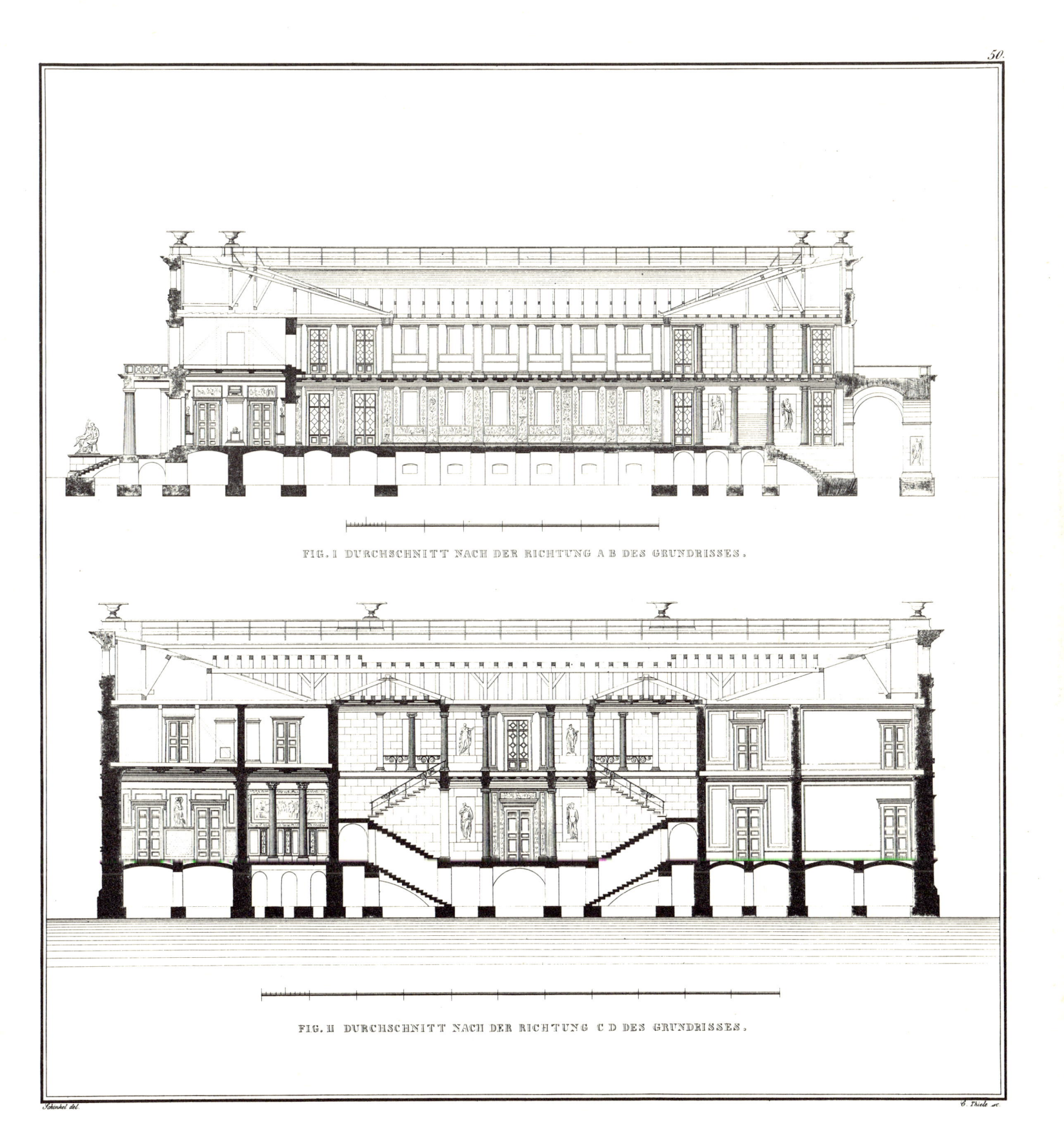

FIG. I DURCHSCHNITT NACH DER RICHTUNG A B DES GRUNDRISSES.

FIG. II DURCHSCHNITT NACH DER RICHTUNG C D DES GRUNDRISSES.

51.

FIG. I. DURCHSCHNITT NACH DER RICHTUNG E F DES GRUNDRISSES.

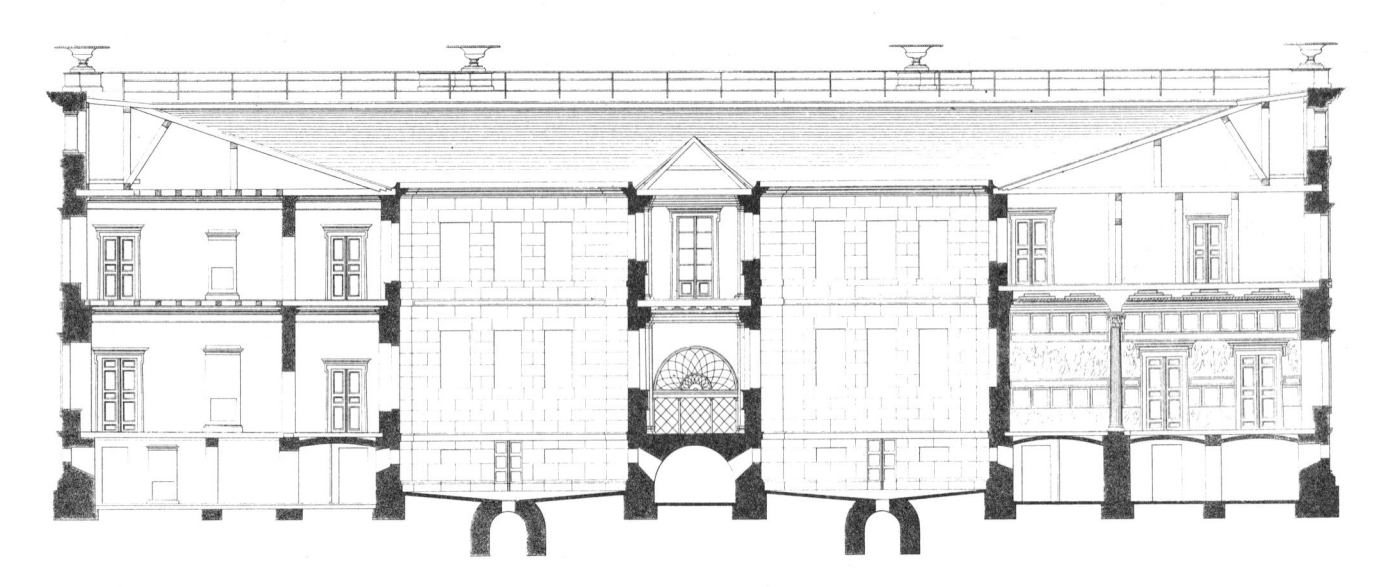

FIG. II. FAÇADE DER WESTSEITE DES SCHLOSSES.

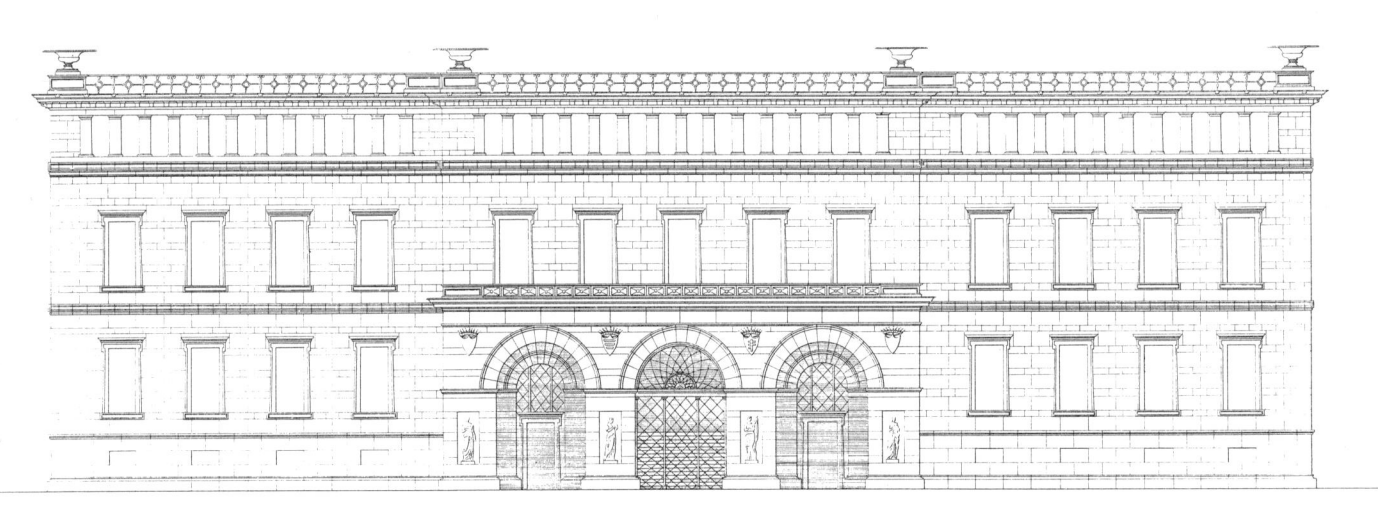

FIG. III. FAÇADE DER OSTSEITE DES SCHLOSSES.

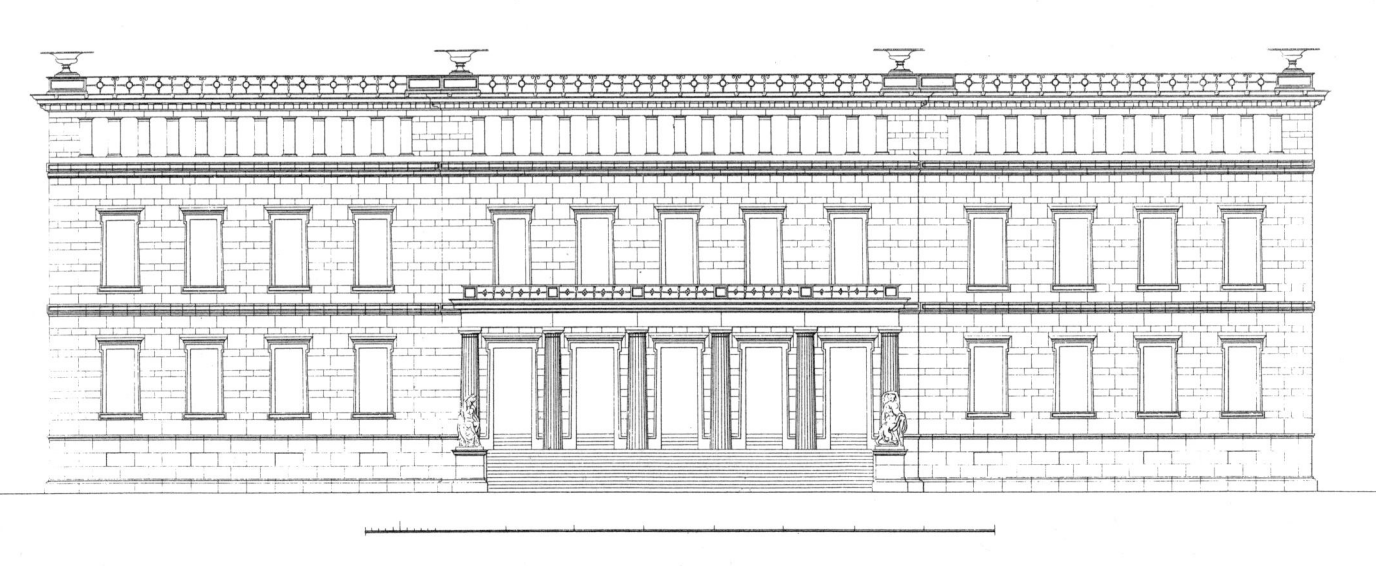

Schinkel del. O. Thiele sc.

EIN THEIL DER LANGEN GALLERIE. ANSTOSSENDER CORRIDOR AM VESTIBULE.

BIBLIOTHEK-SAAL MIT DEN BÜCHERSCHRÆNKEN.

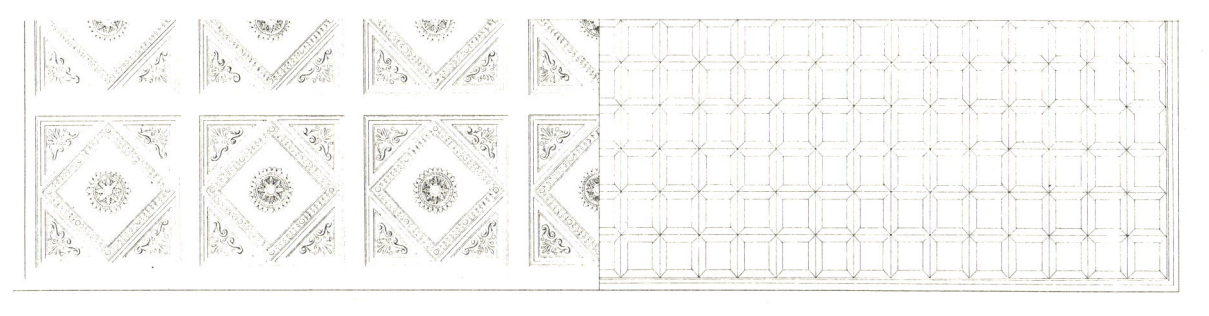

EIN THEIL DES PLATFONDS. EIN THEIL DES FUSSBODENS.

DURCHSCHNITT DES SPEISESAALS.

DURCHSCHNITT DES TANZSAALS.

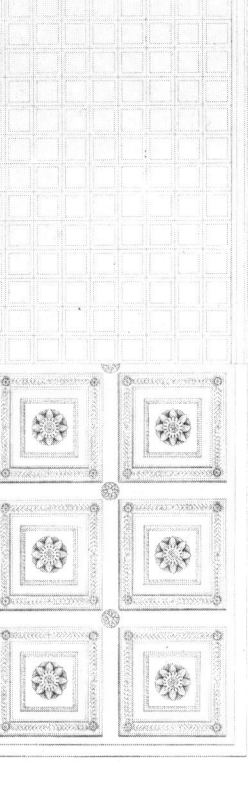

VIERTER THEIL DES PLATFONDS IM SPEISESAAL.

VIERTER THEIL DES PARQUETBODENS IM SPEISESAAL.

VIERTER THEIL DES PLATFONDS IM TANZSAAL.

VIERTER THEIL DES PARQUETBODENS IM TANZSAAL.

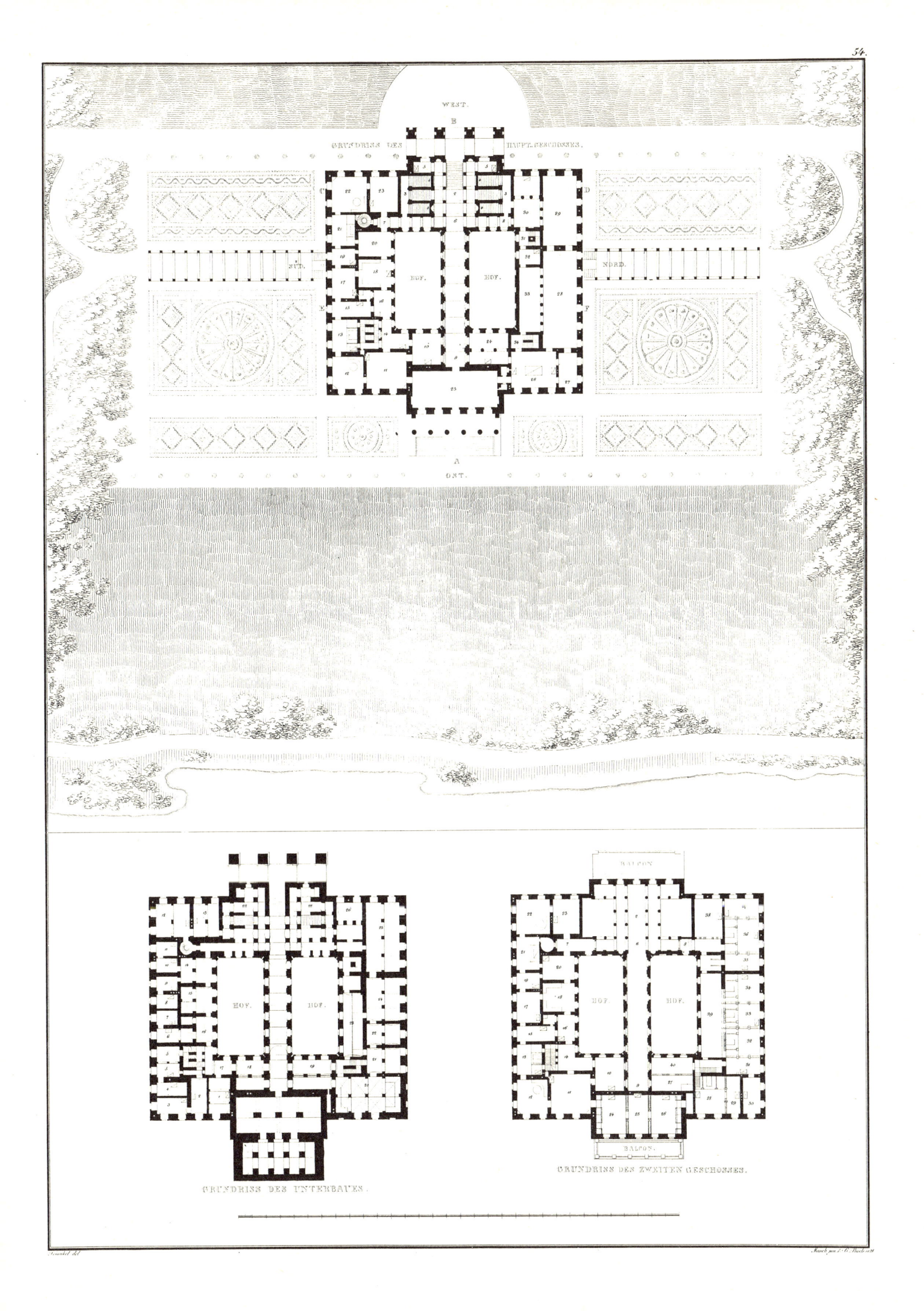

54.

WEST.

GRUNDRISS DES HAUPTGESCHOSSES.

HOF. HOF.

OST.

GRUNDRISS DES UNTERBAUES.

GRUNDRISS DES ZWEITEN GESCHOSSES.

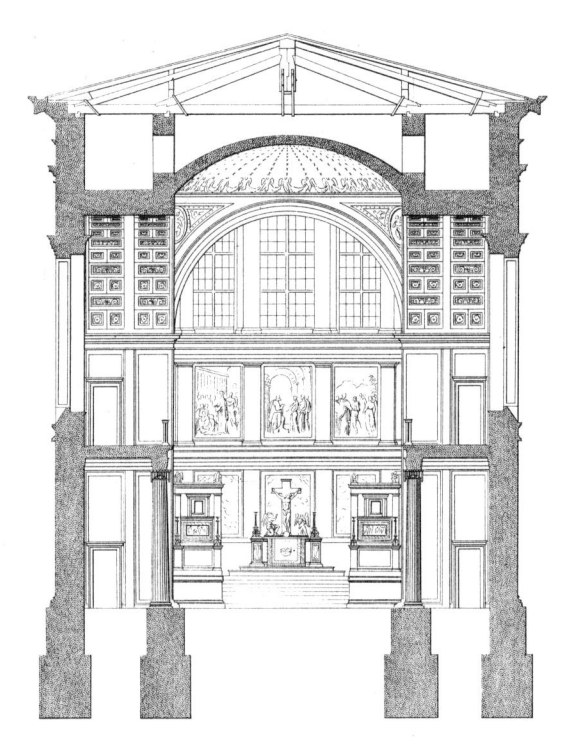

FIG. III. DURCHSCHNITT GEGEN DEN ALTAR GESEHEN. 　　　FIG. IV. DURCHSCHNITT GEGEN DIE EINGANGSPFORTE GESEHEN.

FIG. I. GIEBELSEITE GEGEN DEN MARKT. 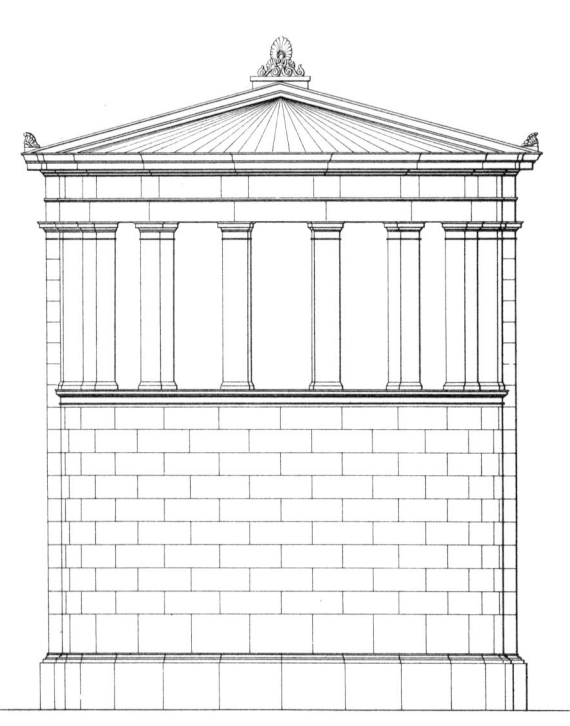　　　FIG. II. NISCHE DES ALTARS.

ENTWURF ZUR KIRCHE AUF DEM WERDERSCHEN MARKT ZU BERLIN.

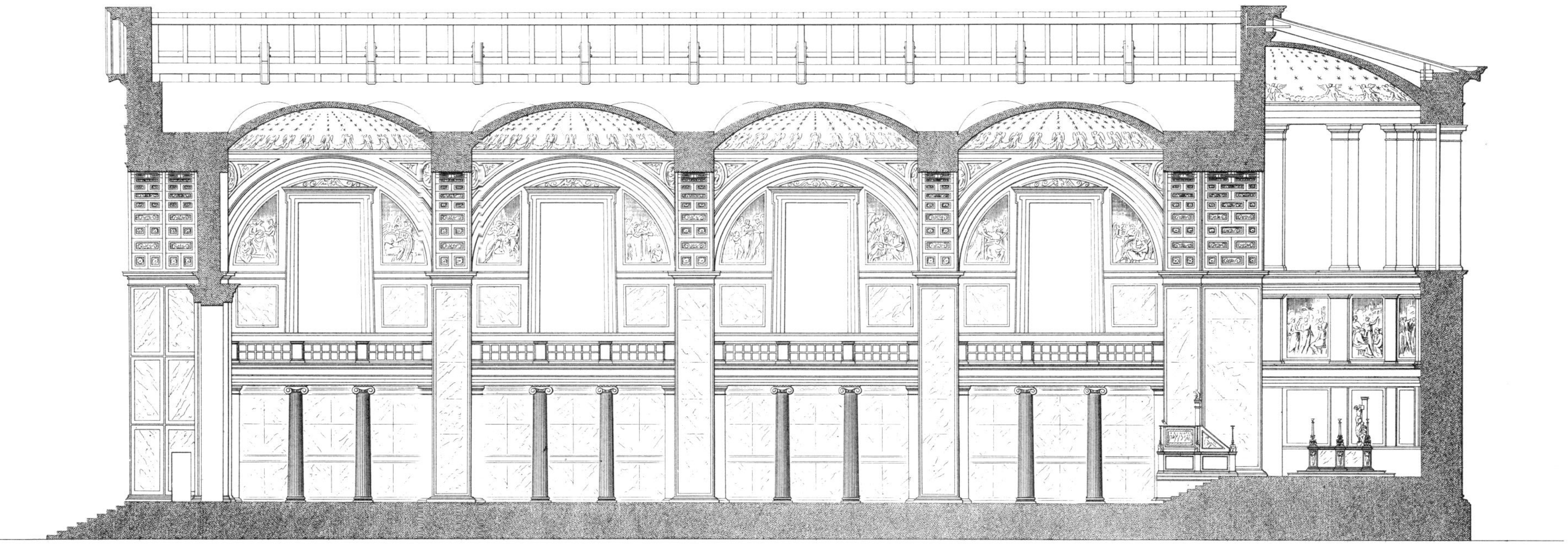

FIG. II. DURCHSCHNITT NACH DER LÄNGE.

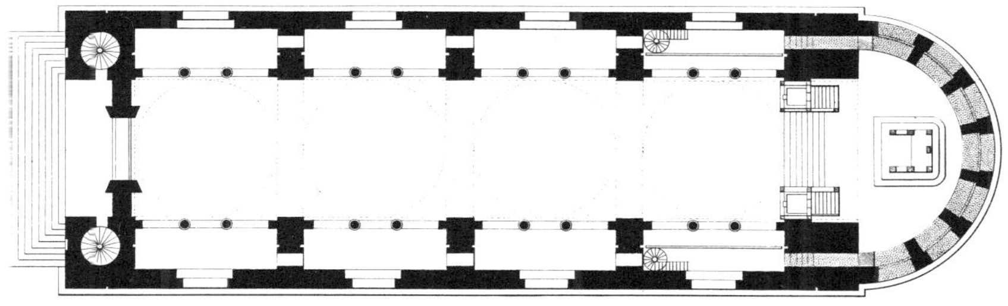

FIG. I. GRUNDRISS DER KIRCHE.

ENTWURF ZUR KIRCHE, AUF DEM WERDERSCHEN MARKT ZU BERLIN.

FIG. I. SEITEN-ANSICHT DER KIRCHE.

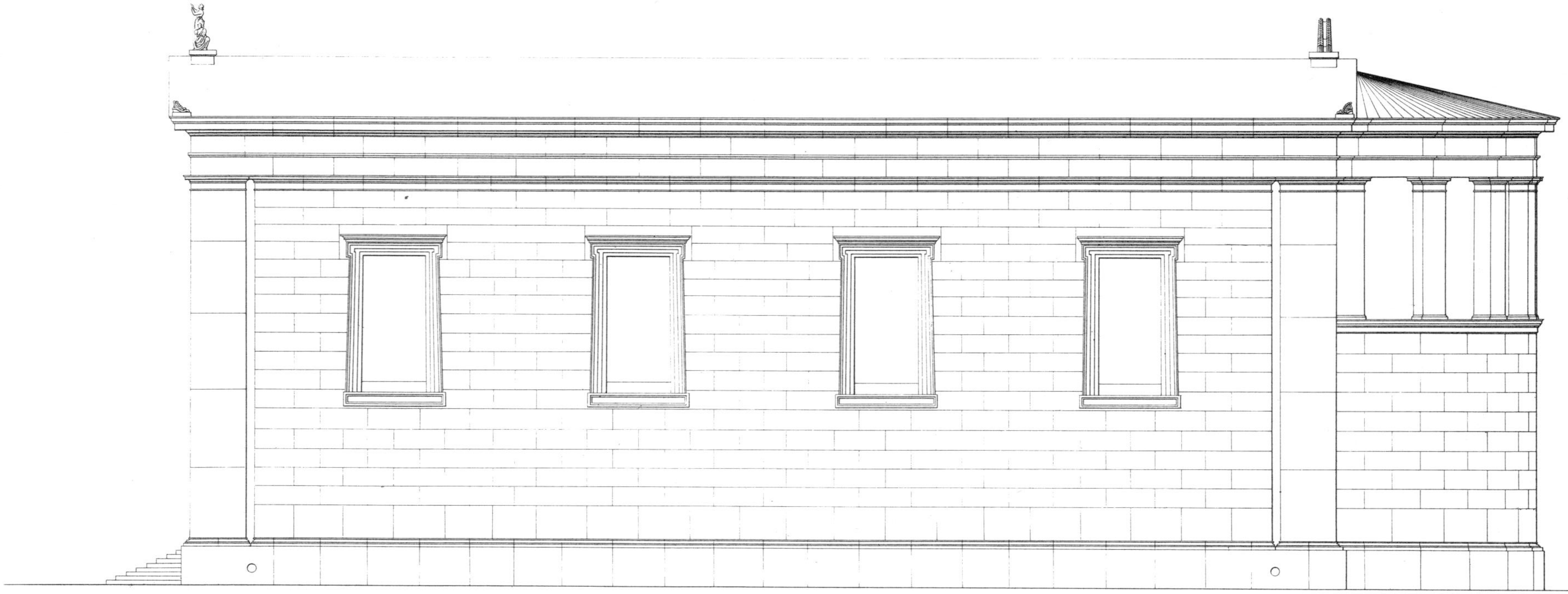

FIG. II. VORDERE ANSICHT DER KANZEL UND DES ALTARS.

SEITEN-ANSICHT VON KANZEL UND ALTAR.

ENTWURF ZUR KIRCHE AUF DEM WERDERSCHEN MARKT ZU BERLIN.

PERSPECTIVISCHE ANSICHT DES INNEREN DER PROJECTIRTEN KIRCHE AUF DEM WERDERSCHEN MARKT ZU BERLIN.

PERSPECTIVISCHE ANSICHT DES LEIPZIGER THORES VON DER ÄUSSEREN SEITE.

ANSICHT DES LEIPZIGER THORES VOM LEIPZIGER PLATZ GESEHN.

ANSICHT EINES THORGEBÄUDES VOM GIEBEL.

DORISCHE ORDNUNG AN DEN THORGEBÄUDEN.

WEG NACH DEM HALLISCHEN THOR.
CHAUSSEE NACH POTSDAM.
CHAUSSEE NACH DEM HOLZGARTEN.
WEG NACH DEM BRANDENBURGER THOR.
LEIPZIGER PLATZ.

GRUNDRISS EINES THORGEBÄUDES.

DURCHSCHNITT DER DORISCHEN GEBÄLKS MIT DEM ECKPILASTER.

VORDERE ANSICHT. SEITENANSICHT.

PERSPECTIVISCHE ANSICHT EINES DENKMALS FÜR DEN GENERAL VON SCHARNHORST.

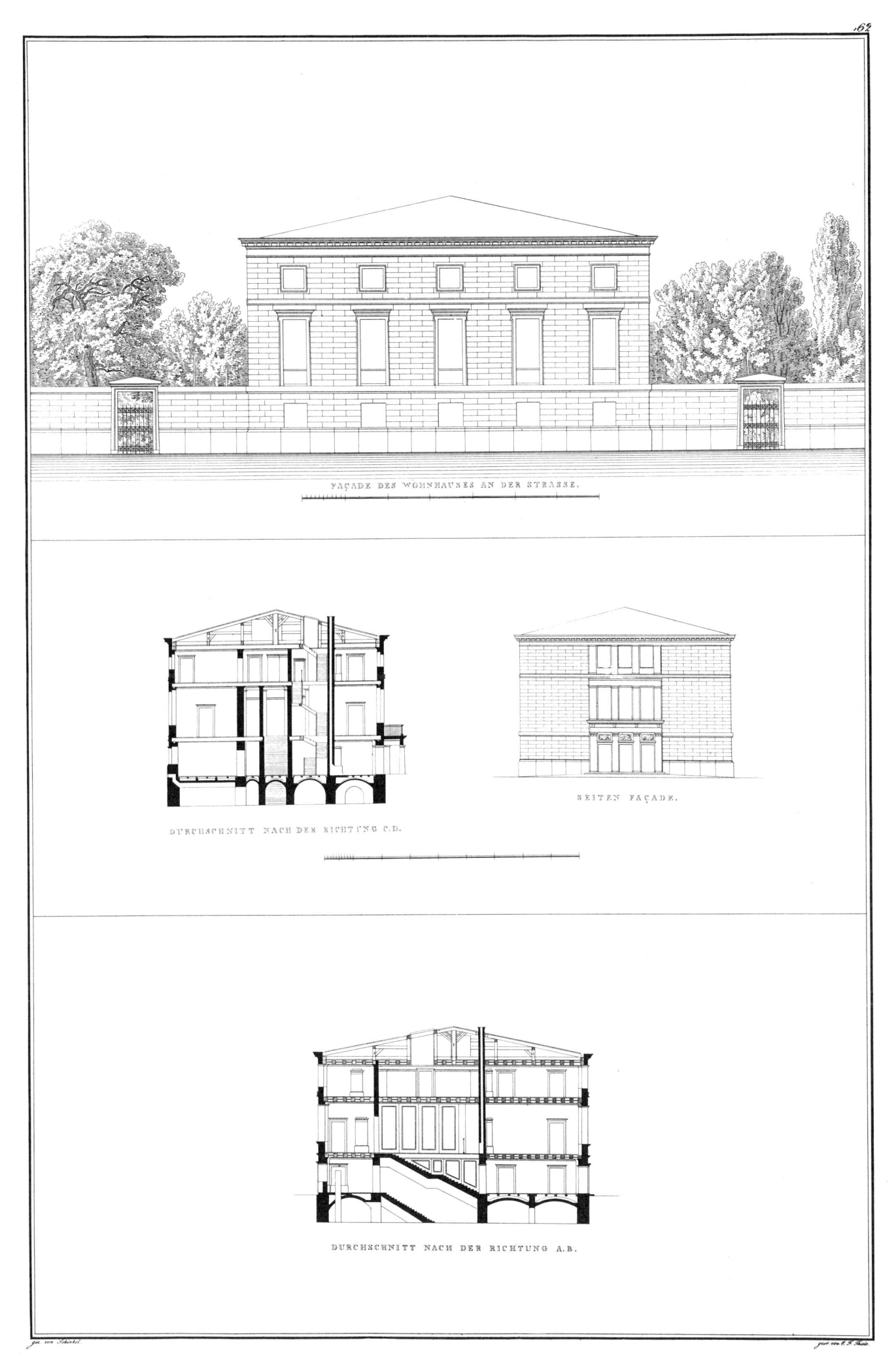

FAÇADE DES WOHNHAUSES AN DER STRASSE.

DURCHSCHNITT NACH DER RICHTUNG C.D.

SEITEN FAÇADE.

DURCHSCHNITT NACH DER RICHTUNG A.B.

ENTWURF ZU EINEM STAEDTISCHEN WOHNGEBAEUDE.

Nº 1.

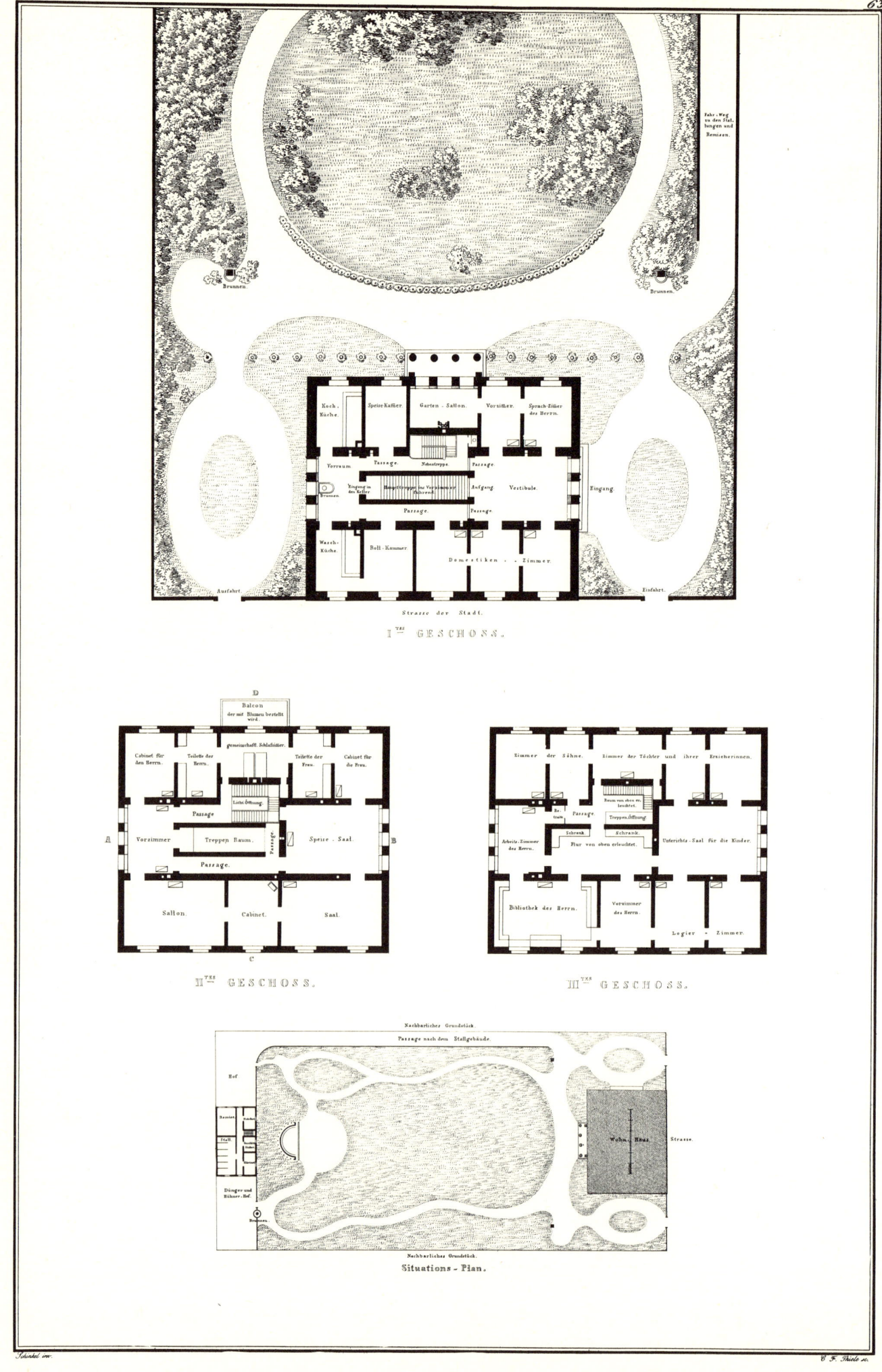

63.

I.tes GESCHOSS.

II.tes GESCHOSS.   III.tes GESCHOSS.

Situations-Plan.

Schinkel inv.   C. F. Thiele sc.

ENTWURF ZU EINEM STAEDTISCHEN WOHNGEBAEUDE.

FAÇADE AN DER STRASSE.

PERSPECTIVISCHE ANSICHT DES VESTIBULS.

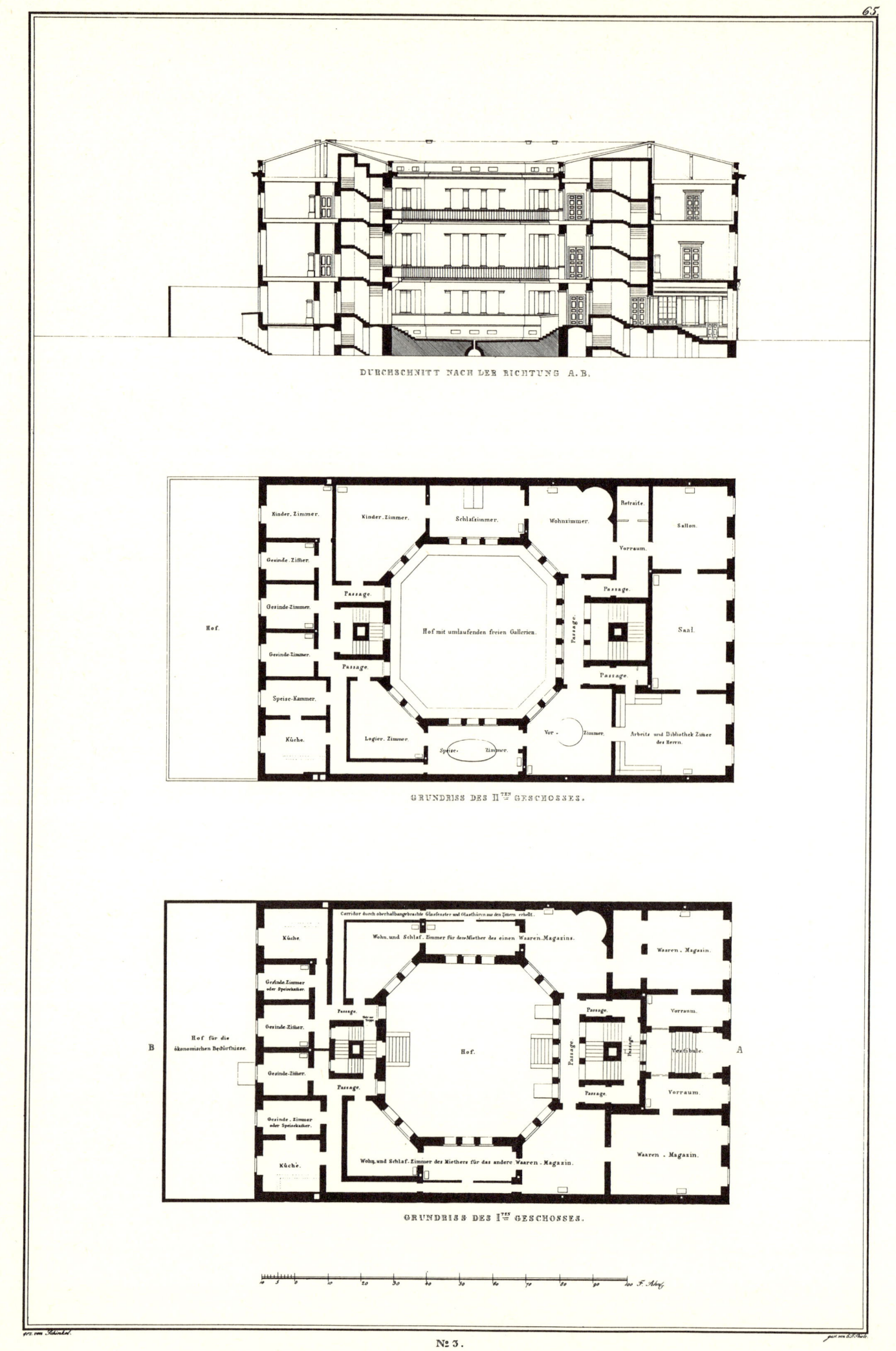

DURCHSCHNITT NACH DER RICHTUNG A.B.

GRUNDRISS DES II.ten GESCHOSSES.

GRUNDRISS DES I.ten GESCHOSSES.

N.º 3.
ENTWURF ZU EINEM STAEDTISCHEN WOHNGEBAEUDE.

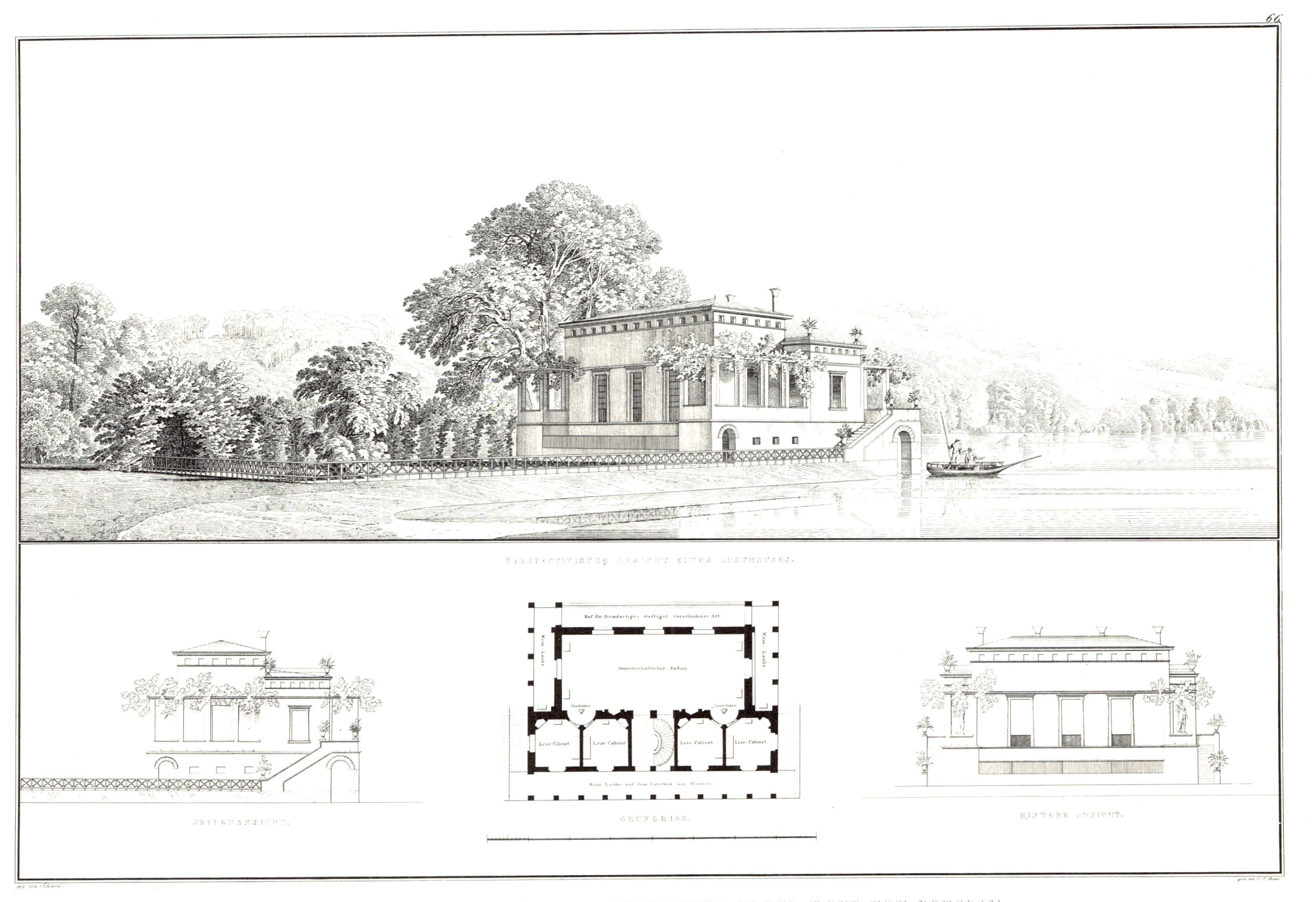

PERSPECTIVISCHE ANSICHT EINES LUSTHAUSES.

HINTERE ANSICHT.

GRUNDRISS.

Wein-Laube.
Leeres Cabinet
Saal für dramatische, Geselligkeit verbindender Art
Gesellschaftlicher Salon
Leeres Cabinet
Leeres Cabinet
Leeres Cabinet
Wein-Laube auf dem Casterton am Wasser.
Wein-Laube.

VORDERANSICHT.

PERSPECTIVISCHE ANSICHT EINES LUSTHAUSES IN DER NÄHE VON POTSDAM.

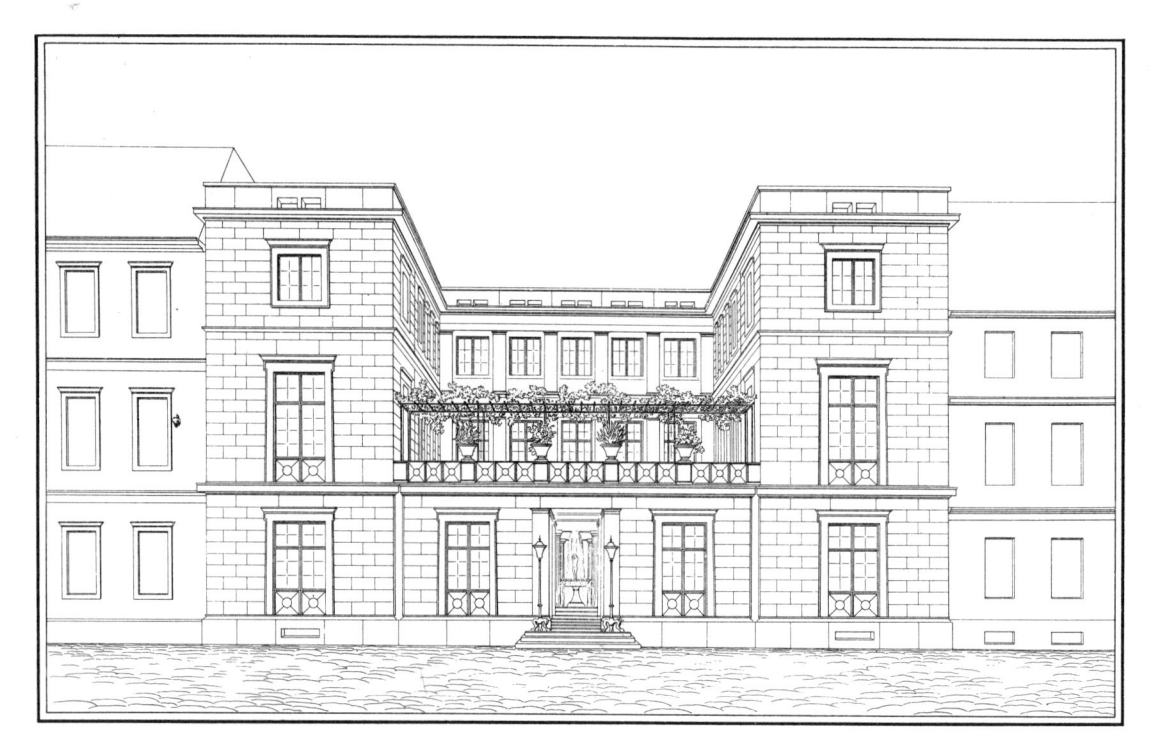

PERSPECTIVISCHE ANSICHT DES HAUSES VON DER STRASSE.

PERSPECTIVISCHE ANSICHT DES MIT EINER SÆULENLAUBE UMGEBENEN HOFS.

ENTWURF ZU EINEM STÆDTISCHEN WOHNGEBÆUDE.

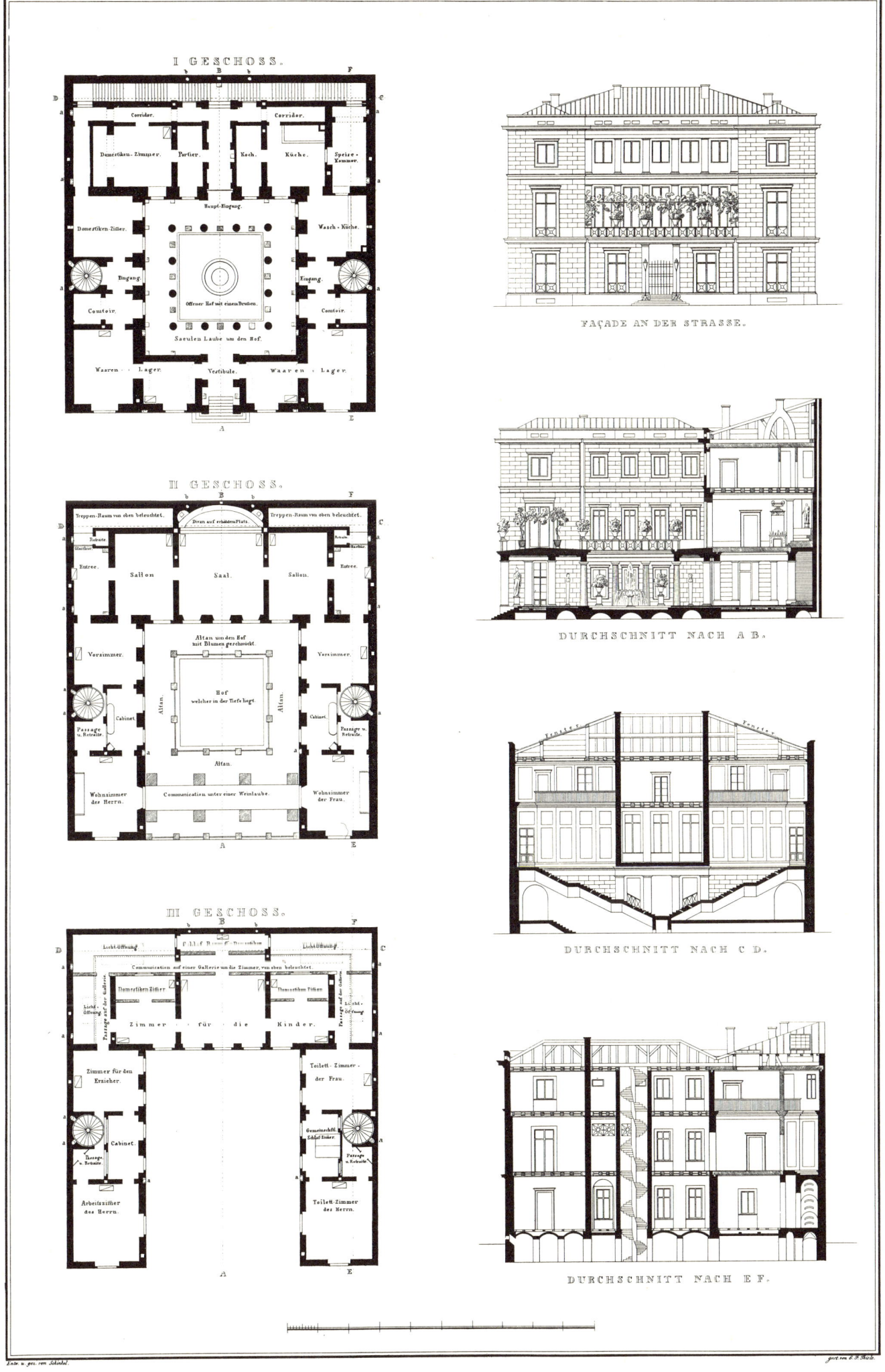

68.

I GESCHOSS.

II GESCHOSS.

III GESCHOSS.

FAÇADE AN DER STRASSE.

DURCHSCHNITT NACH A B.

DURCHSCHNITT NACH C D.

DURCHSCHNITT NACH E F.

ENTWURF ZU EINEM STÆDTISCHEN WOHNGEBÆUDE.

FAÇADE.

PERSPECTIVISCHE ANSICHT DES VESTIBULS UND DER TREPPE.

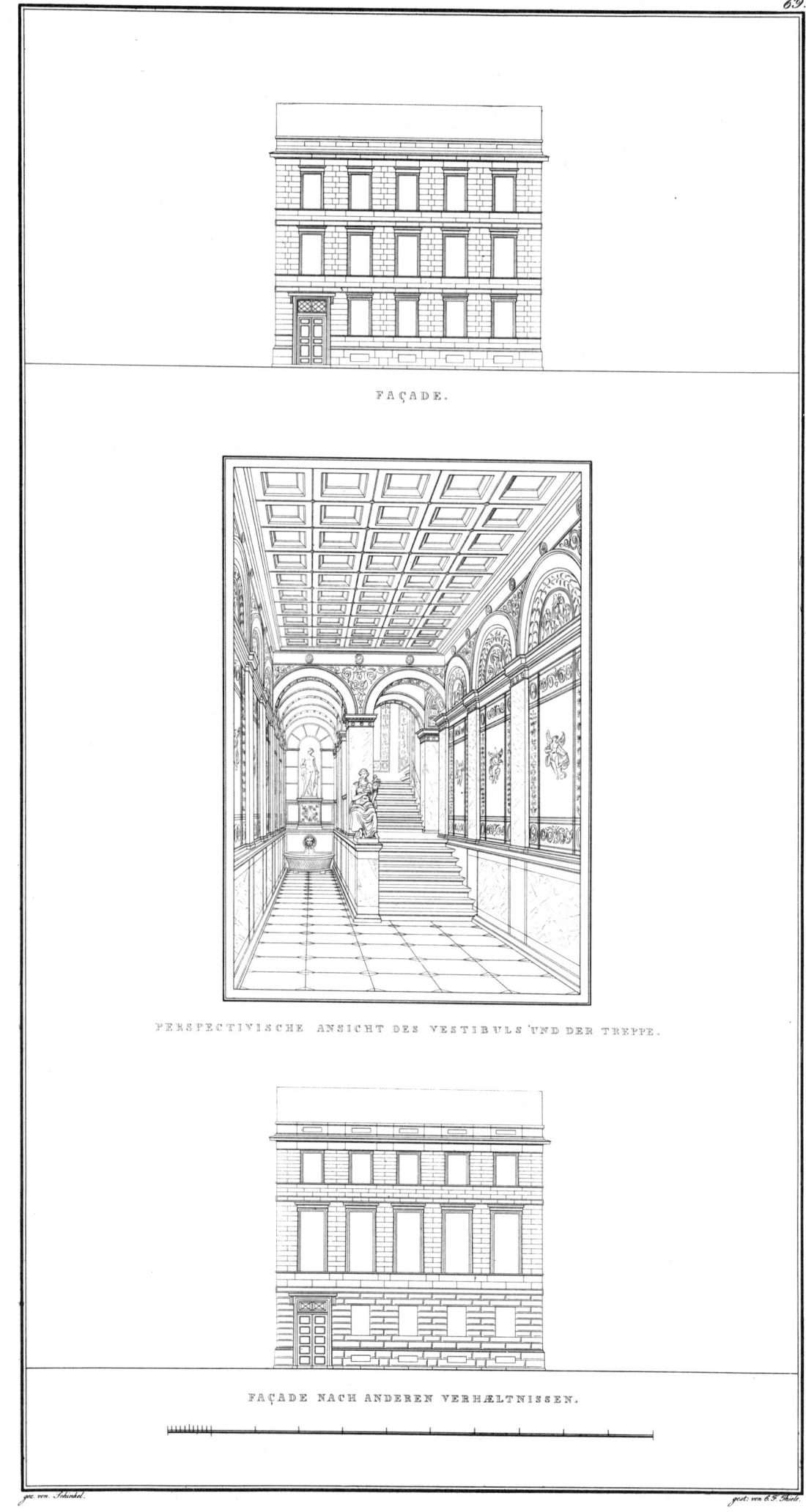

FAÇADE NACH ANDEREN VERHÆLTNISSEN.

ENTWURF ZU EINEM STÆDTISCHEN WOHNGEBÆUDE.

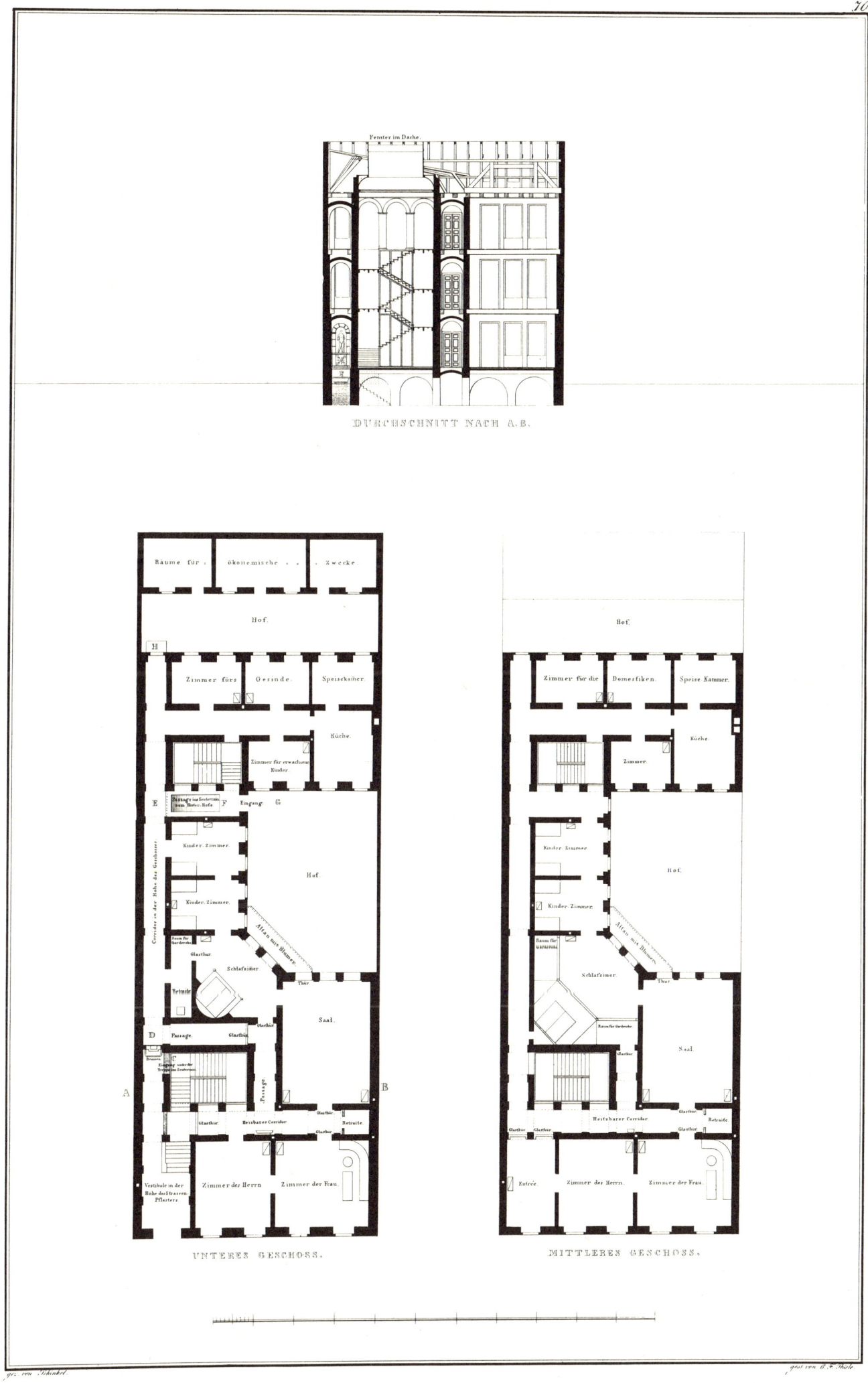

DURCHSCHNITT NACH A.B.

UNTERES GESCHOSS.

MITTLERES GESCHOSS.

ENTWURF ZU EINEM STÄDTISCHEN WOHNGEBÄUDE.

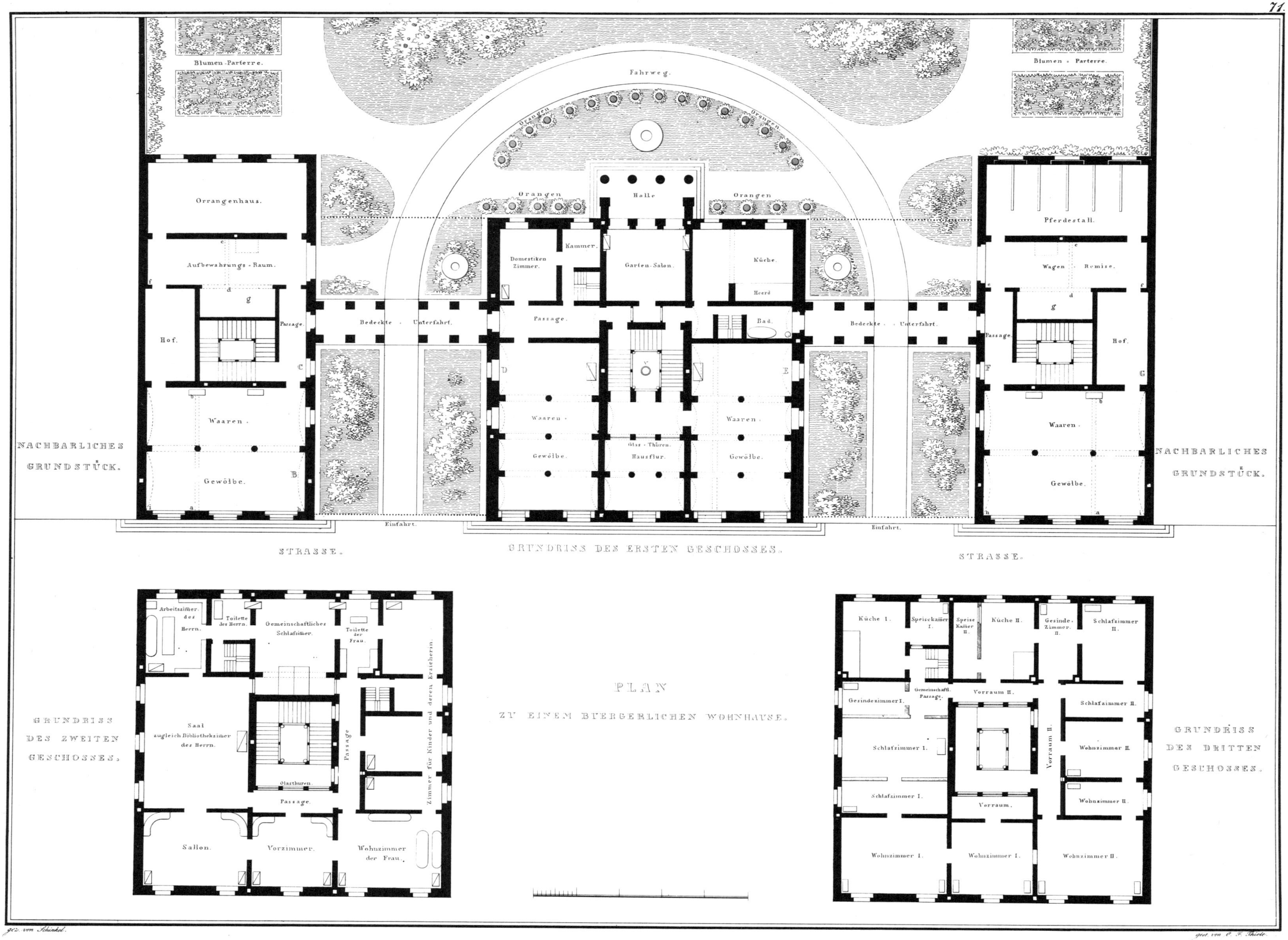

ENTWURF ZU EINEM STÆDTISCHEN WOHNGEBÆUDE.

GRUNDRISS DES ERSTEN GESCHOSSES.

GRUNDRISS DES ZWEITEN GESCHOSSES.

GRUNDRISS DES DRITTEN GESCHOSSES.

PLAN ZU EINEM BÜRGERLICHEN WOHNHAUSE.

NACHBARLICHES GRUNDSTÜCK. NEBENGEBÄUDE. EINFAHRT. FACADE DES HAUPTGEBÄUDES. EINFAHRT. NEBENGEBÄUDE. NACHBARLICHES GRUNDSTÜCK.

DURCHSCHNITT DER GANZEN ANLAGE NACH DER RICHTUNG A B C D E F G DES GRUNDRISSES.

ENTWURF ZU EINEM STÄDTISCHEN WOHNGEBÄUDE.

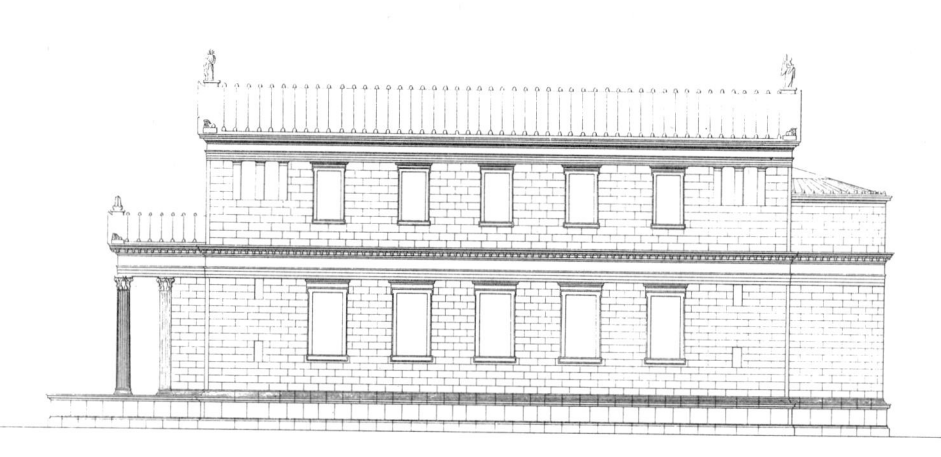

75.

SEITEN-ANSICHT.

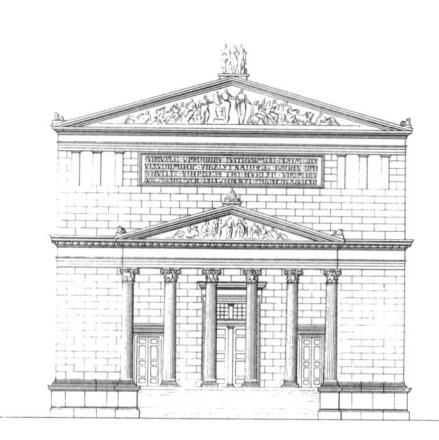

GIEBEL-ANSICHT. 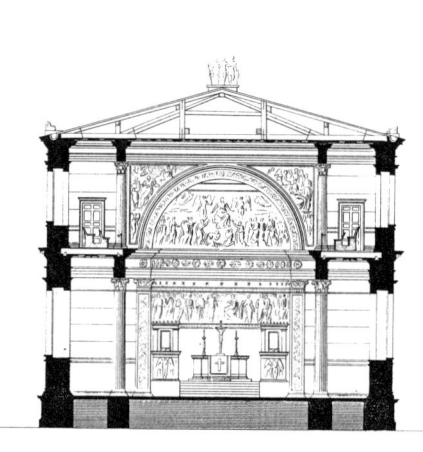   DURCHSCHNITT NACH DER RICHTUNG A.B.

GRUNDRISS.

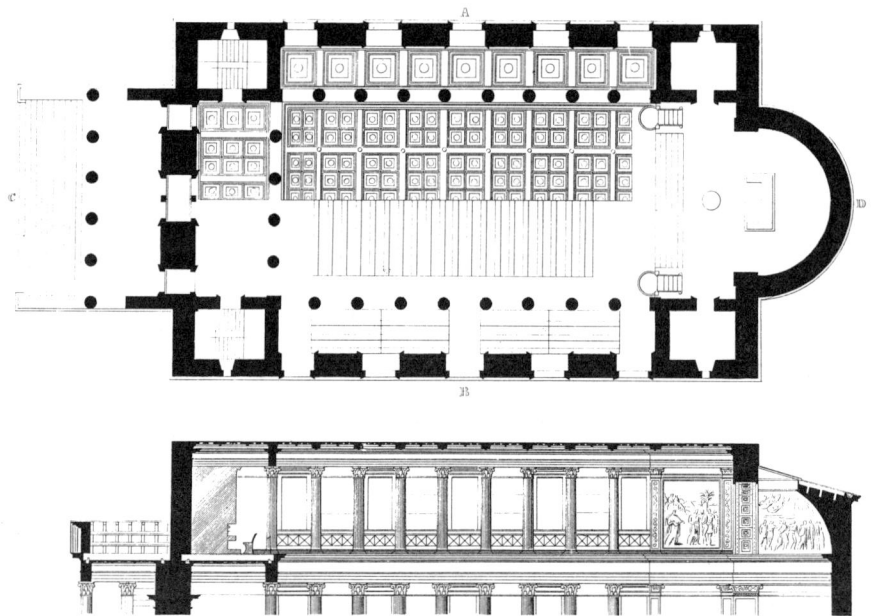

DURCHSCHNITT NACH DER RICHTUNG C.D.

ENTWURF EINER KIRCHE FÜR DEN MARKTPLATZ VON POTSDAM.

74.

ANSICHT DER KIRCHE VON DER SEITE DES EINGANGES.

ANSICHT DES ALTAR-TISCHES.　　ANSICHT DER KANZEL.　　SEITEN-ANSICHT DES ALTAR-TISCHES.

ENTWURF EINER KLEINEN KIRCHE VON QUADRATISCHER FORM DES GRUNDRISSES.

DURCHSCHNITT NACH DER RICHTUNG EF.

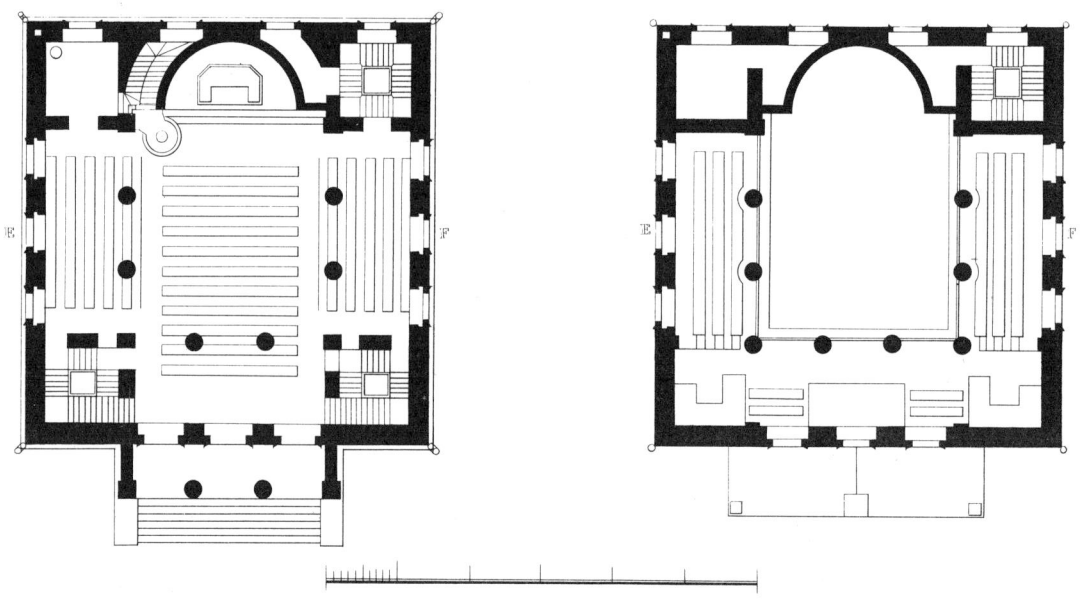

GRUNDRISS IN DER HOEHE A.B.   GRUNDRISS IN DER HOEHE C.D.

ENTWURF EINER KLEINEN KIRCHE VON QUADRATISCHER FORM DES GRUNDRISSES.
No 2.

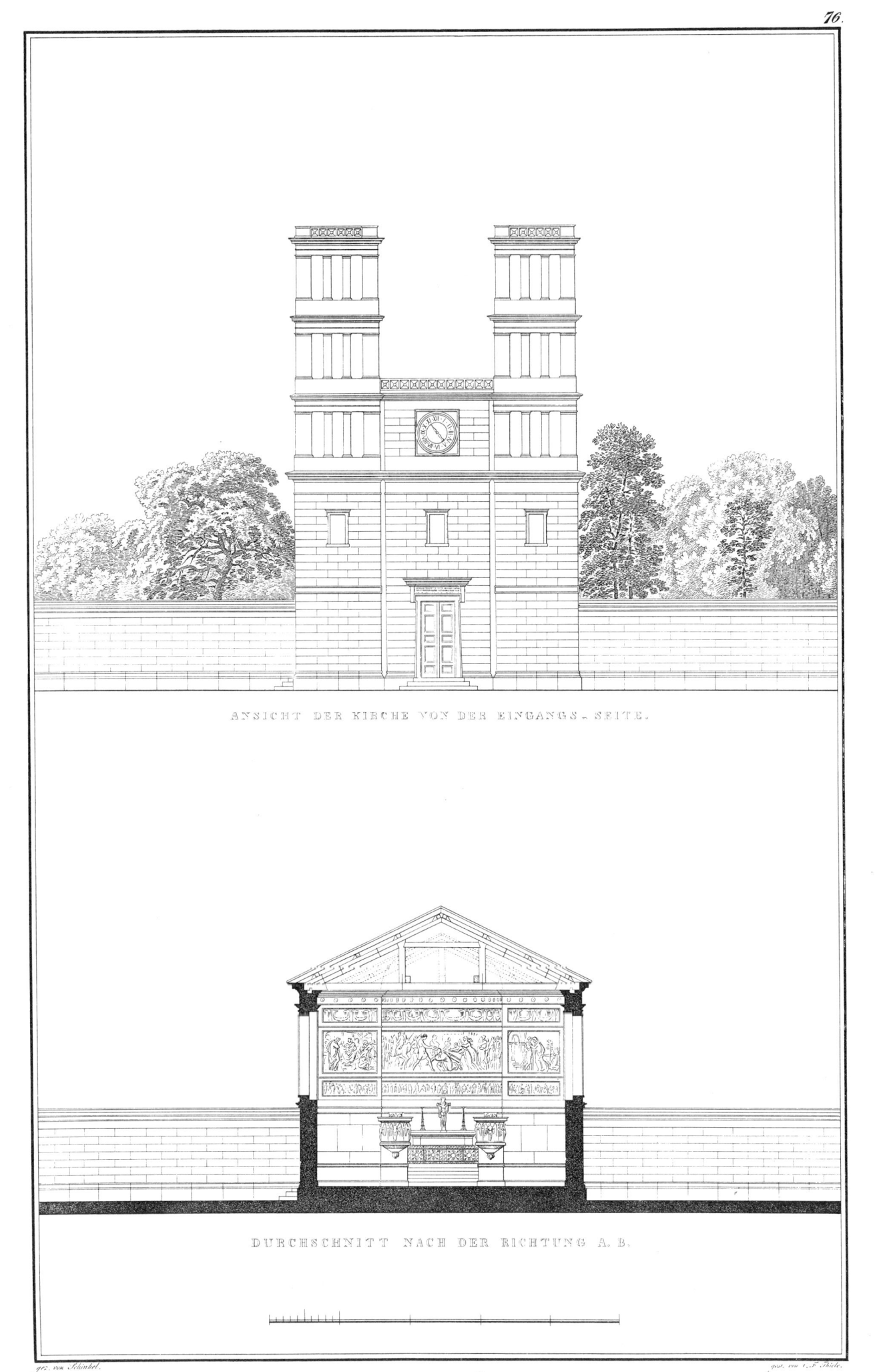

76.

ANSICHT DER KIRCHE VON DER EINGANGS-SEITE.

DURCHSCHNITT NACH DER RICHTUNG A. B.

ENTWURF EINER KLEINEN KIRCHE FÜR DEN KREIS VON MALMEDI.

No. 1.

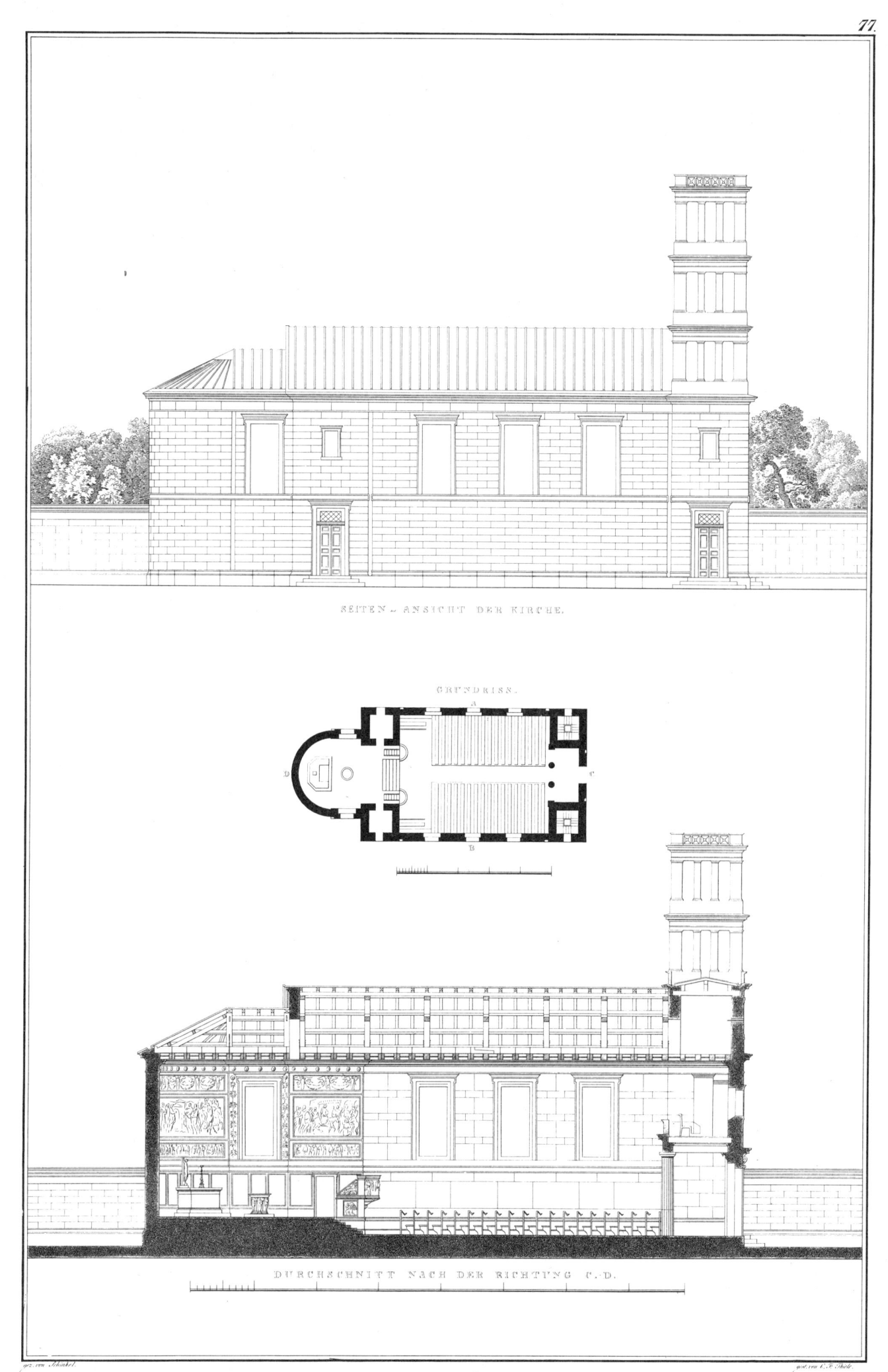

SEITEN-ANSICHT DER KIRCHE.

GRUNDRISS.

DURCHSCHNITT NACH DER RICHTUNG C-D.

ENTWURF EINER KLEINEN KIRCHE FÜR DEN KREIS VON MALMEDI.
N° 2.

ANSICHT DER HINTERSEITE.   SEITEN-ANSICHT.   ANSICHT DER THURMSEITE.

EIN STÜCK DER DECKE.

DURCHSCHNITT NACH DER RICHTUNG A B.   A. GRUNDRISS.   DURCHSCHNITT NACH C D.
DURCHSCHNITT NACH DER RICHTUNG E F.   DURCHSCHNITT NACH DER RICHTUNG A B.
                                                                GEGEN DEN EINGANG GESEHEN.

ENTWURF EINER KLEINEN KIRCHE MIT EINEM THURM.

gez. von Schinkel.   gest. von E. F. Thiele.

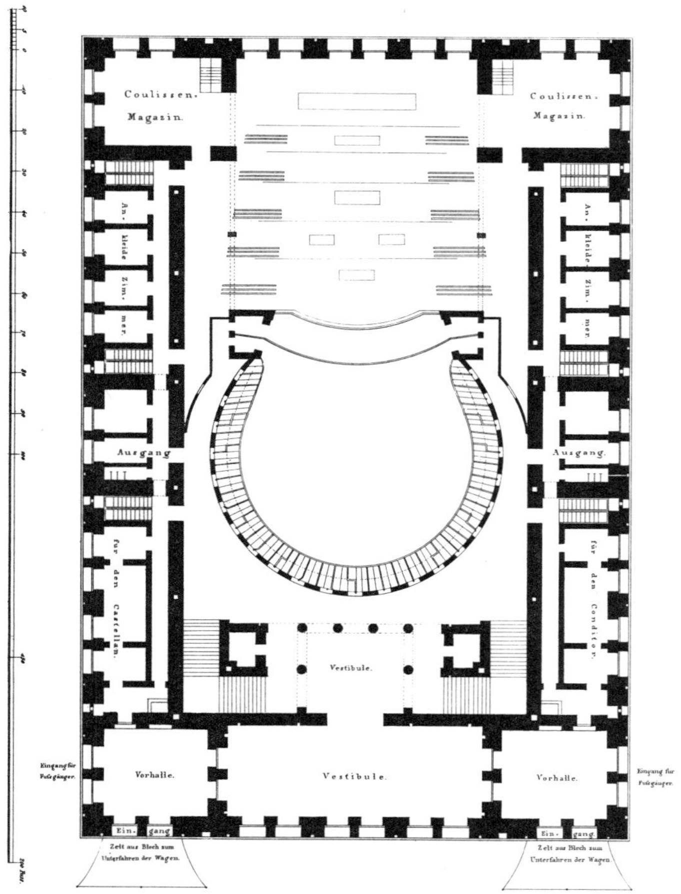

GRUNDRISS C.

GRUNDRISS B.

Garde-robe. Ankleide-Zimmer.
Saalen
Foyer
Foyer
Saalen
Garde-robe. Ankleide-Zimmer.

GRUNDRISS A.

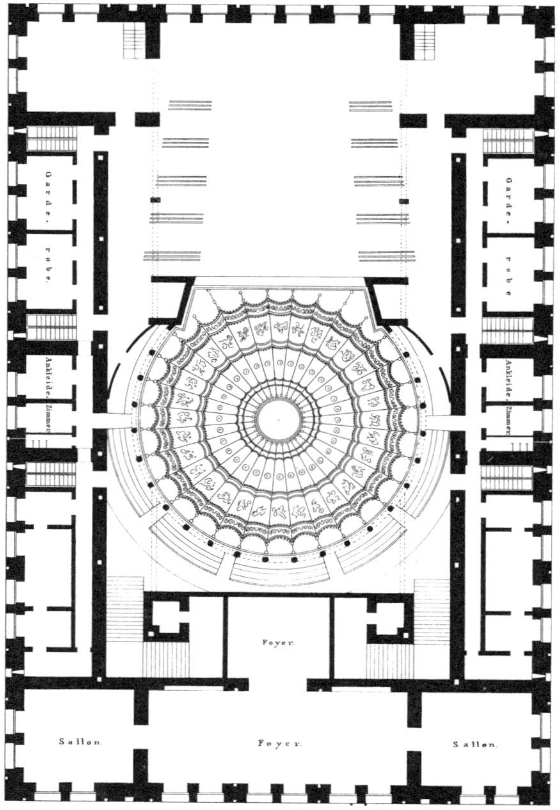

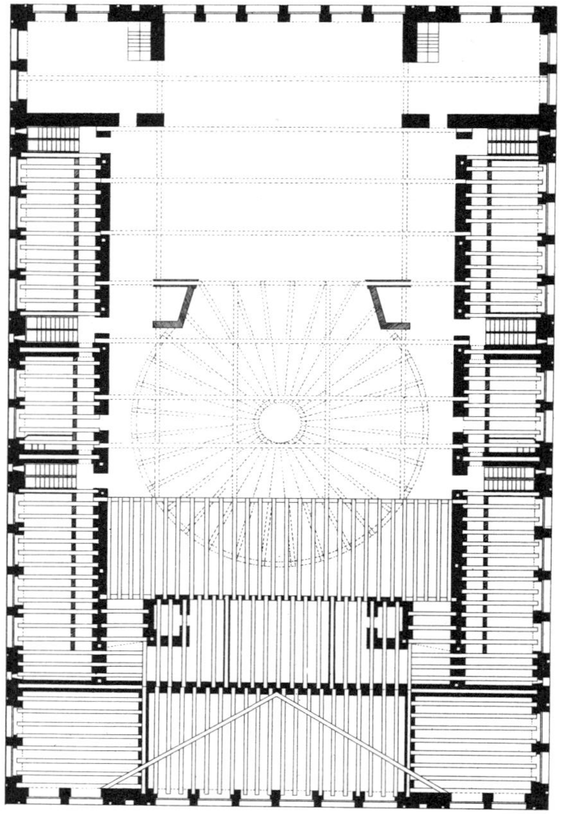

Coulissen-Magazin. An-kleide Zim-mer. Ausgang für den Conditor. Vorhalle.
Vestibule.
Vestibule.
Coulissen-Magazin. An-kleide Zim-mer. Ausgang für den Castellan. Vorhalle.

GRUNDRISSE DES THEATERS IN HAMBURG. N° 1.

AUFRISS DER EINGANGS-SEITE DES THEATERS IN HAMBURG.
N° 2.

ARCHITECTUR DER FAÇADE NACH GROESSEREM MAASSTABE
DES THEATERS IN HAMBURG.
N° 3.

LÆNGEN-FAÇADE DES THEATERS.

Construction des Daches über dem Malersaal.

DURCHSCHNITT NACH DER RICHTUNG A.B. DES GRUNDRISSES.

Partie X des Vestibüls in grösserem Maassstabe.

DURCHSCHNITT NACH DER RICHTUNG C.D. DES GRUNDRISSES.

DURCHSCHNITTE DES THEATERS IN HAMBURG.
Nº 4.

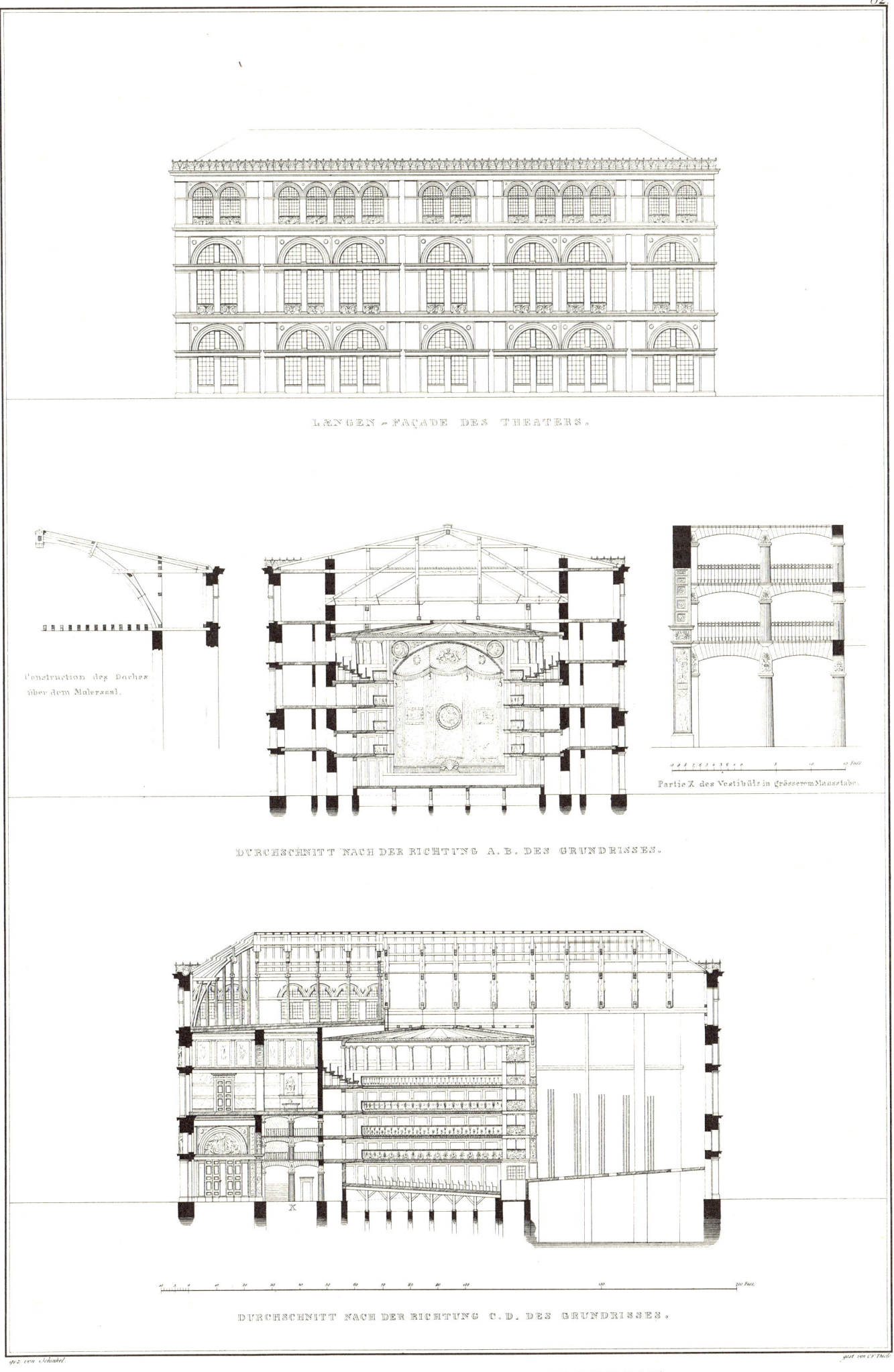

ANSICHT DES PROSCENIUM, DER DARANSTOSSENDEN LOGEN UND DIE PERSPECTIVISCHE ANSICHT DES THEATERS ALS SCENENBILD.

aa Breite des Proscenium. bb Logen zunächst dem Proscenium. cc Logen im runden Raume.

N°. 5.

FAÇADE.

DURCHSCHNITT NACH DER RICHTUNG C. D.

GRUNDRISS.

STRASSE.

Nachbar — Vestibule — Vorzimmer — Cabinet — Cabinet — Hof — Billard — Speisesaal — Hof — Zimmer — Zimmer — Hof — Speisezimmer — Hof — Tanzsaal — Tribune für Musiker — Hof — Sallon — Hof — Zimmer der Damen — Cabinet — Zimmer — Sallon — Nachbar — Hof

DURCHSCHNITT NACH DER RICHTUNG A. B.

DAS CASINO IN POTSDAM.

PERSPECTIVISCHE AYSICHT DES AEUSSEREN DER KIRCHE AUF DEM WERDERSCHEN MARKT IN BERLIN.

FAÇADE DER THÜRME.

GRUNDRISS.

KIRCHE AUF DEM WERDERSCHEN MARKT IN BERLIN.

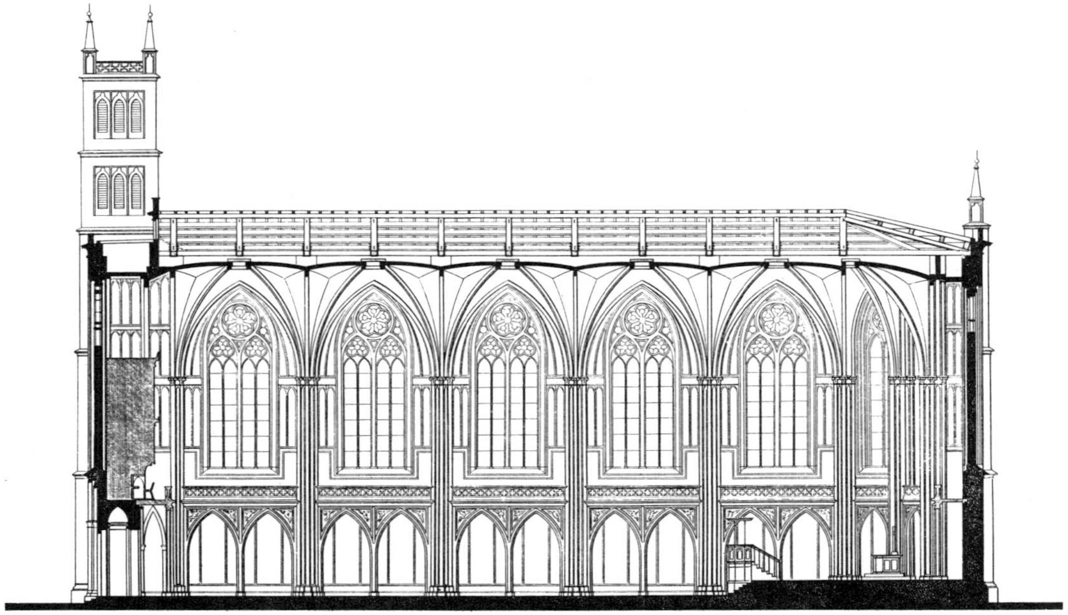

LÄNGEN-DURCHSCHNITT NACH DER LINIE A-B.

DURCHSCHNITT NACH DER LINIE C-D MIT DER ANSICHT EINER WAND WODURCH DAS GEBÄUDE IN ZWEI KIRCHEN ABGETHEILT IST.

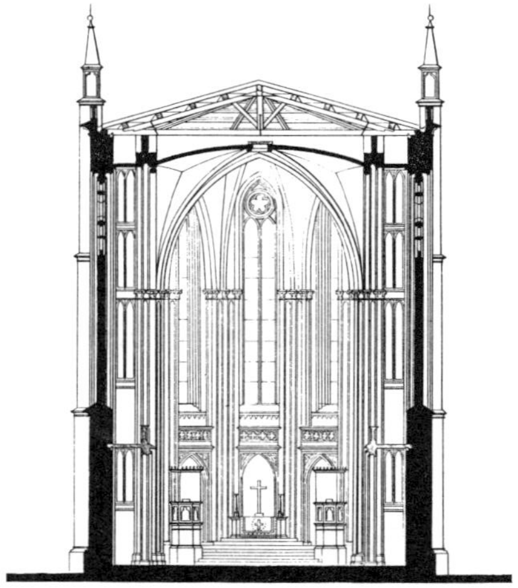

DURCHSCHNITT NACH DER LINIE C-D GEGEN DEN ALTAR GESEHEN.

DURCHSCHNITT NACH DER LINIE C-D GEGEN DEN EINGANG GESEHEN.

KIRCHE AUF DEM WERDERSCHEN MARKT IN BERLIN.

PERSPECTIVISCHE ANSICHT DES INNEREN DER KIRCHE AUF DEM WERDERSCHEN MARKT IN BERLIN.

PORTAL DER KIRCHE AUF DEM WERDERSCHEN MARKT IN BERLIN.

FENSTER ZWISCHEN DEN THÜRMEN. FENSTER AN DER ALTARNISCHE.

FENSTER DER KIRCHE AUF DEM WERDERSCHEN MARKT IN BERLIN.

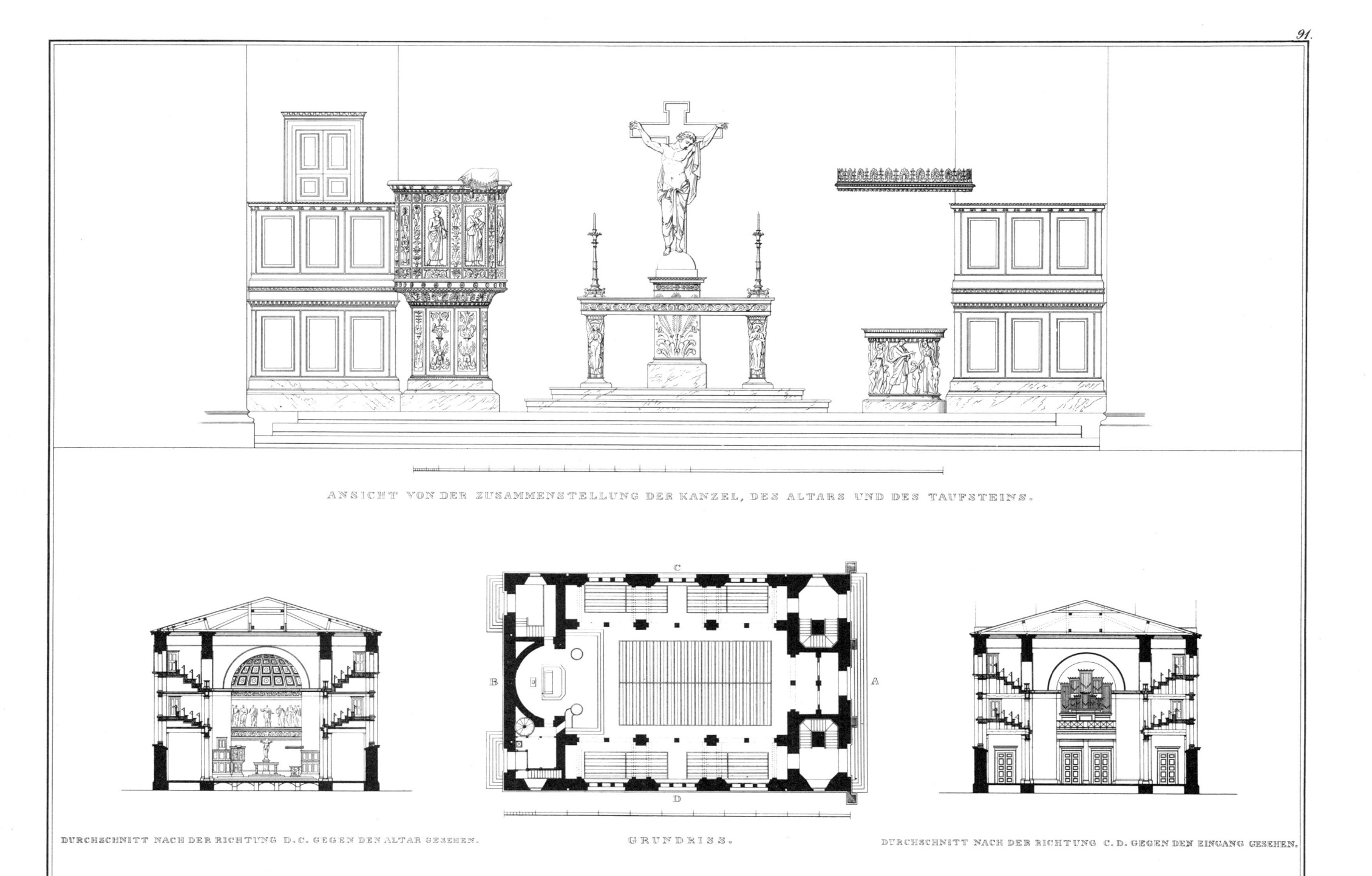

DURCHSCHNITT NACH DER RICHTUNG D.C. GEGEN DEN ALTAR GESEHEN.   ANSICHT VON DER ZUSAMMENSTELLUNG DER KANZEL, DES ALTARS UND DES TAUFSTEINS.

GRUNDRISS.   DURCHSCHNITT NACH DER RICHTUNG C.D. GEGEN DEN EINGANG GESEHEN.

KIRCHE ZU STRAUPITZ IN DER LAUSITZ.

gez. von Schinkel.   gest. von C. F. Thiele.

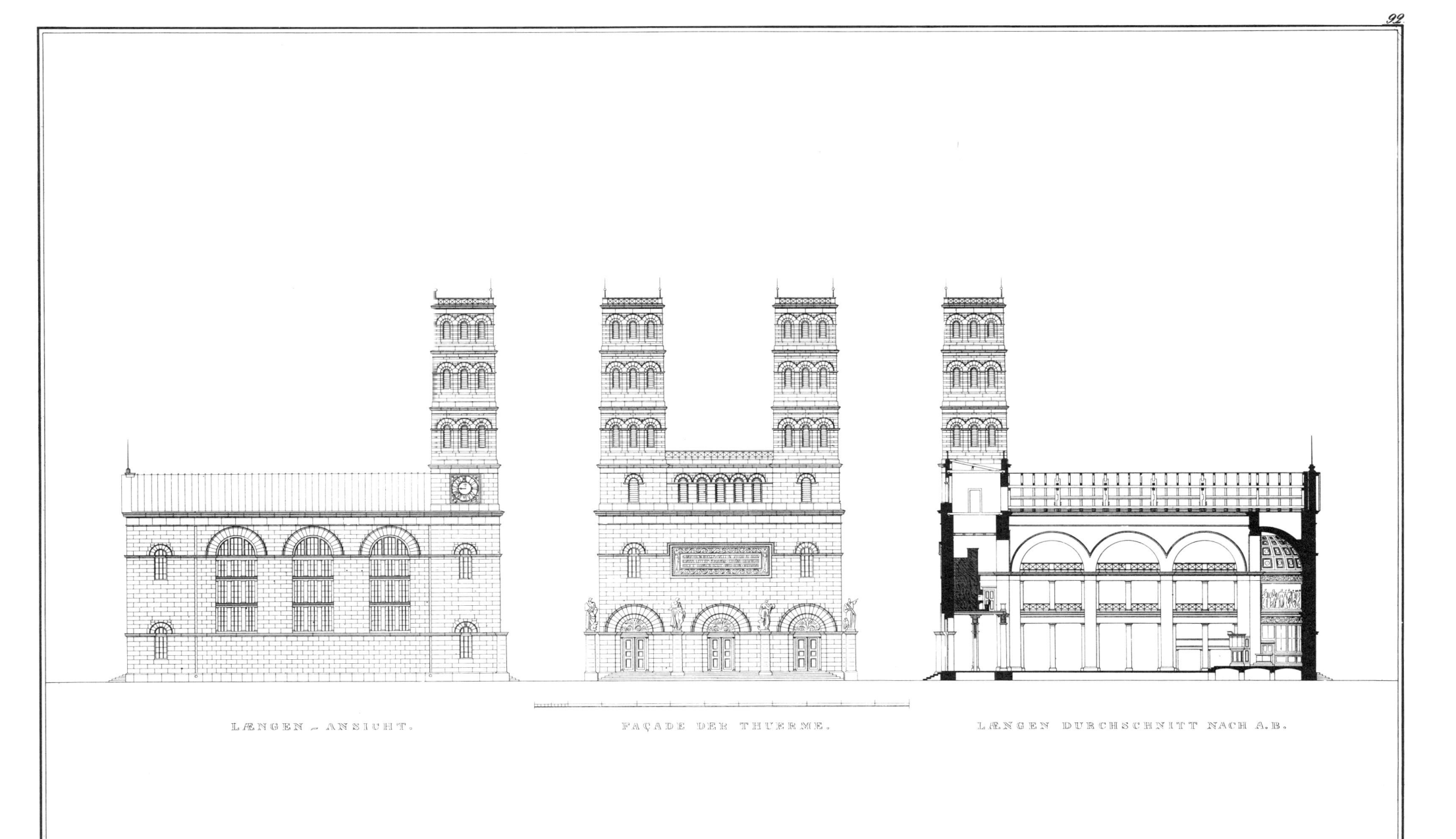

LÆNGEN-ANSICHT. FAÇADE DER THUERME. LÆNGEN DURCHSCHNITT NACH A.B.

KIRCHE ZU STRAUPITZ IN DER LAUSITZ.

DURCHSCHNITT NACH DER RICHTUNG A.B.

GIEBEL-SEITE MIT DEN EINGÄNGEN.

ENTWURF ZU EINER KIRCHE IN DER ORANIENBURGER-VORSTADT BEI BERLIN.
Nº 1.

LANGE-SEITE.

DURCHSCHNITT NACH DER RICHTUNG C. D.

ENTWURF ZU EINER KIRCHE IN DER ORANIENBURGER-VORSTADT BEI BERLIN.
N°1.

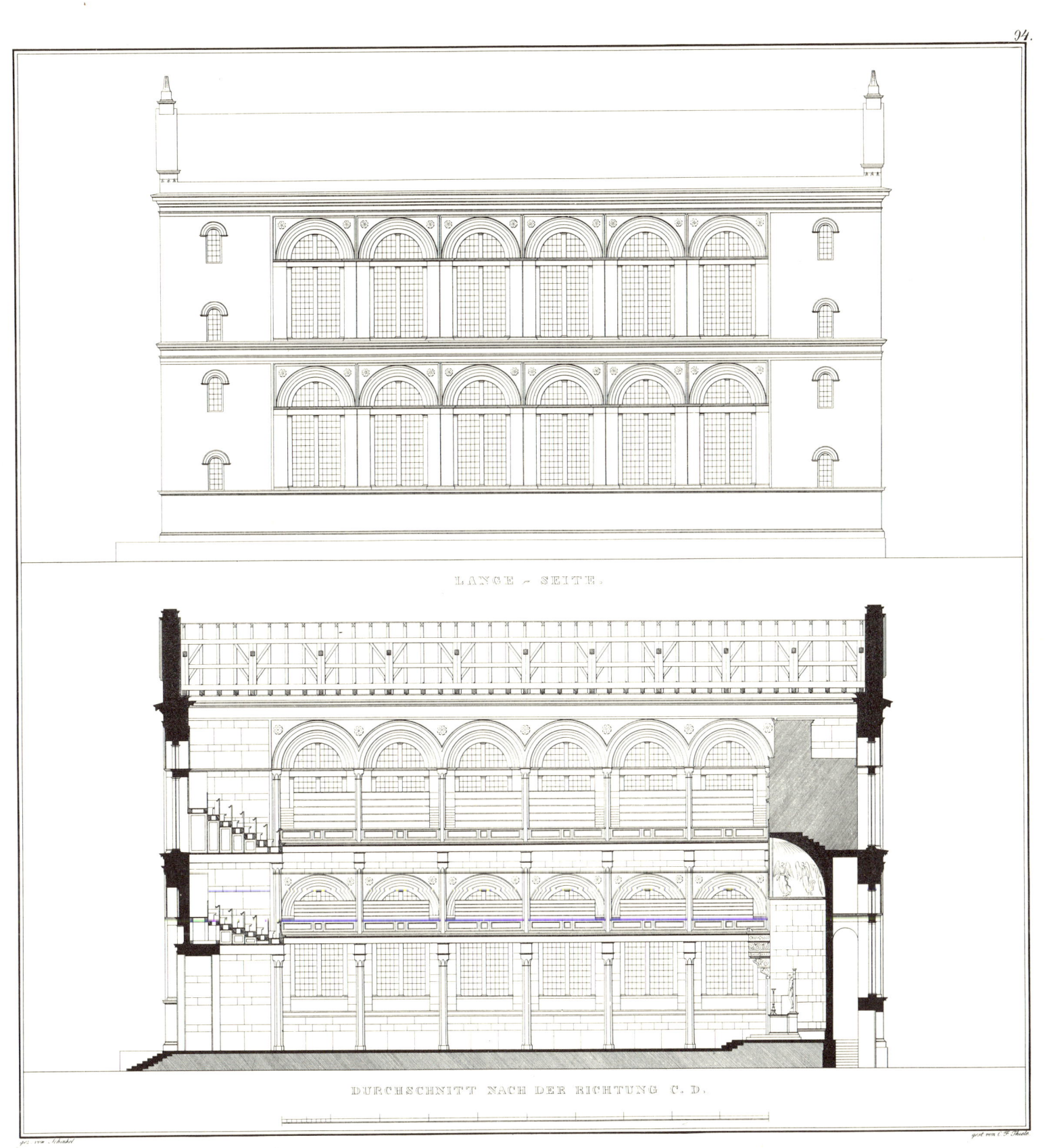

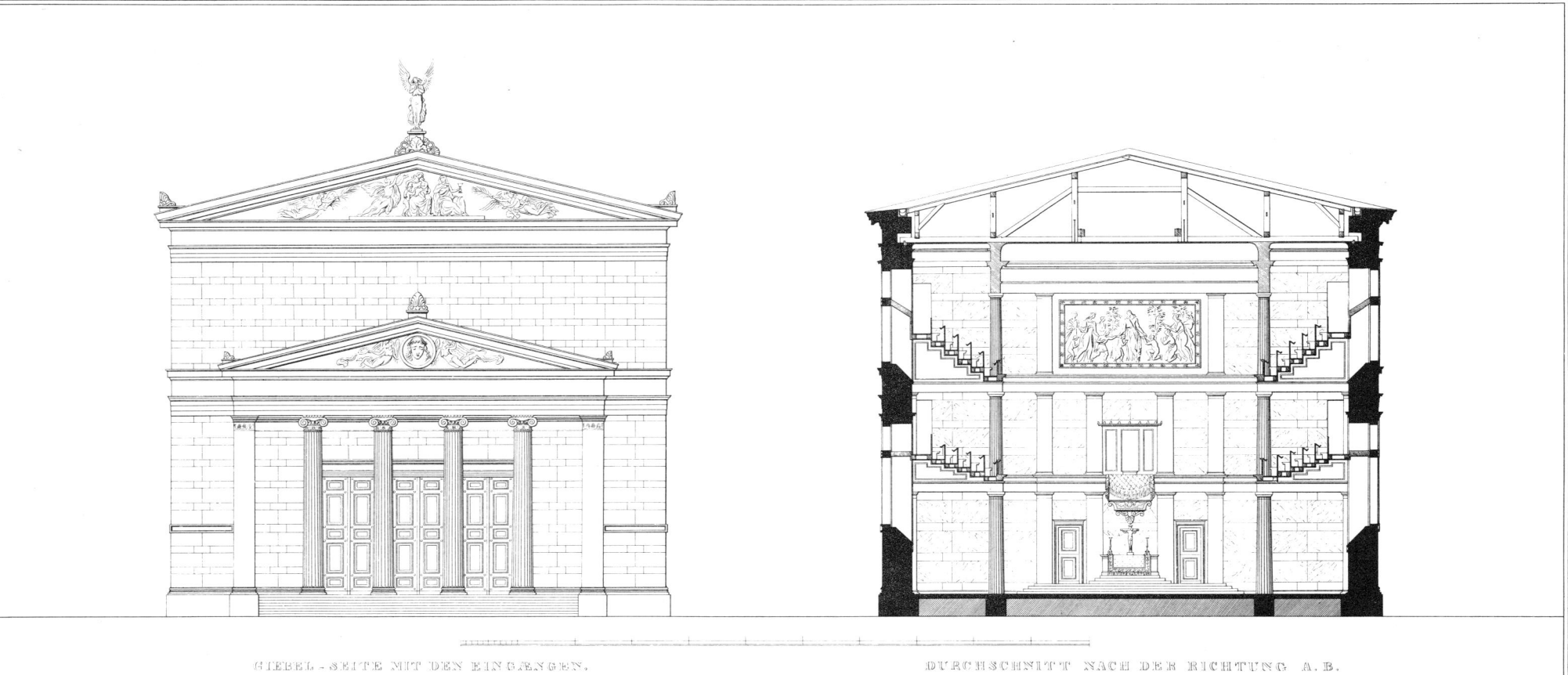

DURCHSCHNITT NACH DER RICHTUNG A. B.

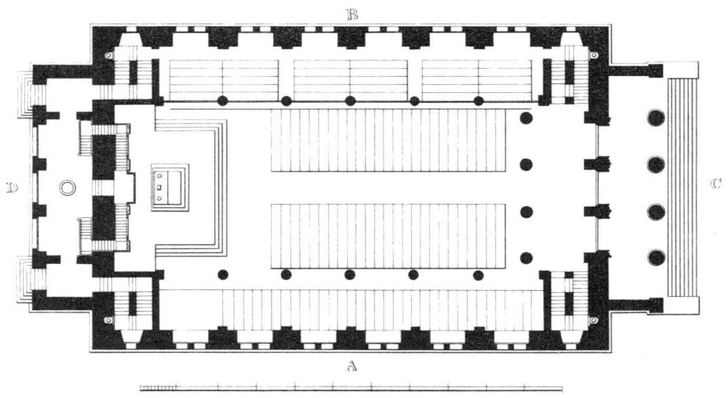

GIEBEL-SEITE MIT DEN EINGÄNGEN.

ENTWURF ZU EINER KIRCHE IN DER ORANIENBURGER VORSTADT BEI BERLIN.

LANGE-SEITE.

DURCHSCHNITT NACH DER RICHTUNG C. D.

ENTWURF ZU EINER KIRCHE IN DER ORANIENBURGER VORSTADT BEI BERLIN.
N° II.

PERSPECTIVISCHE ANSICHT.

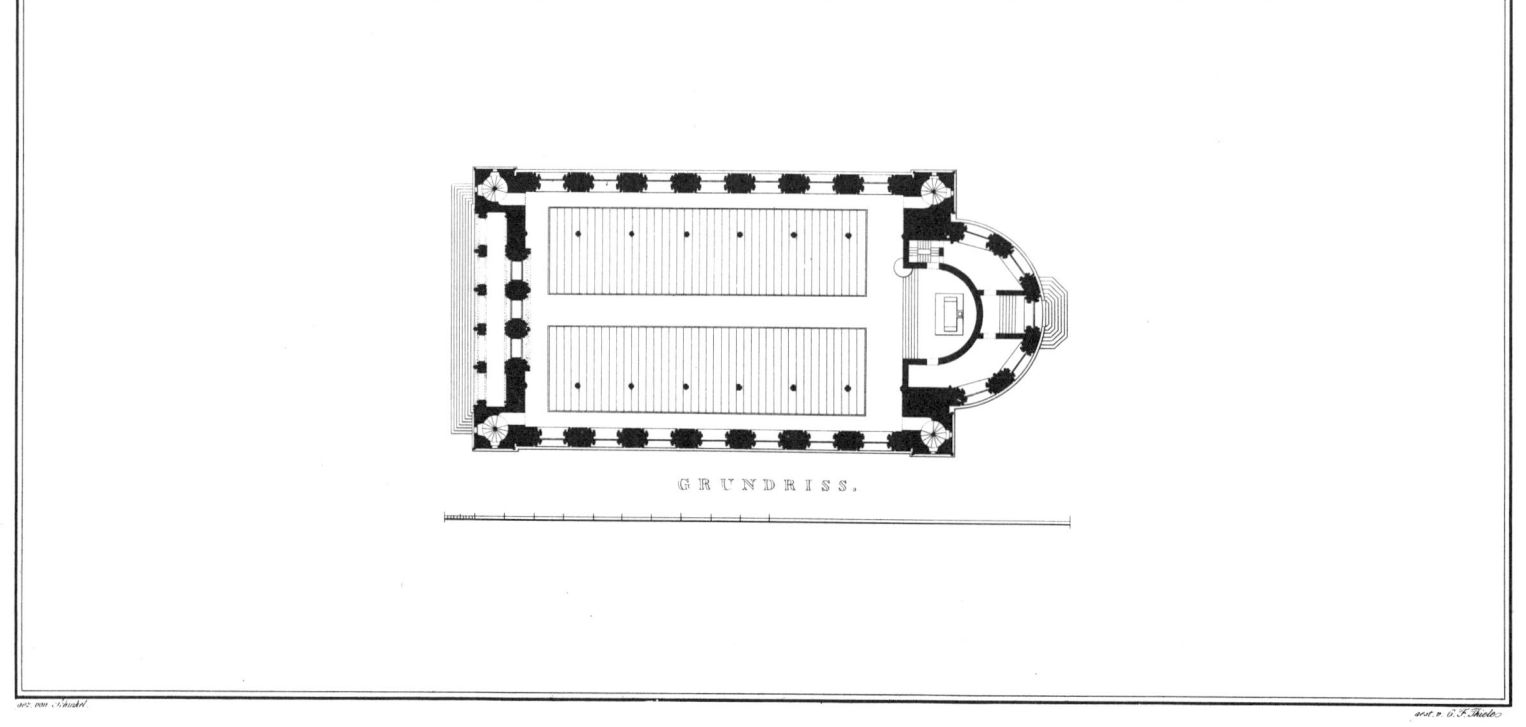

GRUNDRISS.

KIRCHE IN DER ORANIENBURGER VORSTADT BEI BERLIN. NACH DEM ENTWURF N° III.

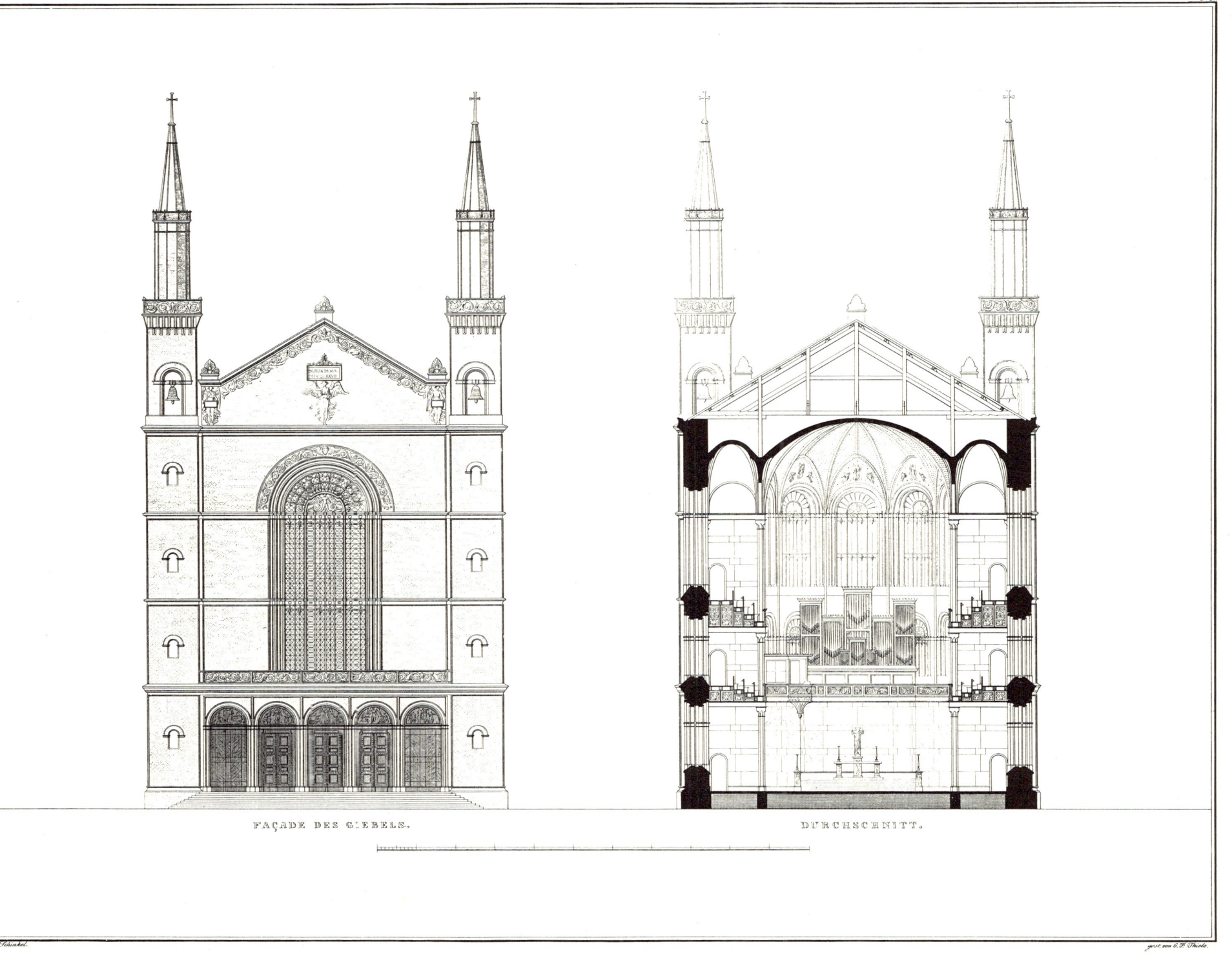

FAÇADE DES GIEBELS. DURCHSCHNITT.

KIRCHE IN DER ORANIENBURGER VORSTADT BEI BERLIN, NACH DEM ENTWURF Nº III.

LÆNGEN-DURCHSCHNITT.

STUECK DER SEITEN-FAÇADE.

KIRCHE IN DER ORANIENBURGER VORSTADT BEI BERLIN, NACH DEM ENTWURF No III.

ANSICHT DER KIRCHE IN DER ORANIENBURGER VORSTADT BEI BERLIN. NACH DEM ENTWURF N° IV.

DURCHSCHNITT DER KIRCHE IN DER ORANIENBURGER VORSTADT BEI BERLIN. NACH DEM ENTWURF Nº IV.

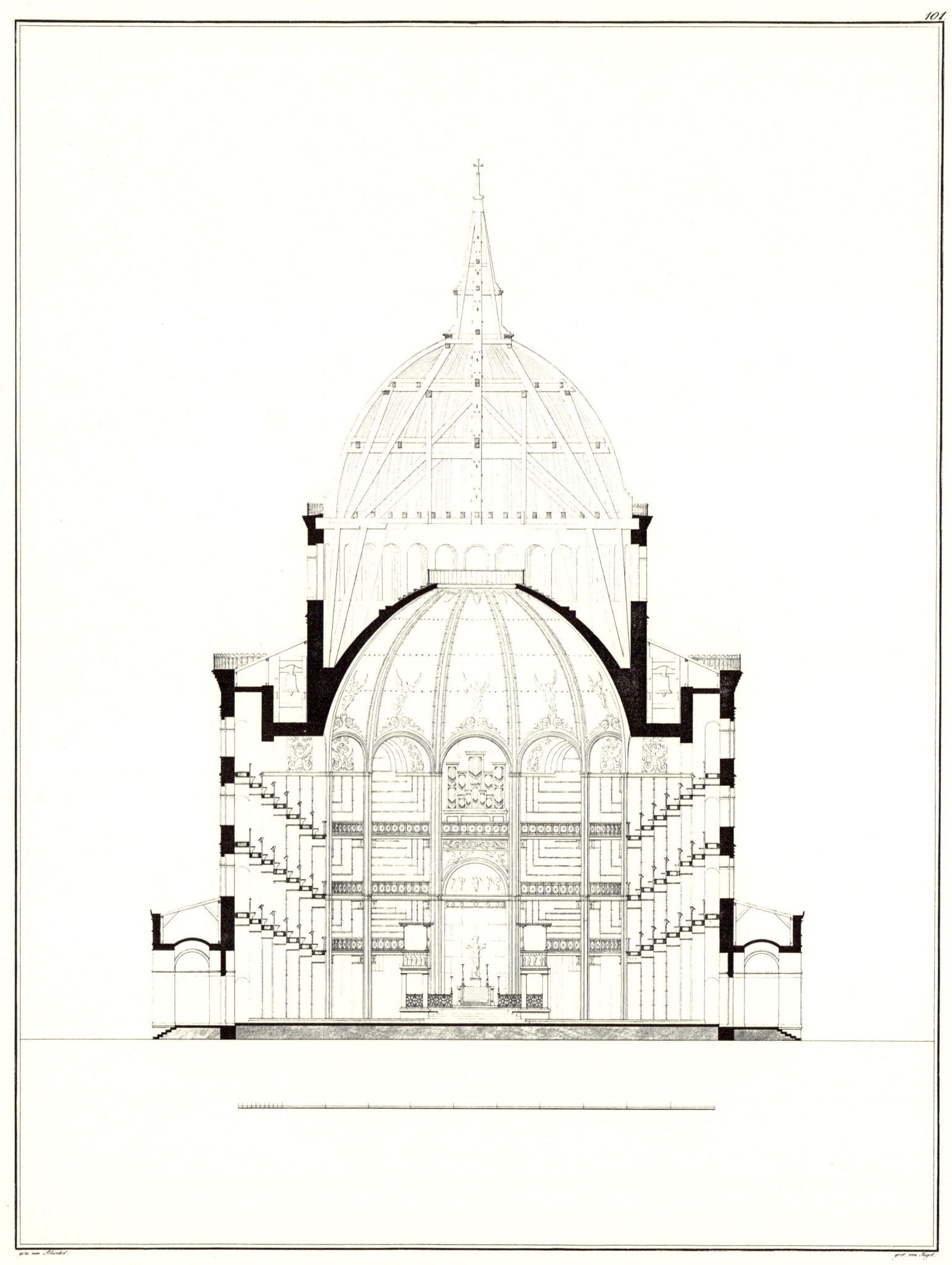

102.

GESIMSS UND ORNAMENTE
AN DER ORGEL.

GESIMSS AM PORTAL.

GESIMSS DER KIRCHE.

KANZEL. ALTAR. KANZEL. PORTAL.

GRUNDRISS.

KIRCHE IN DER ORANIENBURGER VORSTADT BEI BERLIN. NACH DEM ENTWURF N° IV.

PERSPECTIVISCHE ANSICHT DES ENTWURFS No V. EINER KIRCHE IN DER ORANIENBURGER VORSTADT BEI BERLIN.

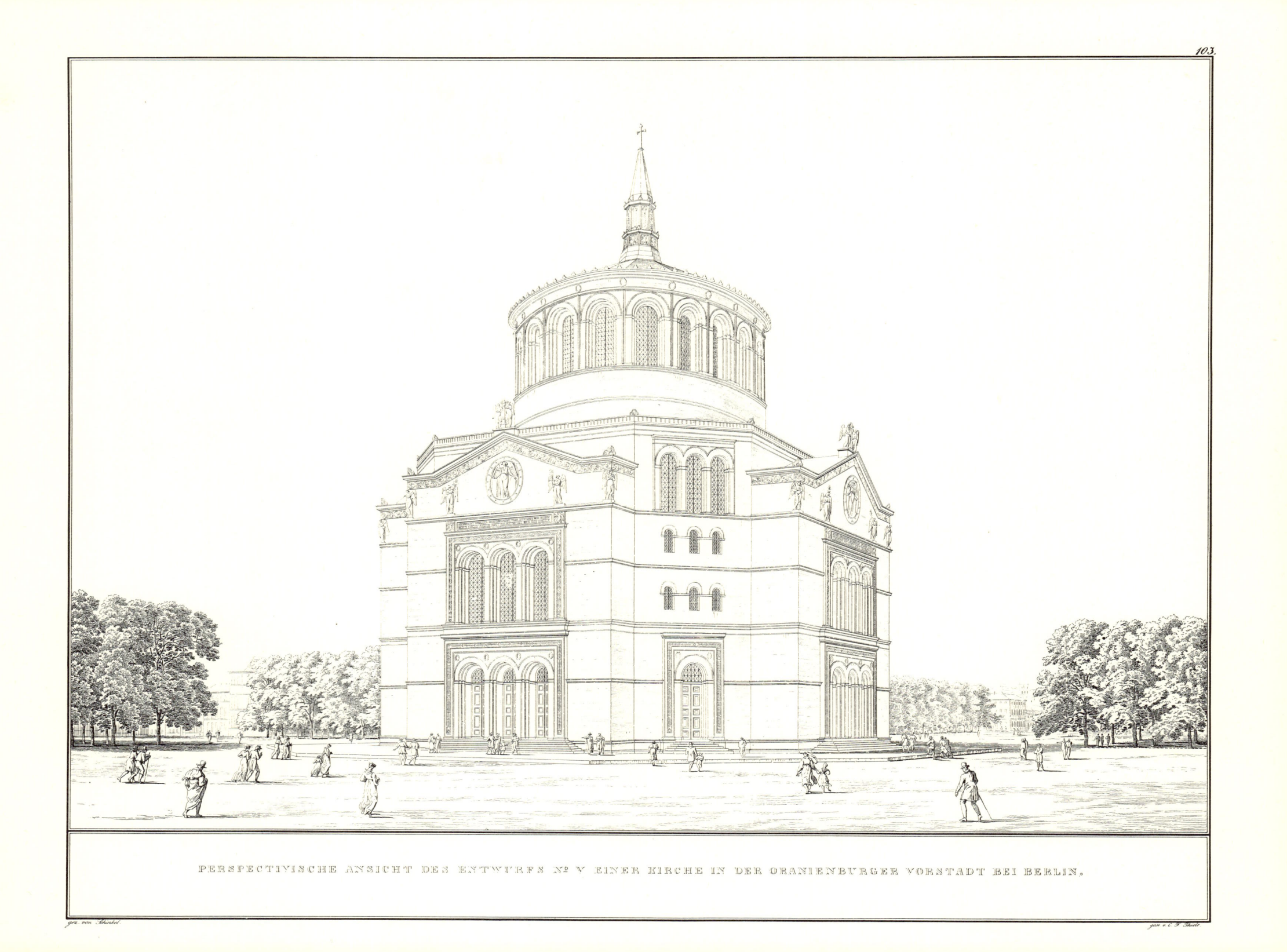

ANSICHT DER KIRCHE IN DER ORANIENBURGER VORSTADT BEI BERLIN, NACH DEM ENTWURF N° V.

DURCHSCHNITT DER KIRCHE IN DER ORANIENBURGER-VORSTADT BEI BERLIN. NACH DEM ENTWURF N° V.

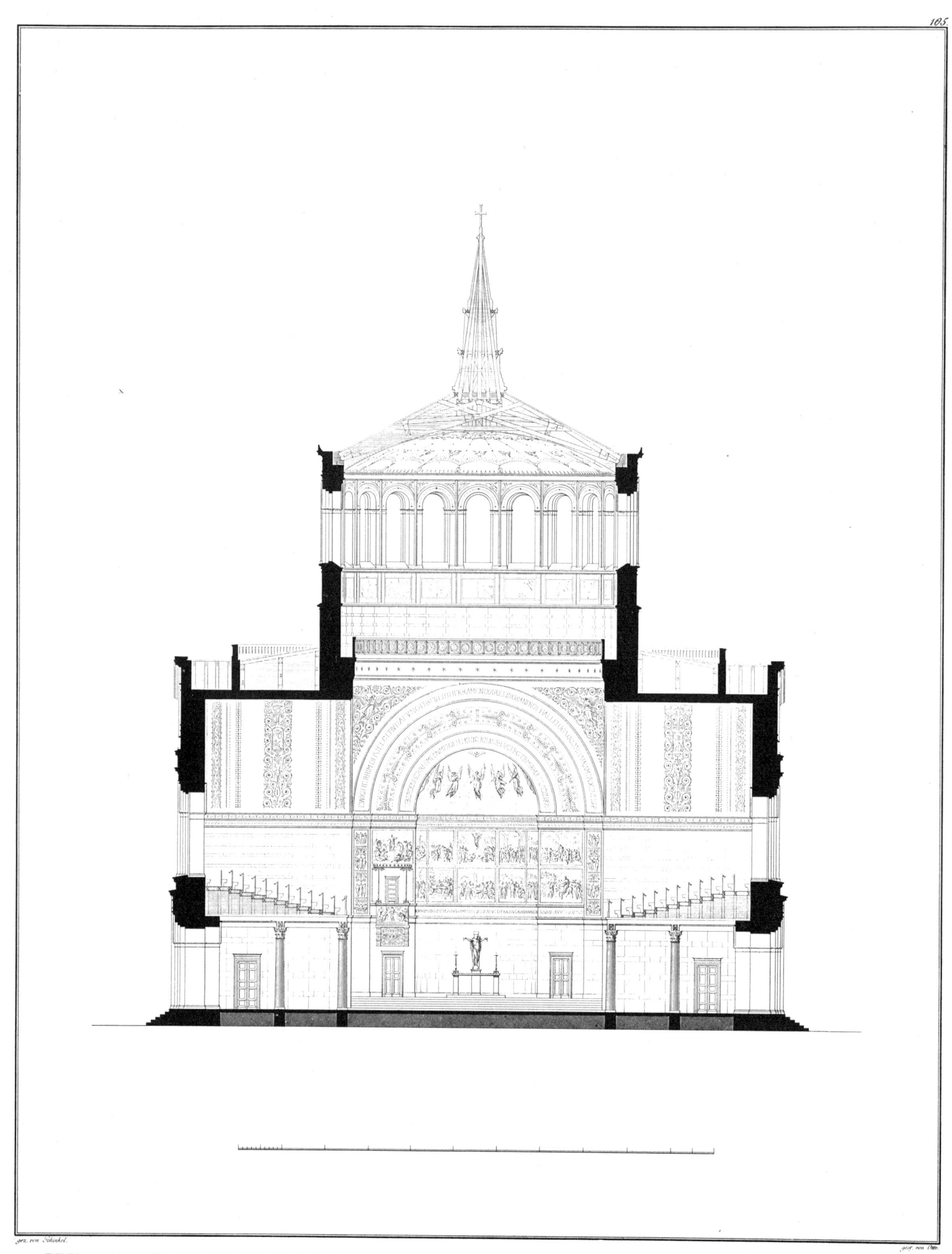

KROENUNG DES GIEBELS.

ECKVERZIERUNG NEBEN DEM GIEBEL.

SEITEN ANSICHT DER KANZEL.

KANZEL.

FENSTER UEBER DEM PORTAL.

GRUNDRISS.

PORTAL DER KIRCHE.

KIRCHE IN DER ORANIENBURGER VORSTADT BEI BERLIN. NACH DEM ENTWURF Nº V.

PERSPECTIVISCHE ANSICHT.

GESELLSCHAFTSHAUS IM FRIEDRICH WILHELMS-GARTEN BEI MAGDEBURG.

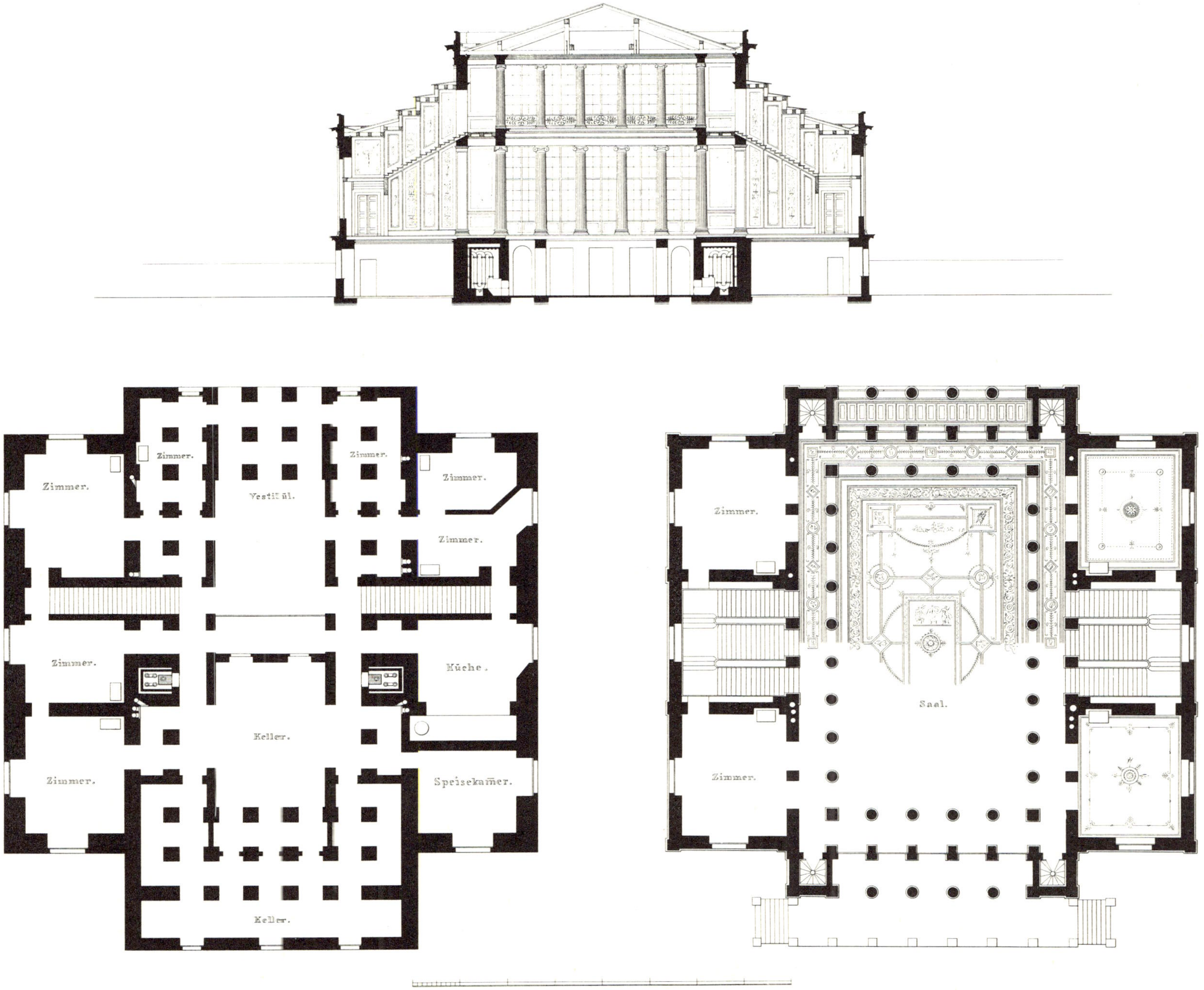

GRUNDRISSE UND DURCHSCHNITT DES GESELLSCHAFTSHAUSES IM FRIEDRICH WILHELMS-GARTEN BEI MAGDEBURG.

SITUATIONS PLAN VON CHARLOTTENHOF MIT DEN GRUNDRISSEN DER GEBAEUDE.

ANSICHT DES SCHORNSTEINS DER DAMPFMASCHINE. ANSICHT DER HALBRUNDEN BANK AUF DER TERRASSE VON CHARLOTTENHOF. SEITENANSICHT DES GEBÄUDES DER DAMPFMASCHINE.

CHARLOTTENHOF.

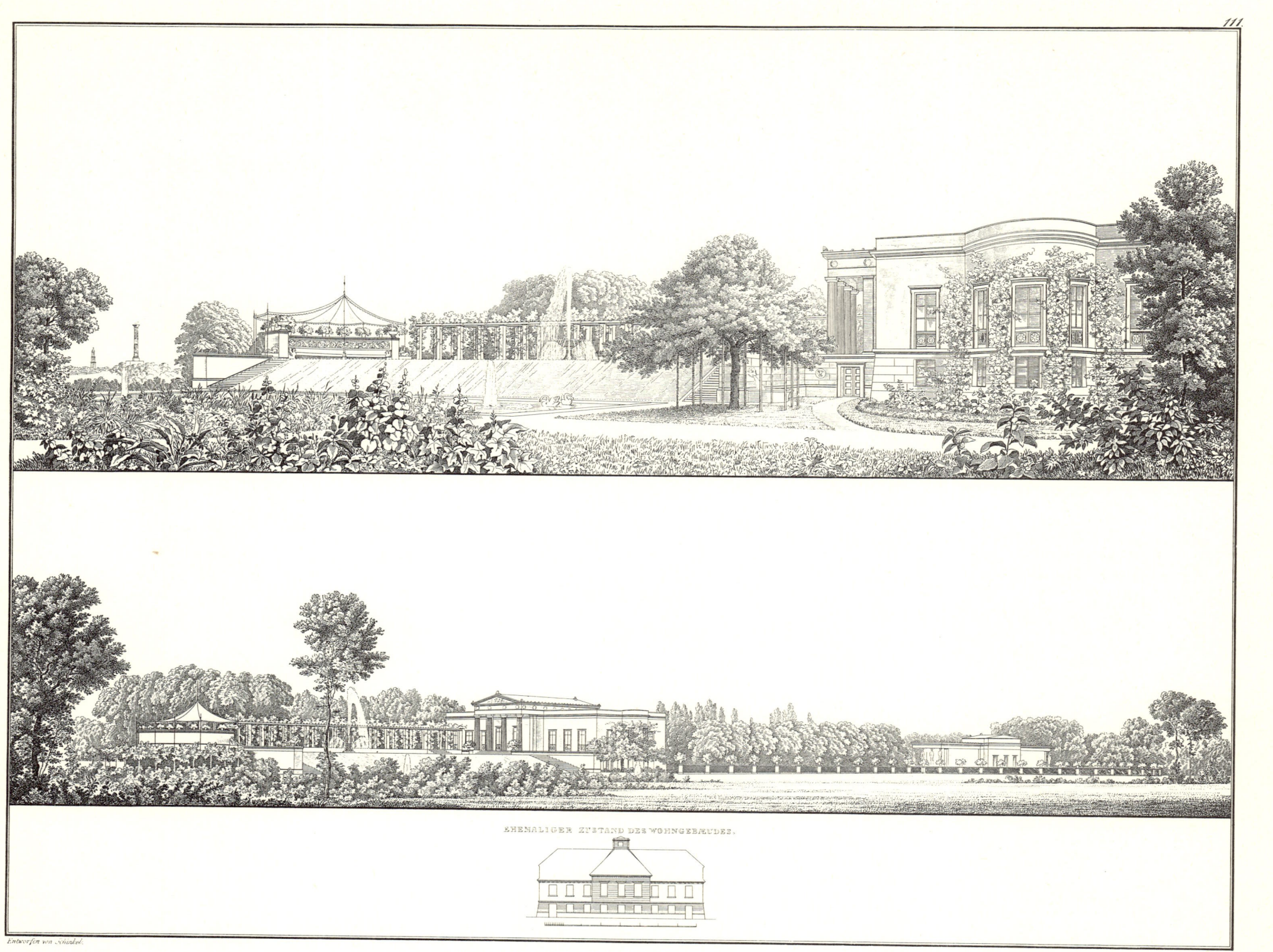

EHEMALIGER ZUSTAND DES WOHNGEBÄUDES.

CHARLOTTENHOF BEI POTSDAM.

FAÇADE GEGEN DIE TERRASSE.

FAÇADE NACH DEN PFLANZENHÆUSERN.

DURCHSCHNITT DURCH VESTIBUELE UND PORTICUS.

DURCHSCHNITT DURCH DAS VESTIBUELE.

CHARLOTTENHOF BEI POTSDAM.

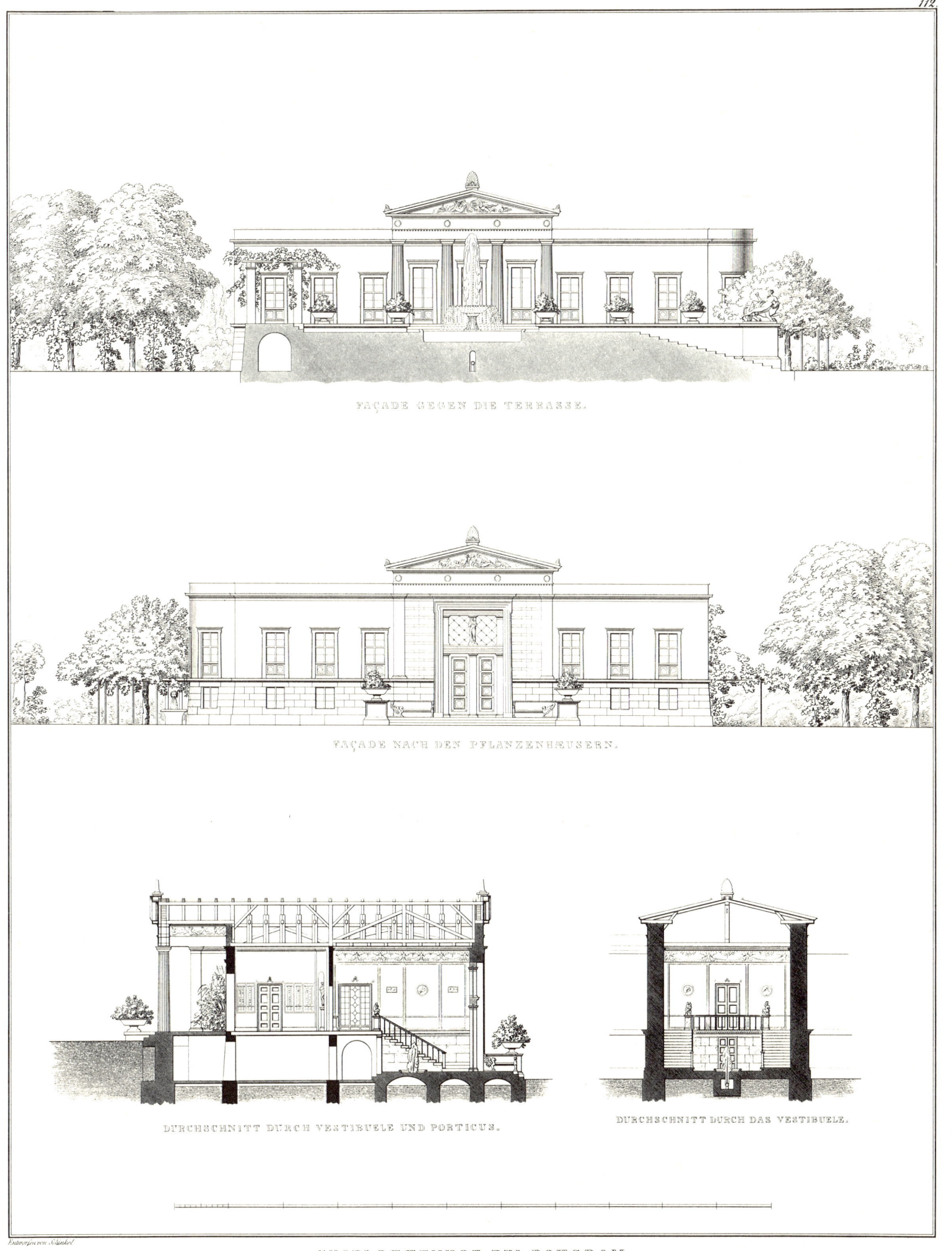

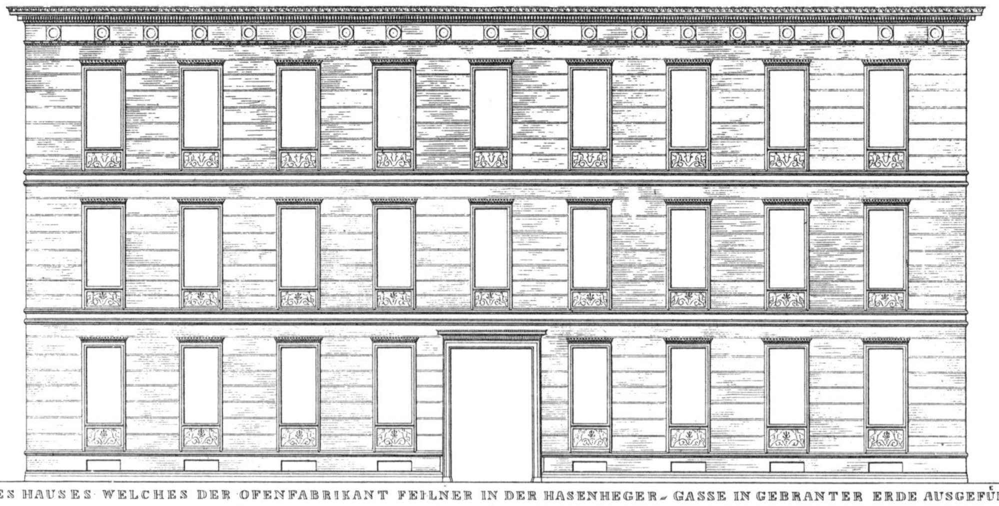

FAÇADE DES HAUSES WELCHES DER OFENFABRIKANT FEILNER IN DER HASENHEGER-GASSE IN GEBRANTER ERDE AUSGEFÜHRT HAT.

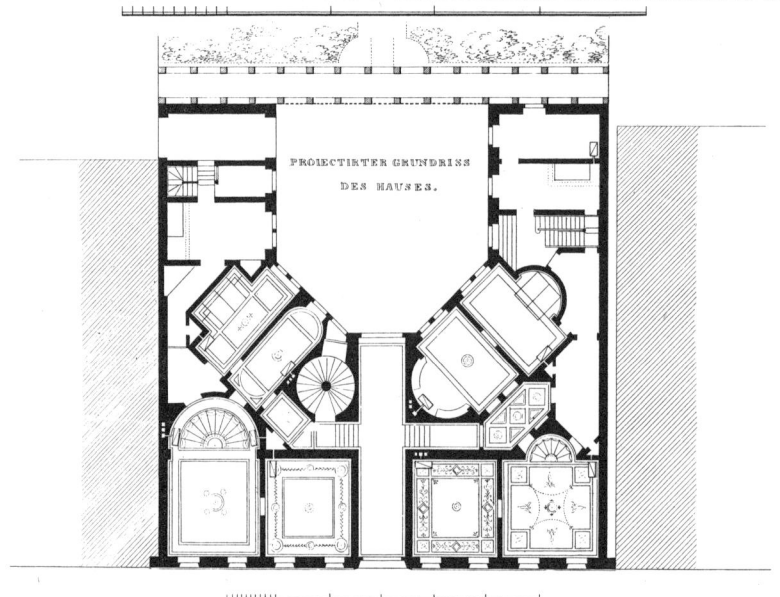

PROJECTIRTER GRUNDRISS DES HAUSES.

ZWEI FENSTER-BRÜSTUNGEN DES HAUSES IN GEBRANTER ERDE AUSGEFÜHRT.

114

HÄLFTE DES DECKEN-STÜCKS DER THÜR-EINFASSUNG.

HÄLFTE EINER INNEREN SEITE DER THÜR-EINFASSUNG.

EIN THEIL DER FAÇADE DES HAUSES DES OFENFABRIKANTEN FEILNER IN BERLIN, AN WELCHEM ALLE ARCHITECTUR-THEILE IN GEBRANTER ERDE AUSGEFÜHRT SIND.

DURCHSCHNITT DER FAÇADE.

gez. von Schinkel.　　　　　　　　　　　gest. von C. F. Thiele.

PERSPECTIVISCHE ANSICHT DES GEBAEUDES DER ALLGEMEINEN BAUSCHULE IN BERLIN.

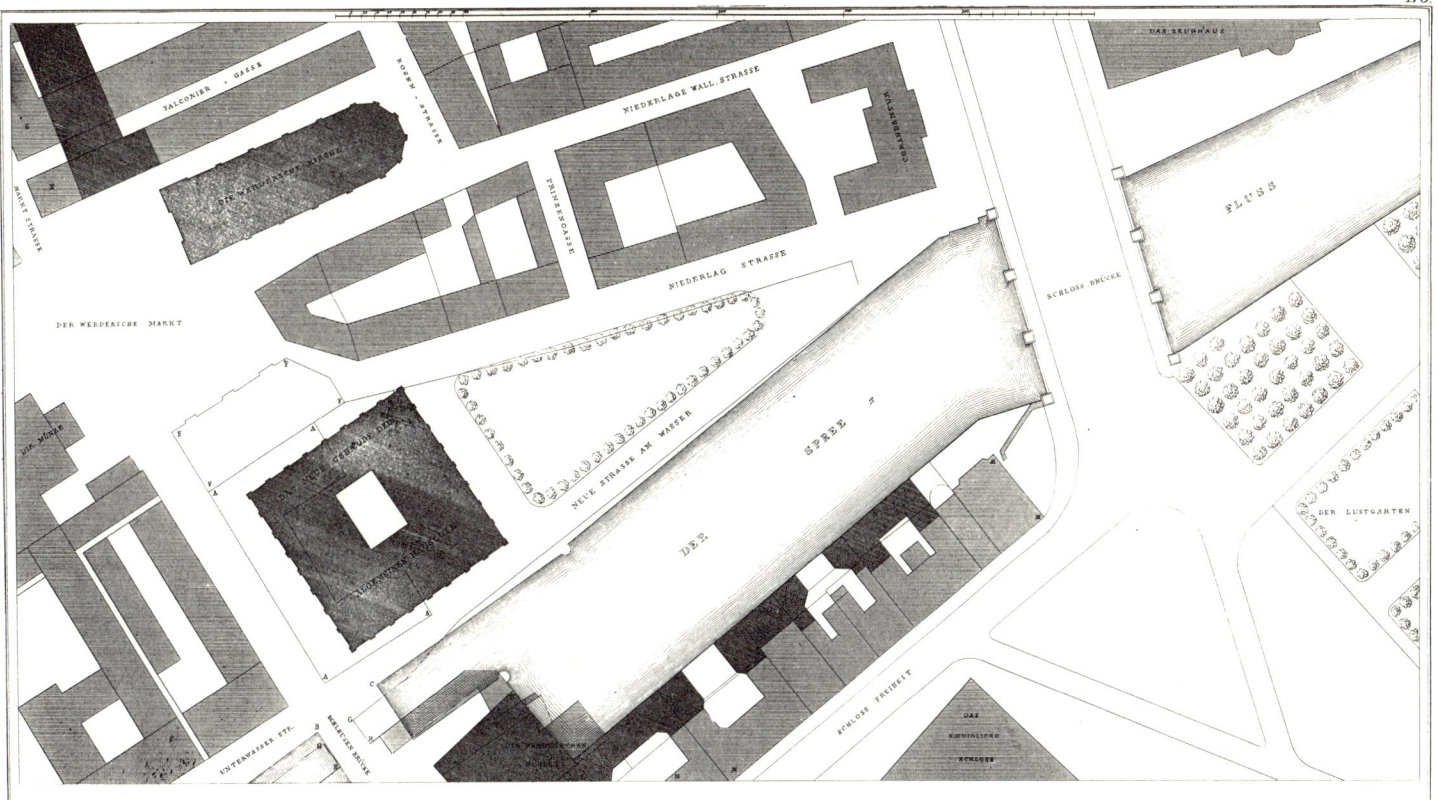

ERSTES HAUPTGESCHOSS.
ENTHÆLT DIE LEHR- UND BIBLIOTHEK-ZIMMER FÜR DIE BAUSCHULE

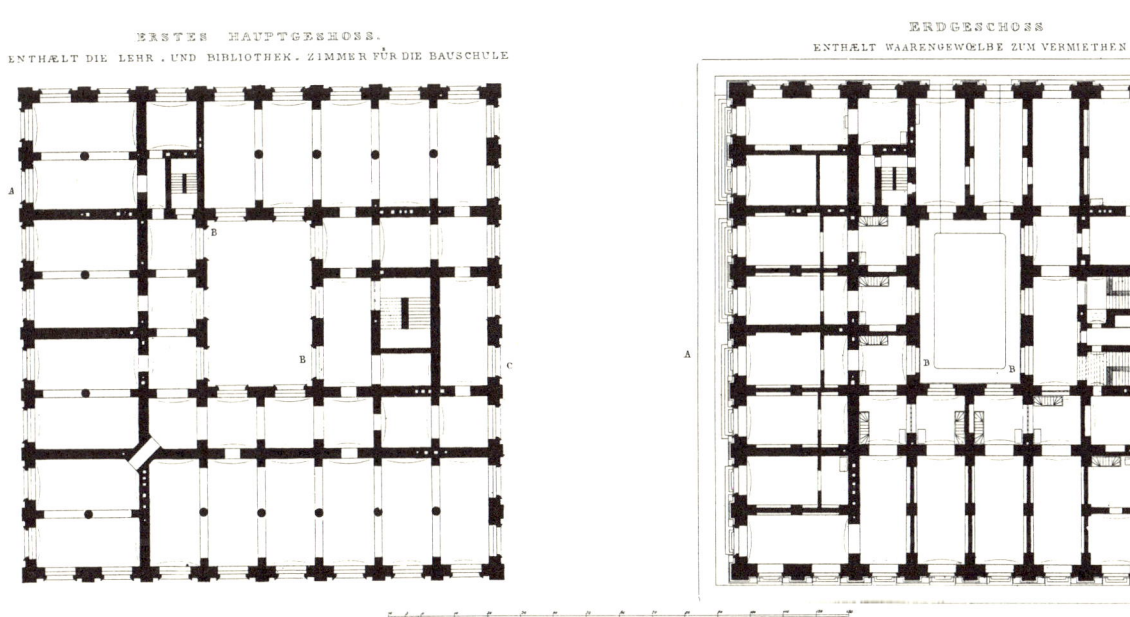

ERDGESCHOSS
ENTHÆLT WAARENGEWŒLBE ZUM VERMIETHEN

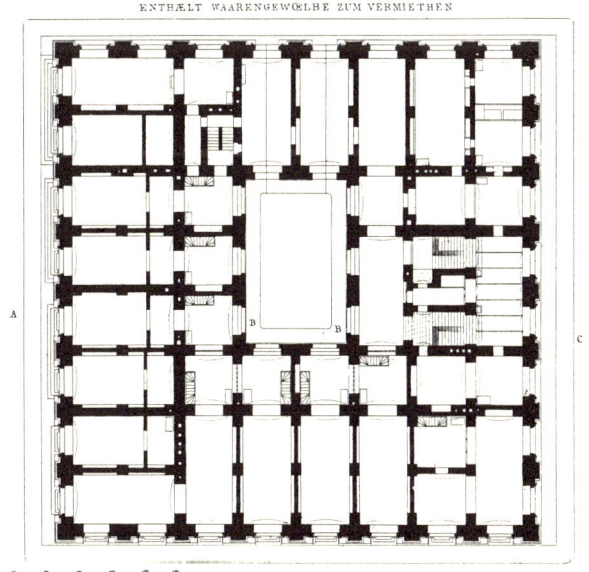

DURCHSCHNITT NACH DER RICHTUNG ABC

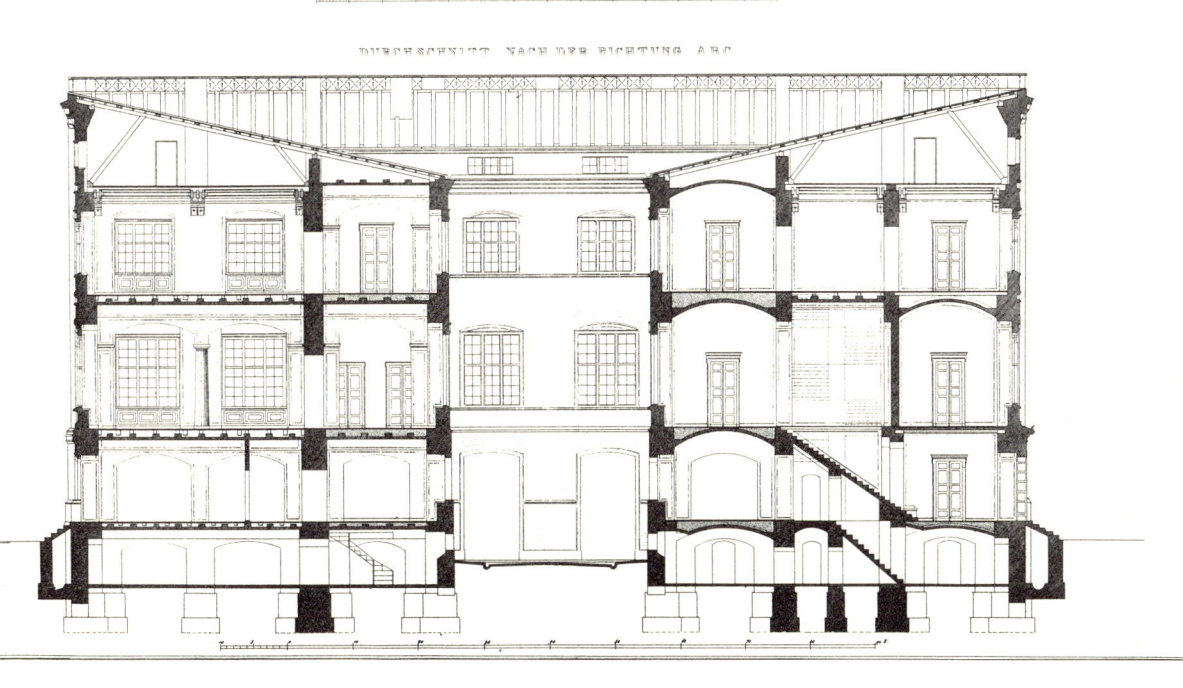

FAÇADE DES ARCADES DER ALLGEMEINEN BAUSCHULE.

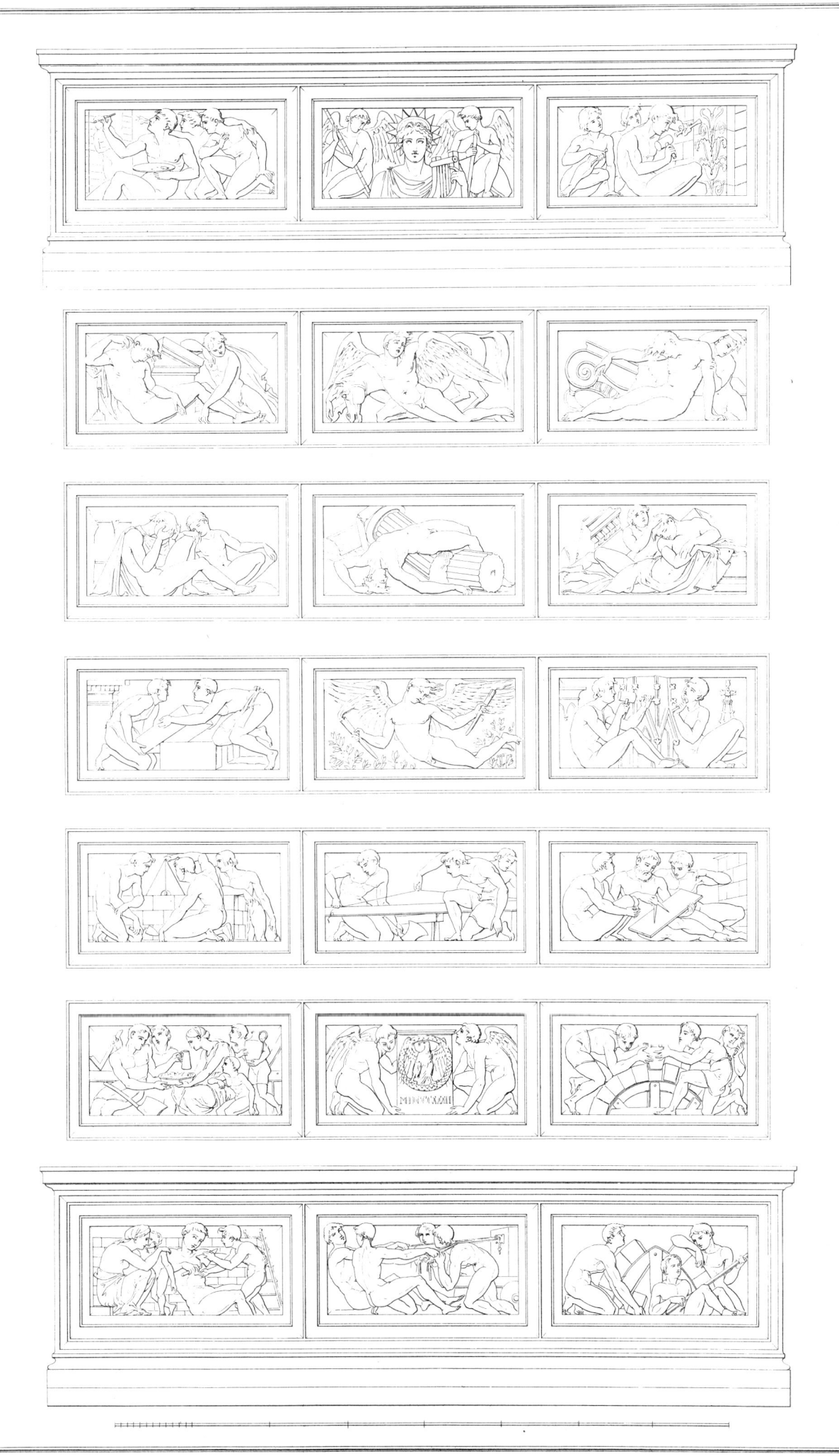

BILDWERKE DER FENSTER BRÜSTUNGEN IN GEBRANNTER ERDE.

PROFIL DES HAUPT-GESIMSES.

HAUPT-GESIMSS.

ORNAMENT AN DER INNEREN SEITE DER FENSTER-EINFASSUNG.

FENSTER UND GURTUNGS-GESIMSSE IN GROSSEREM MAASSTABE. — PROFIL EINES FENSTERS. — AUSFÜLLUNG DER BOGEN-SCHEIBEN DER FENSTER.

Gez. von Schinkel. Gest. von E. Mandel.

EINE DER BEIDEN HAUPTTHÜREN DES GEBÆUDES DER ALLGEMEINEN BAUSCHULE.

PERSPECTIVISCHE ANSICHT DES GEBÄUDES DER NEUEN BAUSCHULE IN BERLIN
VON EINEM NAHEN STANDPUNKTE.

ANSICHT DES ZWEITEN PORTALS MIT SEINEN ORNAMENTEN AN DER NEUEN BAUSCHULE IN BERLIN.

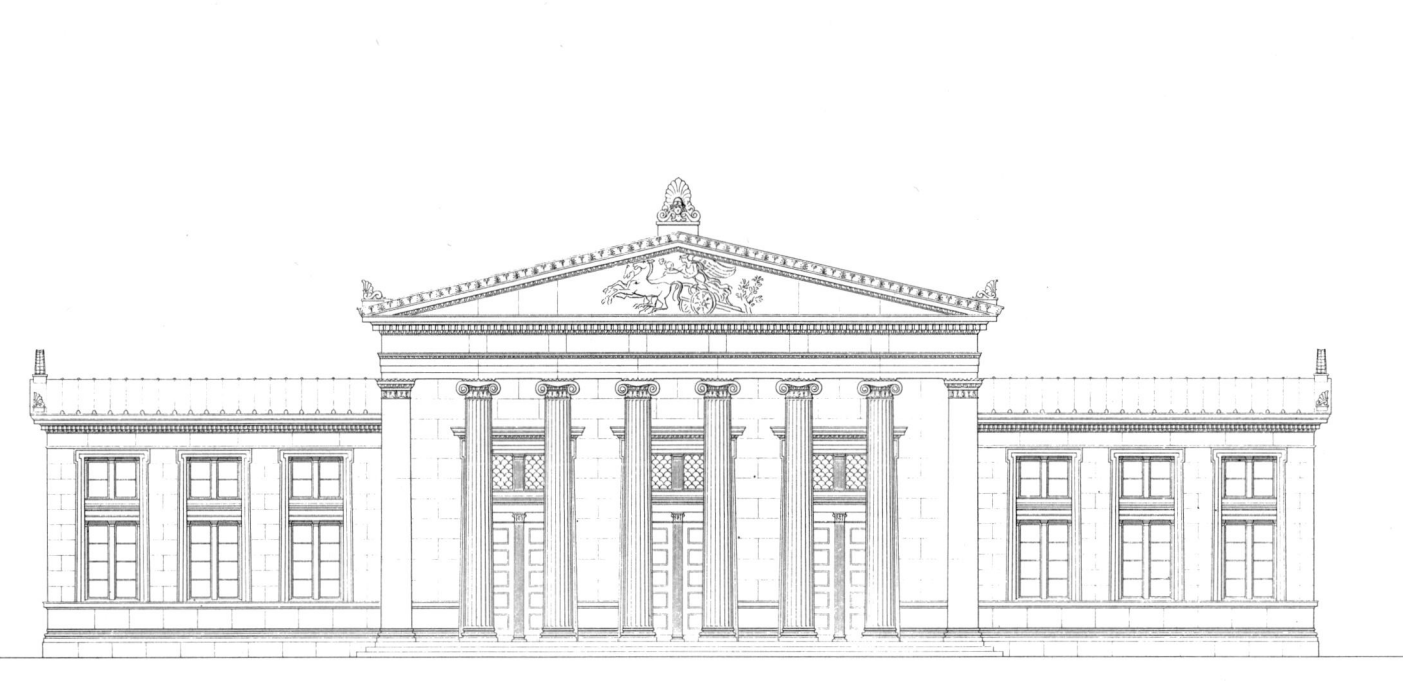

123.

HAUPT-ANSICHT DES NEUEN WACHTHAUSES IN DRESDEN.

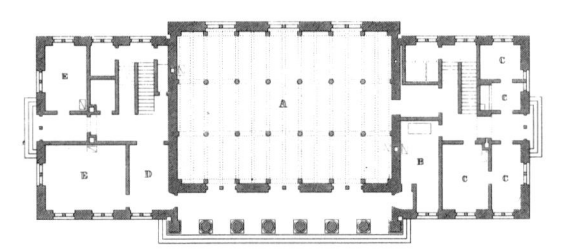

ERSTES-GESCHOSS. 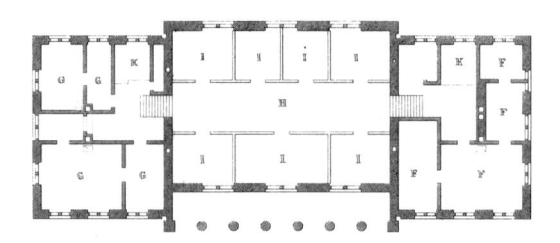   ZWEITES-GESCHOSS.

A. Wachtstube.
B. Officierstube.
C. Wohnung eines Beamten.
D. Passage.
E. Arrestantenzimmer.

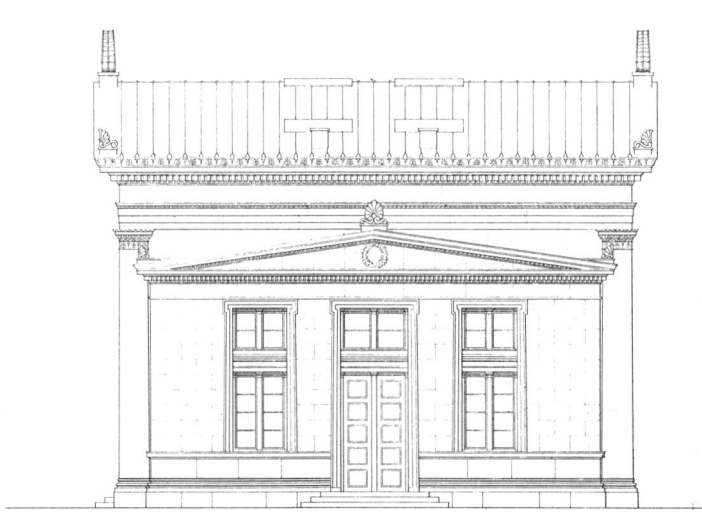

F. Wohnung eines Beamten.
G. Wohnung eines Beamten.
H. Corridor.
I. Aufbewahrungszimmer.
K. Treppenraum.

SEITEN-ANSICHT.

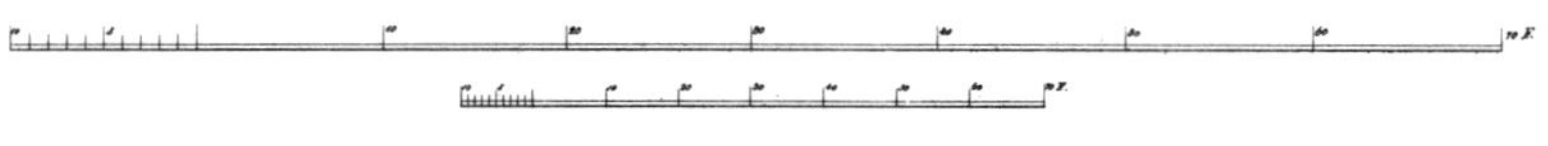

Schinkel Inv.   Schwechten sc.

RATH-HAUS ZU ZITTAU.

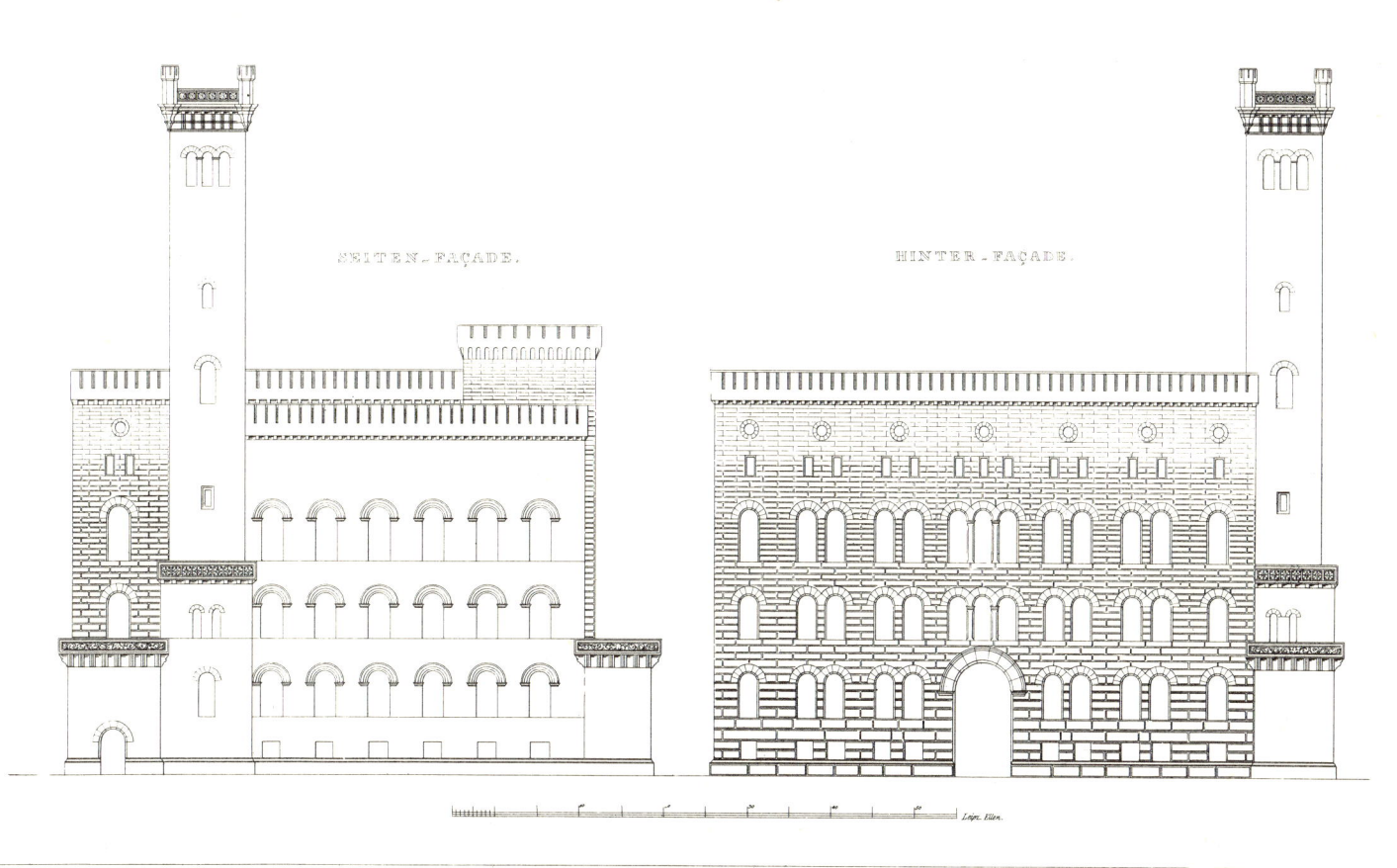

VORDER-FAÇADE.

SEITEN-FAÇADE.   HINTER-FAÇADE.

RATH-HAUS ZU ZITTAU

PROFIL nach AB.

PROFIL nach CD.

Canal.

ZWEITE ETAGE.

Balkon	Polizei Expedition	Calculatur	Archiv

Corridor.

Retirade.

Archiv. | Corridor.

Stadt Schreiberei. | Canzelei. | Vor. Saal. | Conferenz. Saal.

Corridor.

Balkon.

DRITTE ETAGE.

Zur Disposition. | Deputirten Zimmer. | Saal der Stadtverordneten. | Neben Gemach.

Corridor.

Retirade.

Zur Disposition.

Neben Gemach. | Redner Bühne | Grosser Bürger Saal | Vor. Saal.

Balkon.

ERDGESCHOSS.

Zur Feuer Wache. | Durchfahrt. | Depositen Gewölbe.

Alter Thurm | Corridor. | Corridor.

Retirade. | Neben Treppe | Hof.

A | Wohnung | Küche.

des | Corridor. | Corridor.

Keller. | Wirthes. | Durchfahrt. | Disponible Gewölbe.

ERSTE ETAGE.

Cämmerei Casse | Durchfahrt. | Steuer Verwaltung.

Corridor | Corridor.

Retirade. | Flur.

Billard Zimmer | Neben Zimmer.

Corridor. | Corridor.

Wein Stube | Speise Zimmer. | Durchfahrt. | Spaarkasse u. Markt gelder Einnahme.

desgl.

Schinkel inv.

126.

PROFIL DES HAUPTGEBÄUDES.

GRUNDRISS DES I.TEN GESCHOSSES.

VORMALIGE FORM DES GEBÄUDES.

UMGEÄNDERTE FRONTE DES GEBÄUDES.

Schinkel inv. Grünmacher sc.

GRÄFLICH REDERN'SCHES PALAIS IN BERLIN.

SCHLOSS KURNIK
IM GROSSHERZOGTHUM POSEN, DEM GRAFEN DZIALINSKI GEHÖRIG.

GRUNDRISS DES ERSTEN GESCHOSSES.

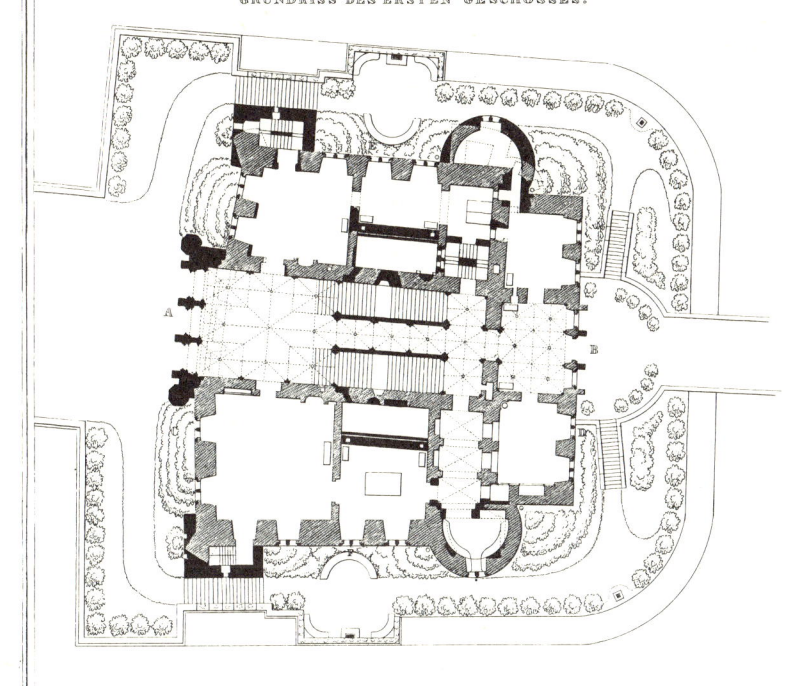

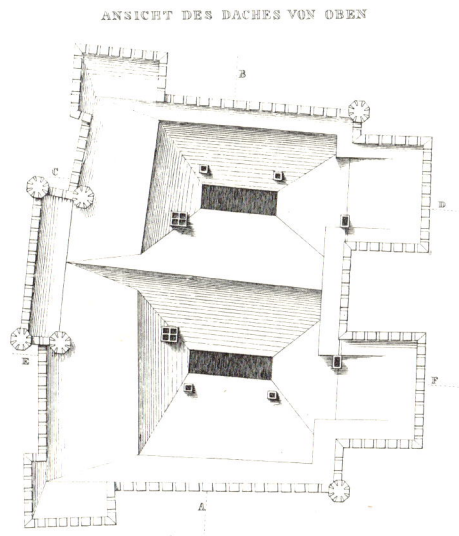

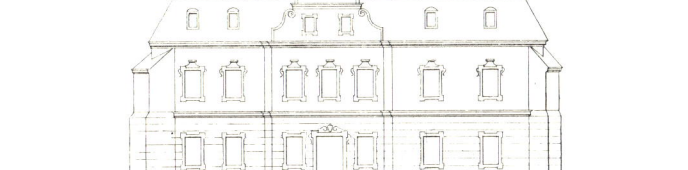

GRUNDRISS DES ZWEITEN GESCHOSSES.

ANSICHT DES DACHES VON OBEN

DURCHSCHNITTE DES DACHES
Nach der Richtung A. B.

Nach der Richtung C. D.

Nach der Richtung E. F.

ALTE FACADE DER SEITE A. DES GRUNDRISSES.

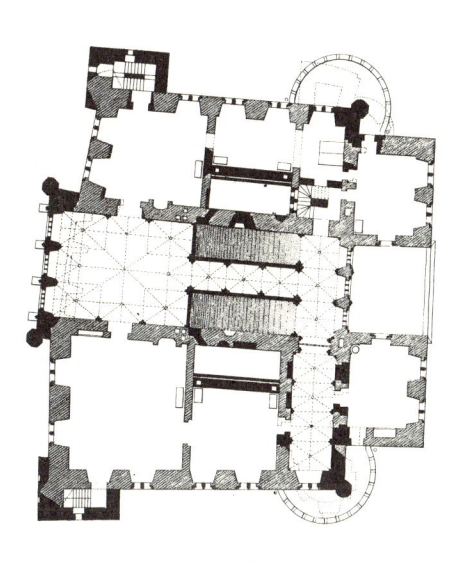

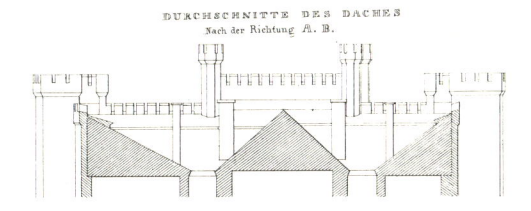

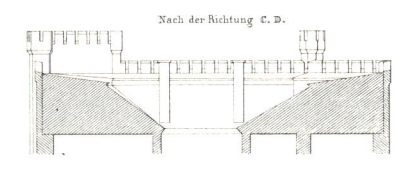

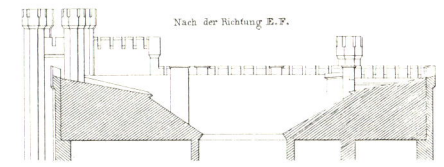

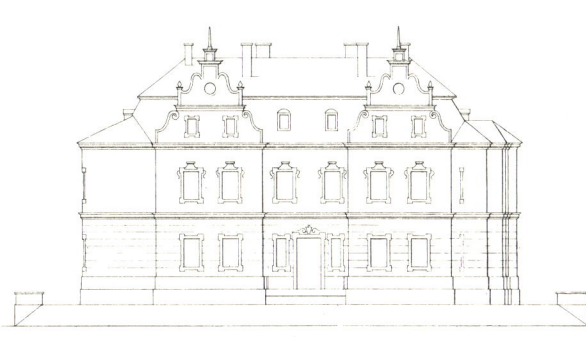

ALTE FACADE DER SEITE B. DES GRUNDRISSES.

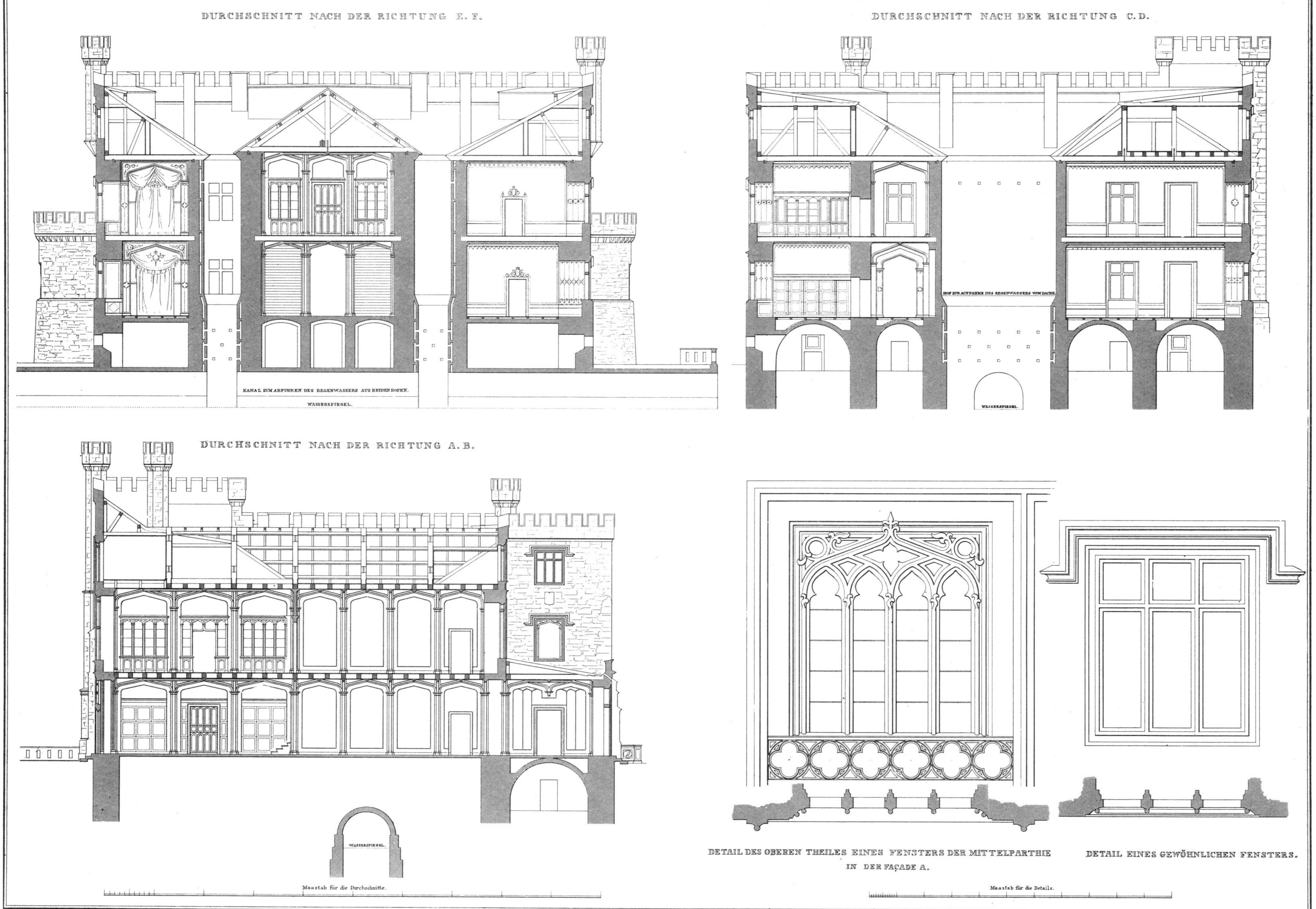

120

DURCHSCHNITT NACH DER RICHTUNG C.D.

DURCHSCHNITT NACH DER RICHTUNG E.F.

DURCHSCHNITT NACH DER RICHTUNG A.B.

DETAIL EINES GEWÖHNLICHEN FENSTERS.

DETAIL DES OBEREN THEILES EINES FENSTERS DER MITTELPARTHIE IN DER FAÇADE A.

Maasstab für das Detail.

Maasstab für die Durchschnitte.

WASSERSPIEGEL.

KANAL ZUM ABFÜHREN DES REGENWASSERS AUS BEIDEN DÄCHERN.

WASSERSPIEGEL.

HOF ZUM AUFFANGEN DES REGENWASSERS VOM DACHE.

WASSERSPIEGEL.

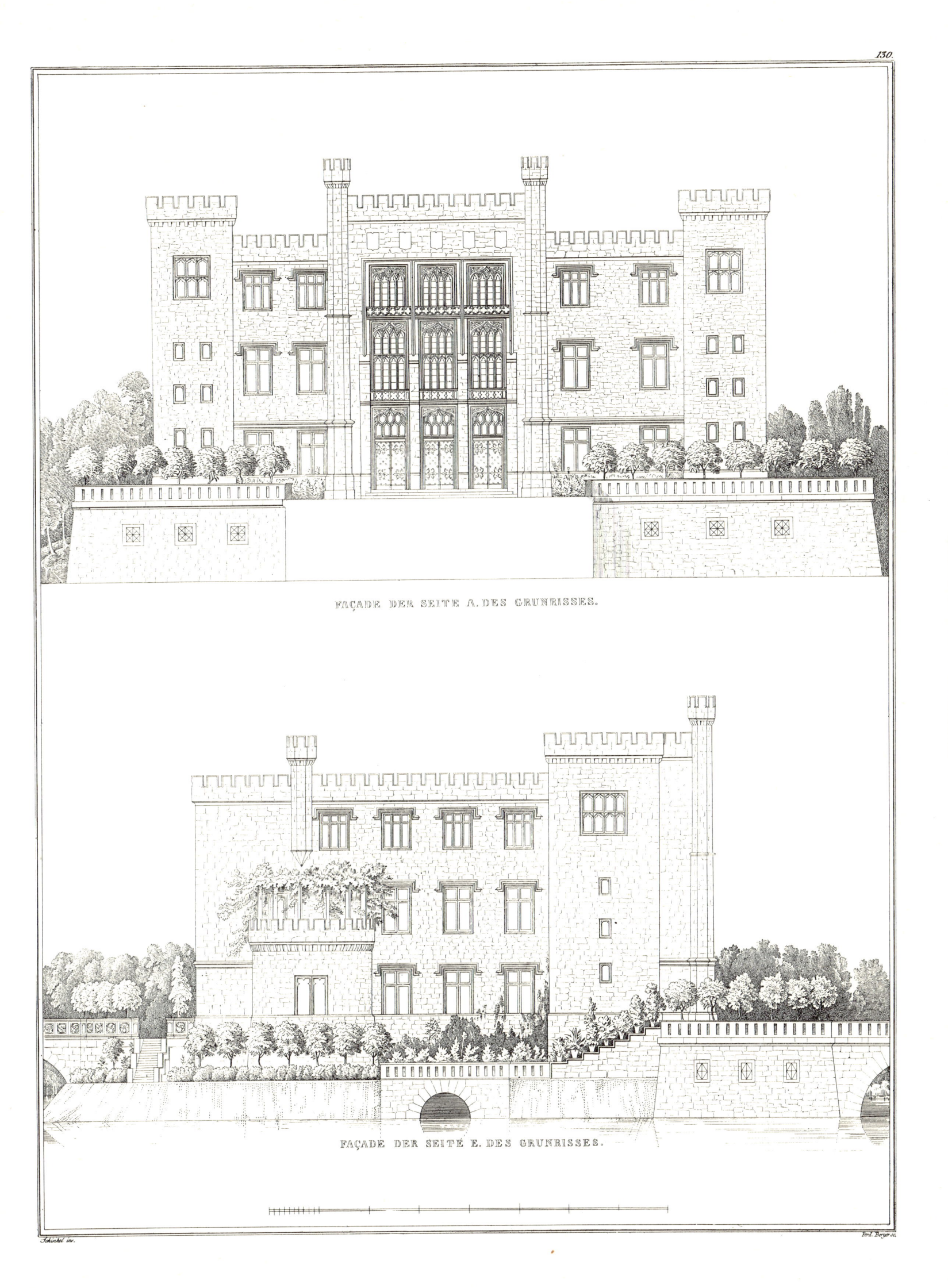

FAÇADE DER SEITE A. DES GRUNRISSES.

FAÇADE DER SEITE E. DES GRUNRISSES.

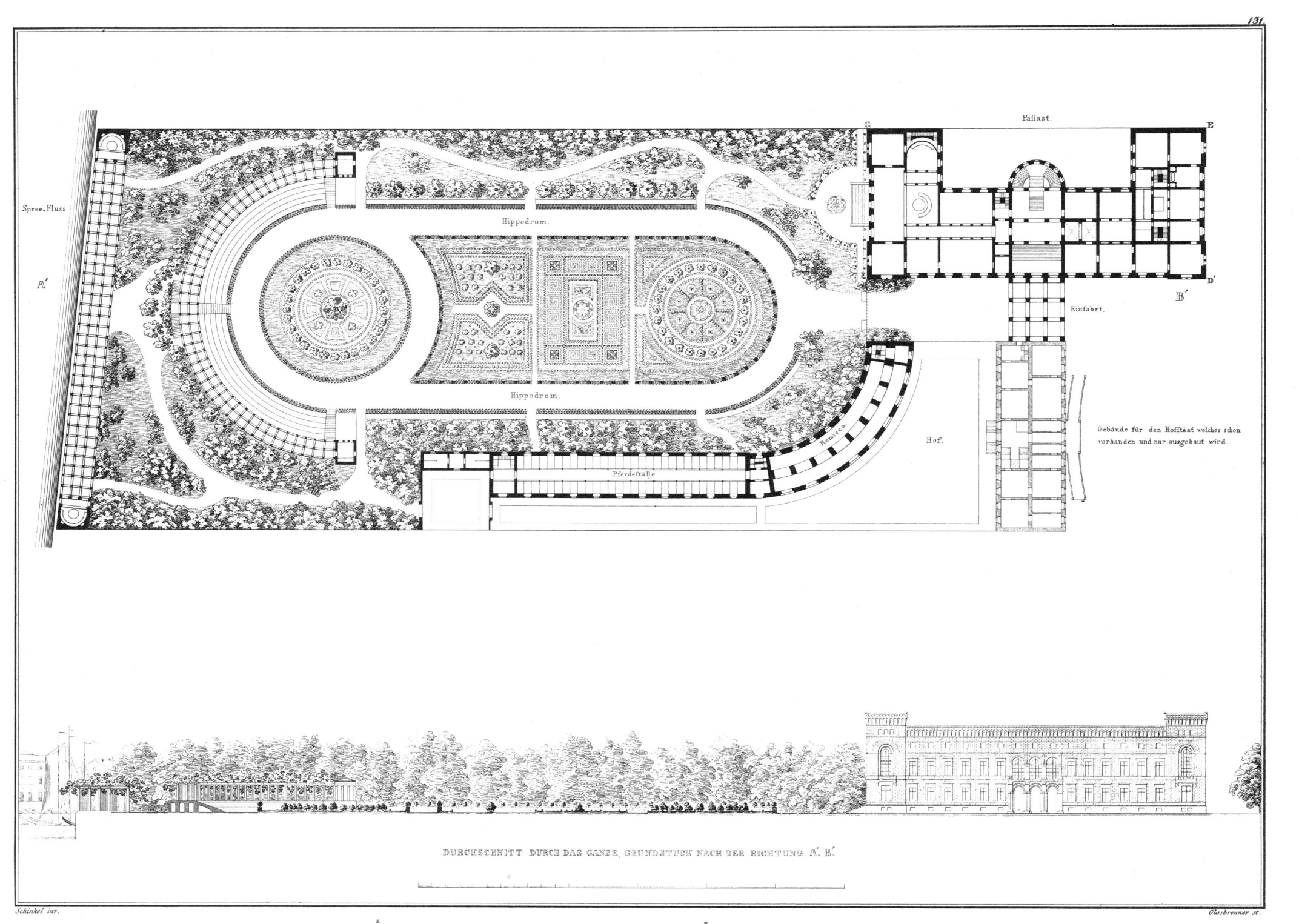

Pallast.

Einfahrt.

Gebäude für den Hofstaat welcher schon vorhanden und nur ausgebaut wird.

Hof.

Remisen.

Pferdestalle.

Hippodrom.

Hippodrom.

Spree-Fluss.

DURCHSCHNITT DURCH DAS GANZE GRUNDSTÜCK NACH DER RICHTUNG A'B'.

ENTWURF FÜR EINEN PALLAST DES PRINZEN WILHELM KÖNIGL. HOHEIT AM PARISER-PLATZ.

Schinkel inv. Glatzkowsky sc.

ENTWURF FÜR EINEN PALLAST DES PRINZEN WILHELM KÖNIGL. HOHEIT AM PARISER PLATZ.

133

F. II.

F. I.

Schinkel inv.

Gaedicke sc.

ENTWURF FÜR EINEN PALLAST DES PRINZEN WILHELM KÖNIGL. HOHEIT AM OPERNPLATZ.

ENTWURF FÜR EINEN PALLAST DES PRINZEN WILHELM KÖNIGL. HOHEIT AM OPERNPLATZ.

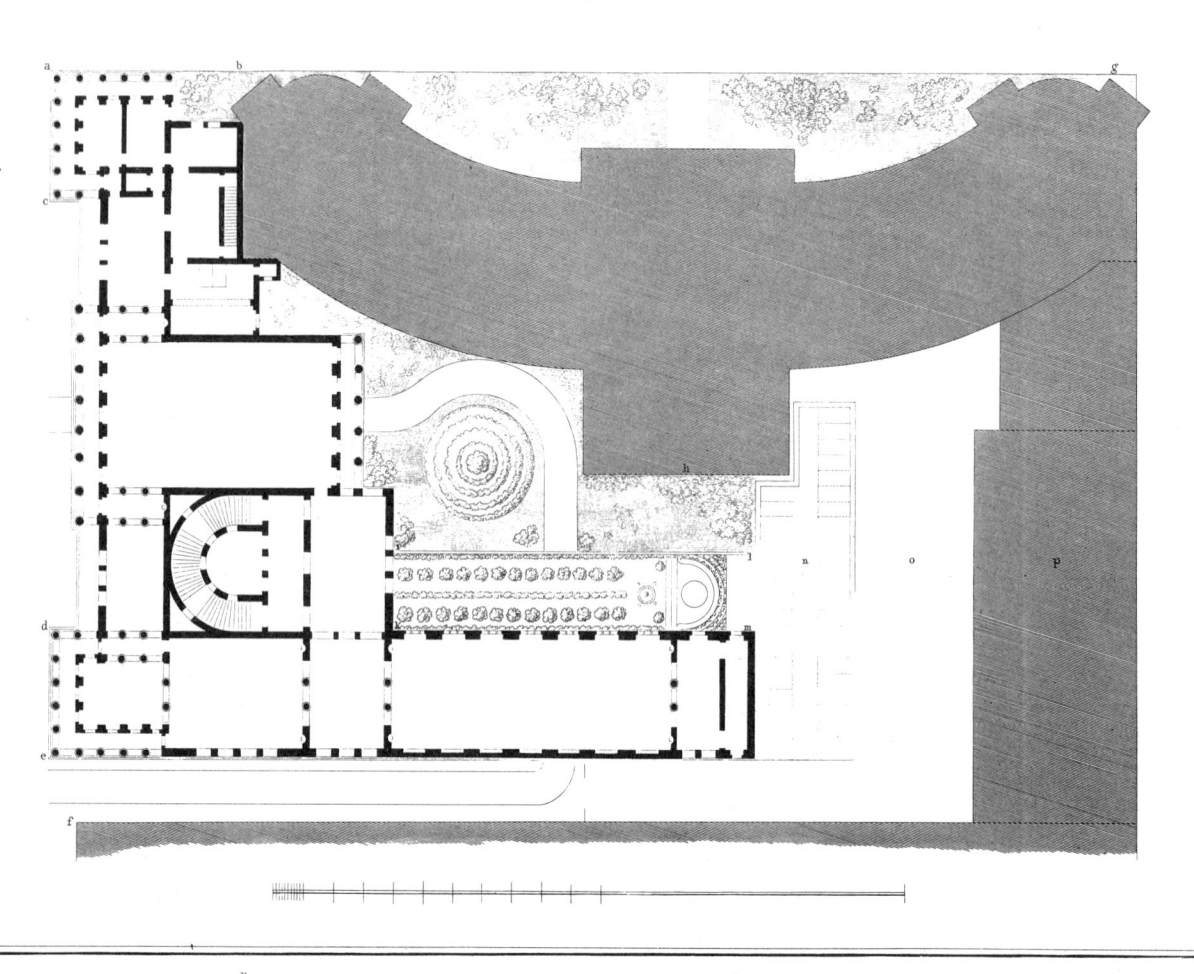

ENTWURF FÜR DAS LANDHAUS DES PRINZEN WILHELM K. H. AUF DEM BABELSBERGE BEI POTSDAM.

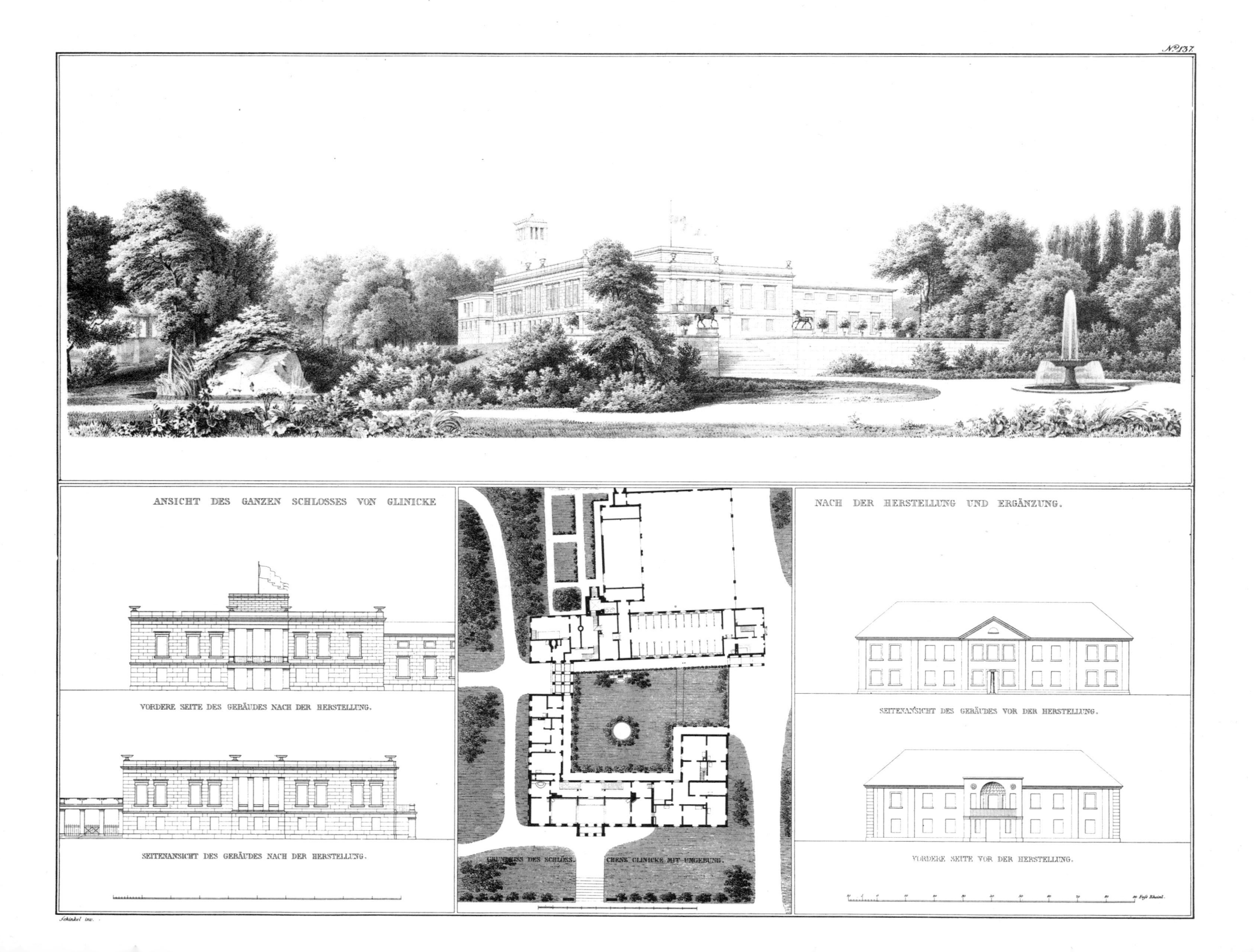

ANSICHT DES GANZEN SCHLOSSES VON GLINICKE

VORDERE SEITE DES GEBÄUDES NACH DER HERSTELLUNG.

SEITENANSICHT DES GEBÄUDES NACH DER HERSTELLUNG.

NACH DER HERSTELLUNG UND ERGÄNZUNG.

SEITENANSICHT DES GEBÄUDES VOR DER HERSTELLUNG.

VORDERE SEITE VOR DER HERSTELLUNG.

Schinkel inv.

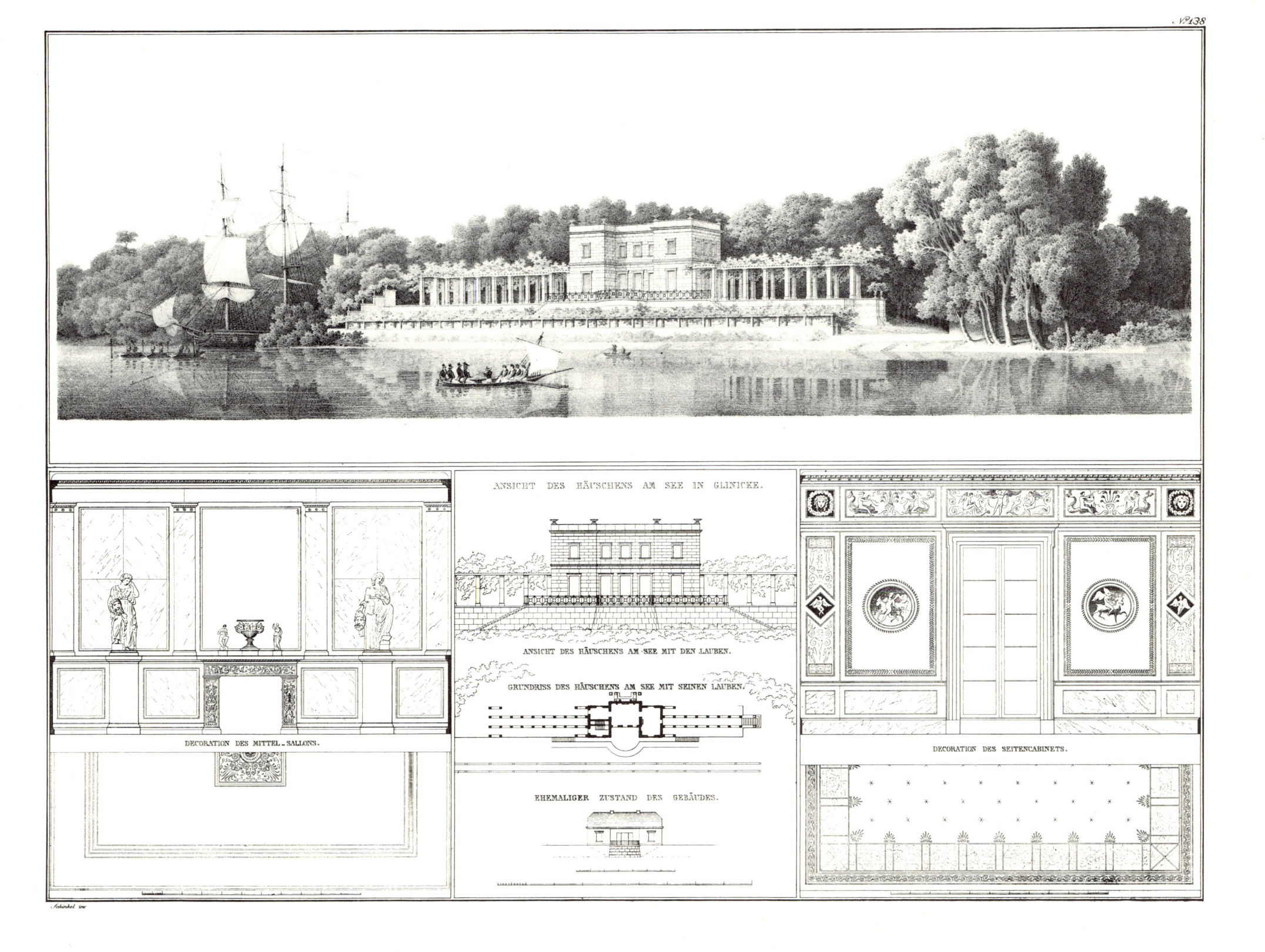

ANSICHT DES HÄUSCHENS AM SEE IN GLINICKE.

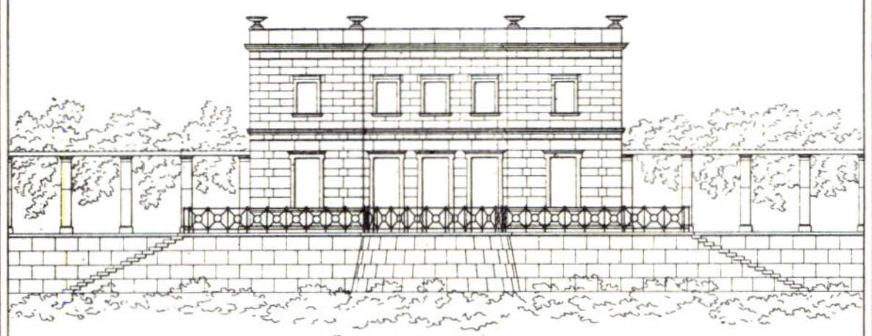

ANSICHT DES HÄUSCHENS AM SEE MIT DEN LAUBEN.

GRUNDRISS DES HÄUSCHENS AM SEE MIT SEINEN LAUBEN.

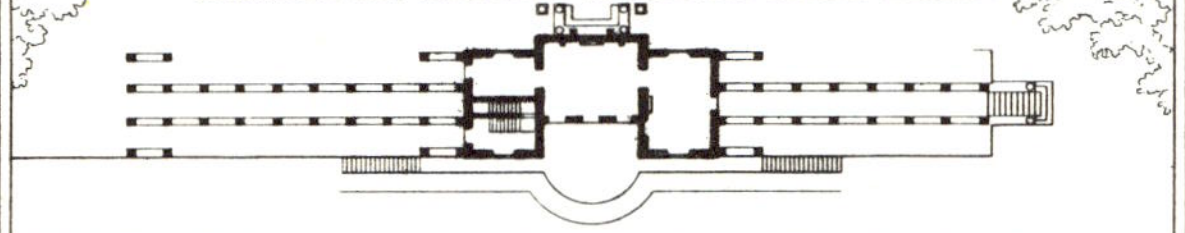

EHEMALIGER ZUSTAND DES GEBÄUDES.

DECORATION DES SEITENCABINETS.

DECORATION DES MITTEL-SALONS.

No 139

ANSICHT DES GRABES DES HERREN VON LANDSBERG IN CHARLOTTENBURG BEI BERLIN VON DER SEITE DES KANALS UND ZWEI DETAILS DER DEKORATION.

SEITEN

LÄNGEN ANSICHT

FRONT DER LANDSEITE

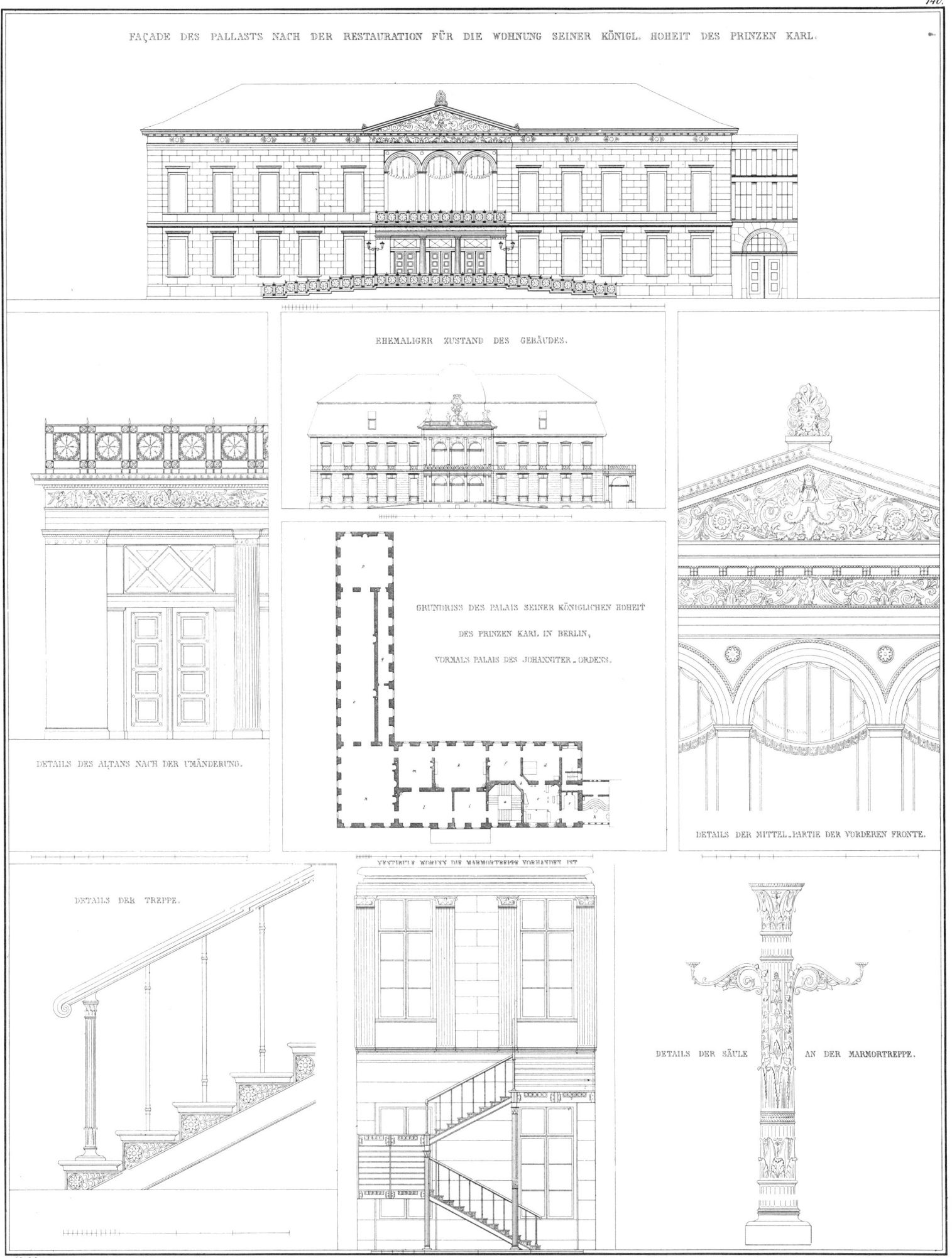

140.

FAÇADE DES PALLASTS NACH DER RESTAURATION FÜR DIE WOHNUNG SEINER KÖNIGL. HOHEIT DES PRINZEN KARL.

EHEMALIGER ZUSTAND DES GEBÄUDES.

DETAILS DES ALTANS NACH DER UMÄNDERUNG.

GRUNDRISS DES PALAIS SEINER KÖNIGLICHEN HOHEIT DES PRINZEN KARL IN BERLIN, VORMALS PALAIS DES JOHANNITER-ORDENS.

DETAILS DER MITTEL-PARTIE DER VORDEREN FRONTE.

DETAILS DER TREPPE.

VESTIBULE WORINN DIE MARMORTREPPE VORHANDEN IST.

DETAILS DER SÄULE AN DER MARMORTREPPE.

Schinkel inv.

GRUNDRISS DES I.ᵗᵉⁿ UND II.ᵗᵉⁿ GESCHOSSES, SITUATIONSPLAN UND PERSPECTIVISCHE ANSICHT DER NEUEN STERNWARTE IN BERLIN.

142.

Fronton der Sternwarte.

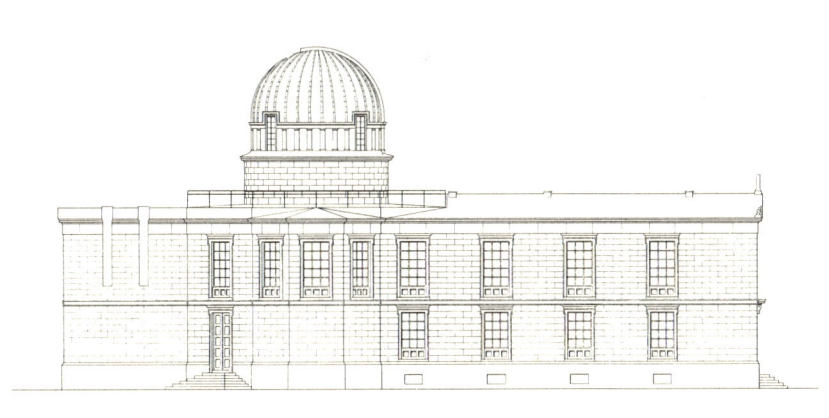

Seiten-Façade der Sternwarte.

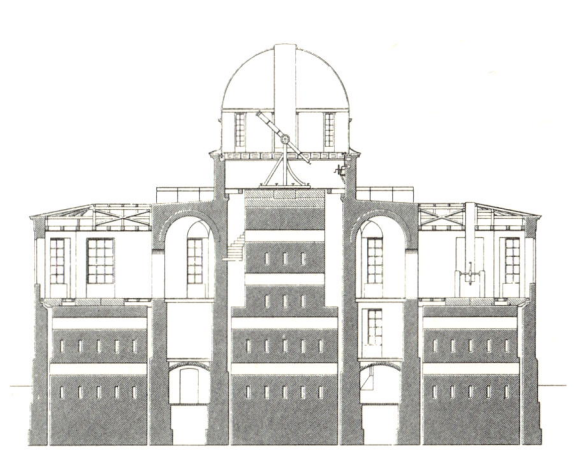

Durchschnitt der Sternwarte.

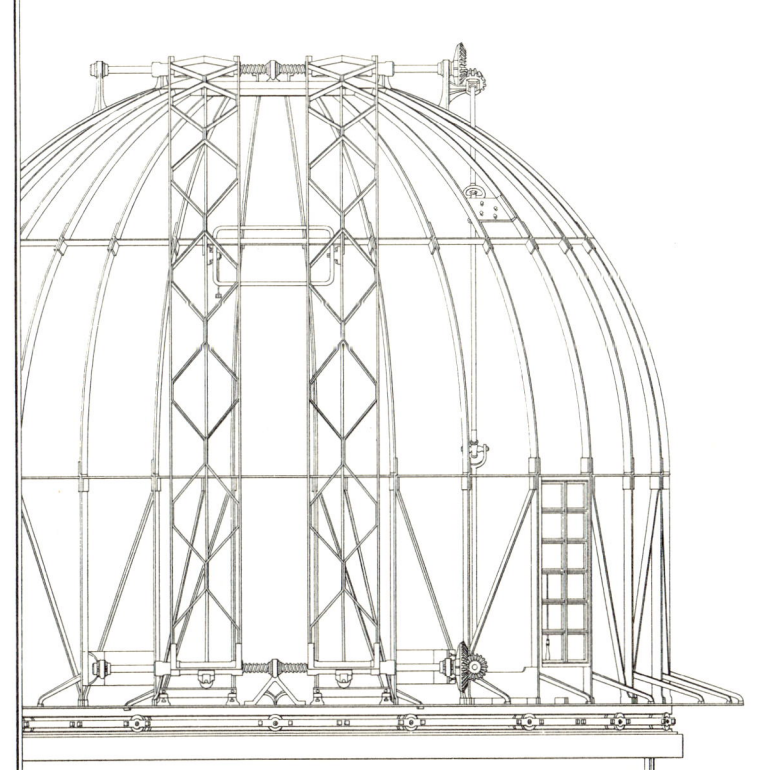

Ansicht der Eisen-Construction und des Maschinenwerks der Drehkuppel.

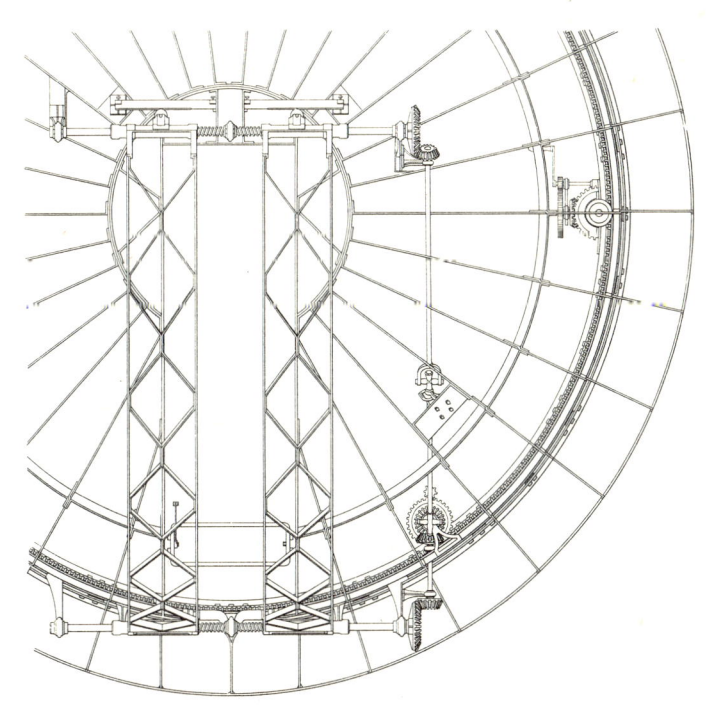

Grundriss der Eisen-Construction und des Maschinenwerks der Drehkuppel auf der Sternwarte.

Schinkel inv.

143.

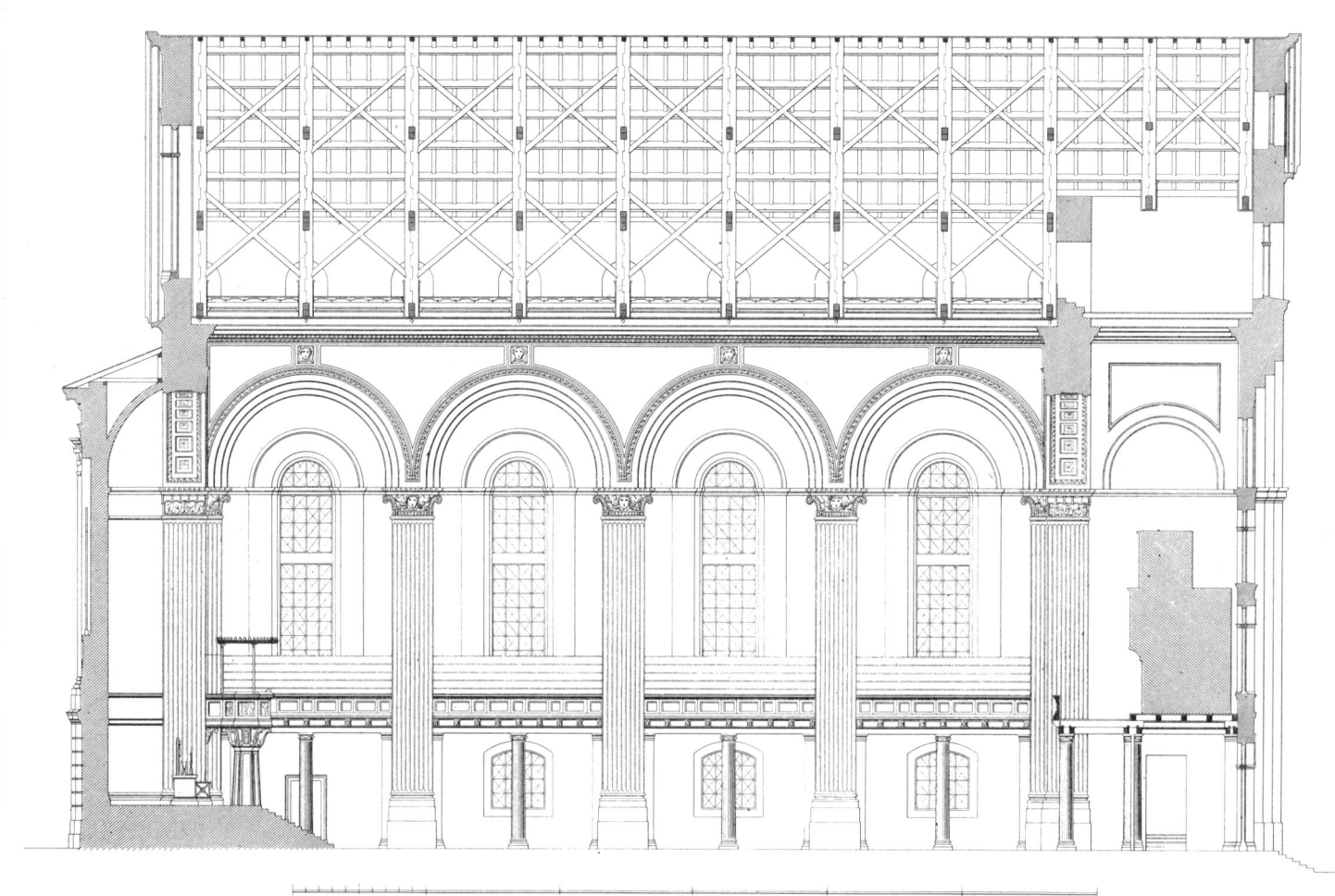

LÄNGENPROFIL DER RESTAURIRTEN KIRCHE VON ZITTAU.

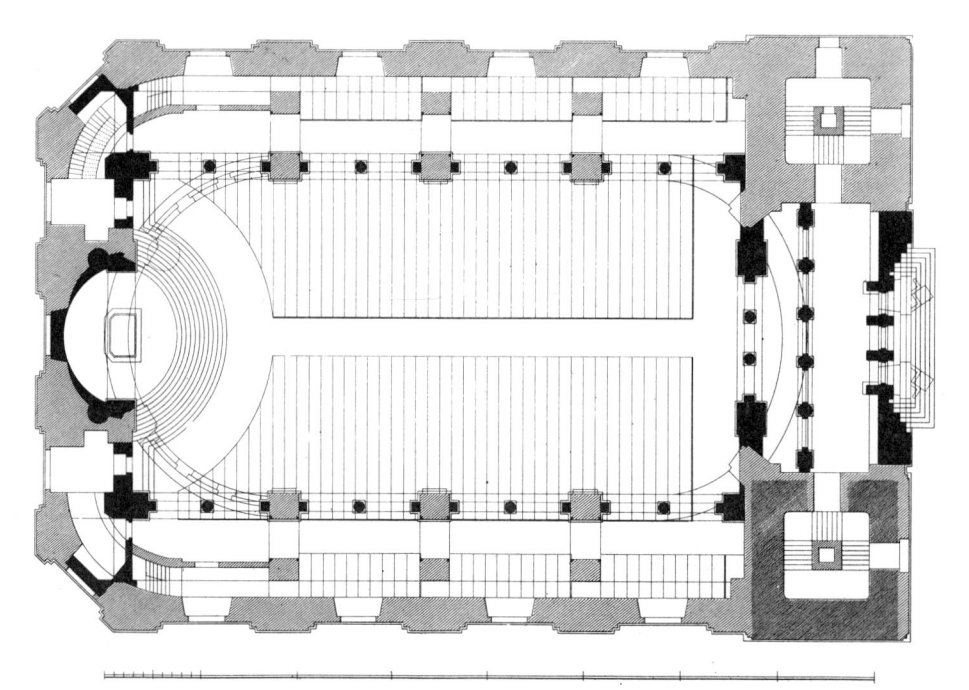

GRUNDRISS DER RESTAURIRTEN KIRCHE VON ZITTAU.

PROFIL DER RESTAURIRTEN KIRCHE ZU ZITTAU.

ALTE FAÇADE UND PROFIL DER KIRCHE VON ZITTAU IM UNRESTAURIRTEN ZUSTANDE.

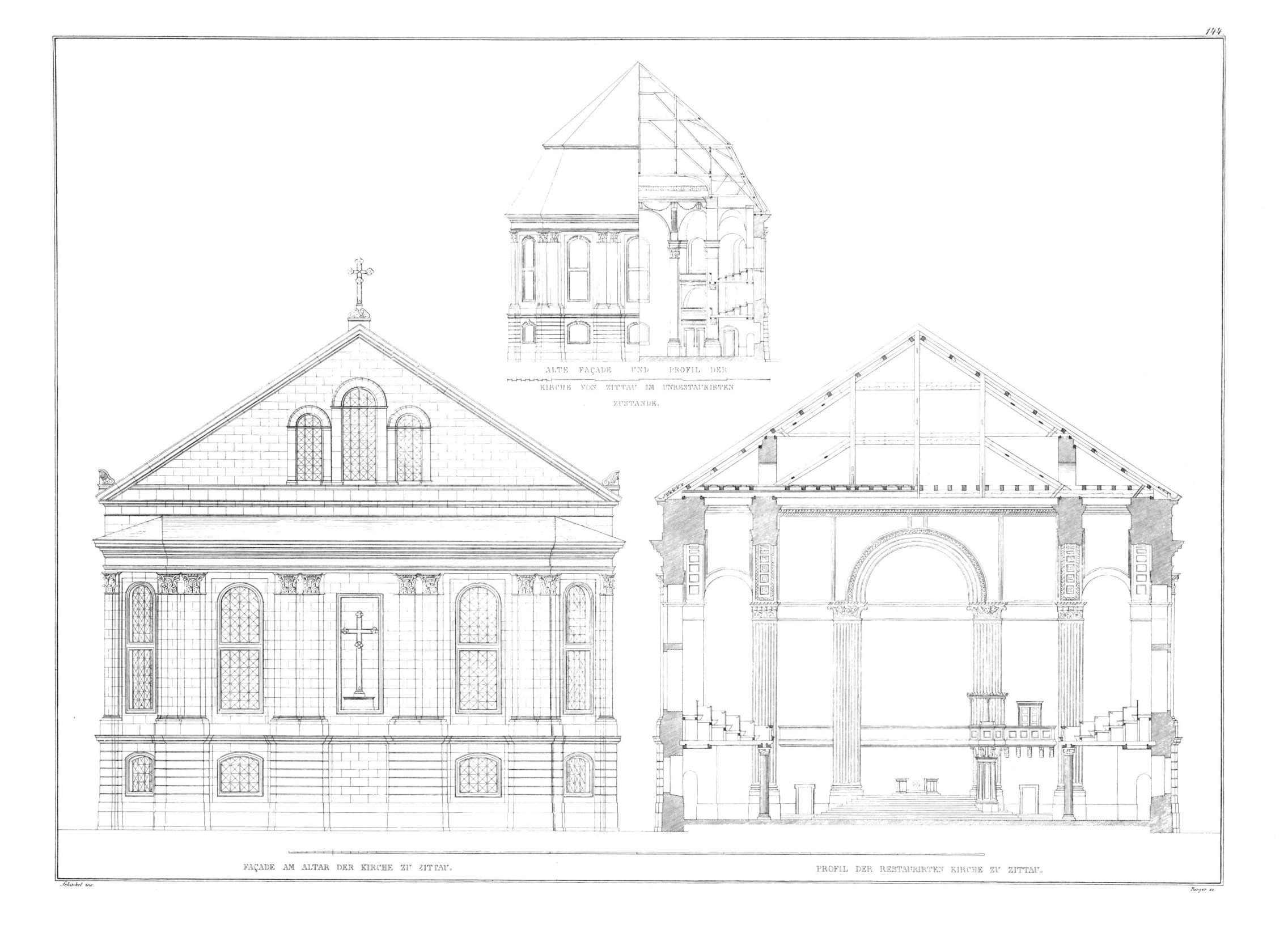

FAÇADE AM ALTAR DER KIRCHE ZU ZITTAU.

145

THURM WIE ER JETZT IN ALTERTHÜMLICHER ART RESTAURIRT WORDEN.

SCHIEFER THURM

SCHIEFER THURM

ALTER THURM IN SEINEM UNVERÄNDERTEN ZUSTANDE

EHEMALIGER ZUSTAND DER THURMFAÇADE DER KIRCHE IN ZITTAU.

PROFIL DURCH DIE RESTAURIRTEN THÜRME UND DEN ANGRÄNZENDEN THEIL DER KIRCHE.

FAÇADE DER THURMSEITE AN DER RESTAURIRTEN S. JOHANNIS-KIRCHE ZU ZITTAU.

PERSPECTIVISCHE ANSICHTEN DES NEUEN THORS BEI DER CHARITÉ IN BERLIN.

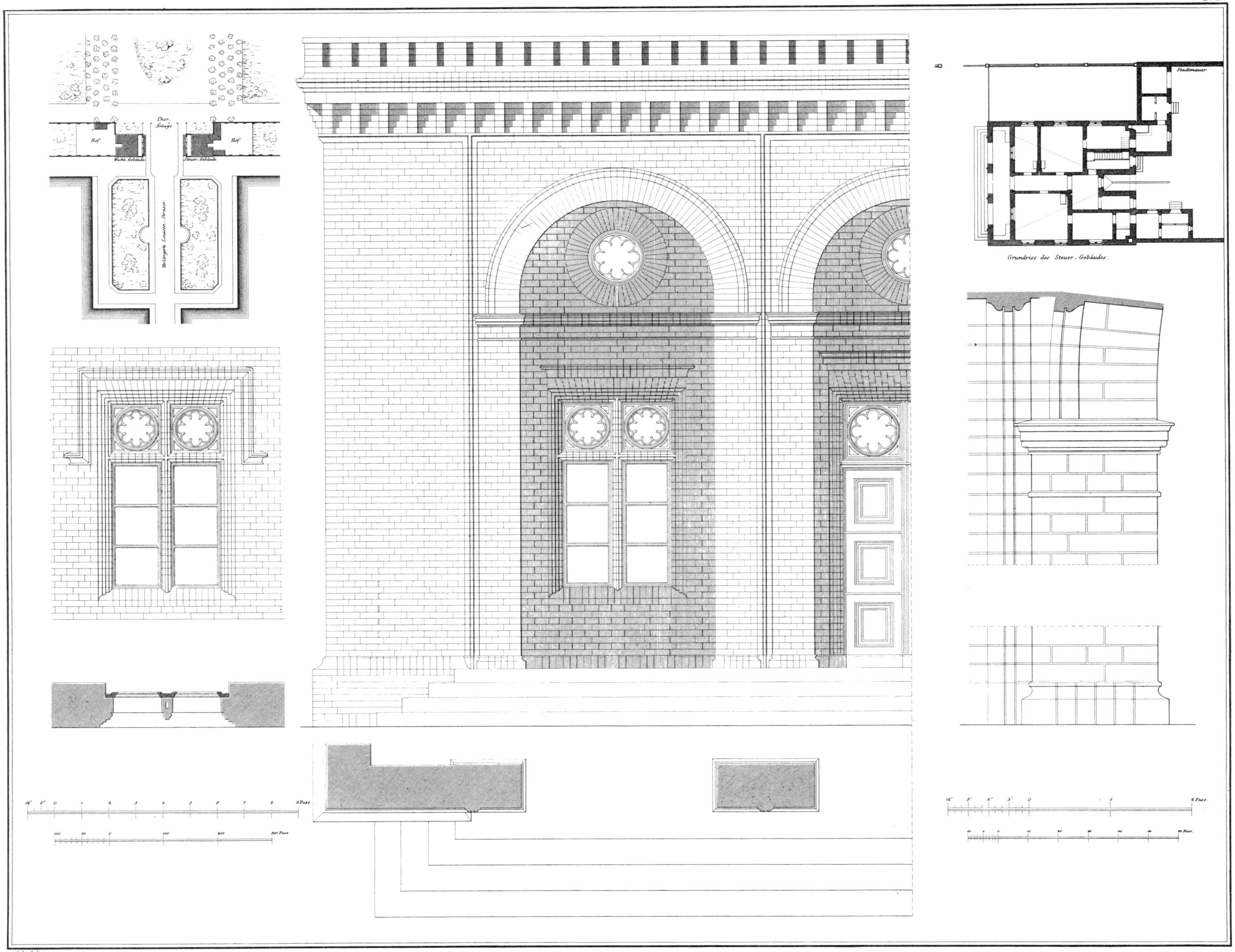

SITUATIONSPLAN, GRUNDRISS UND DETAILS DER ARCHITECTUR DES NEUEN THORS BEI DEM CHARITÉ-GEBÄUDE IN BERLIN.

PERSPECTIVISCHE ANSICHT DER NEUEN PACKHOFS-GEBAEUDE VON DER SCHLOSSBRÜCKE GESEHN.

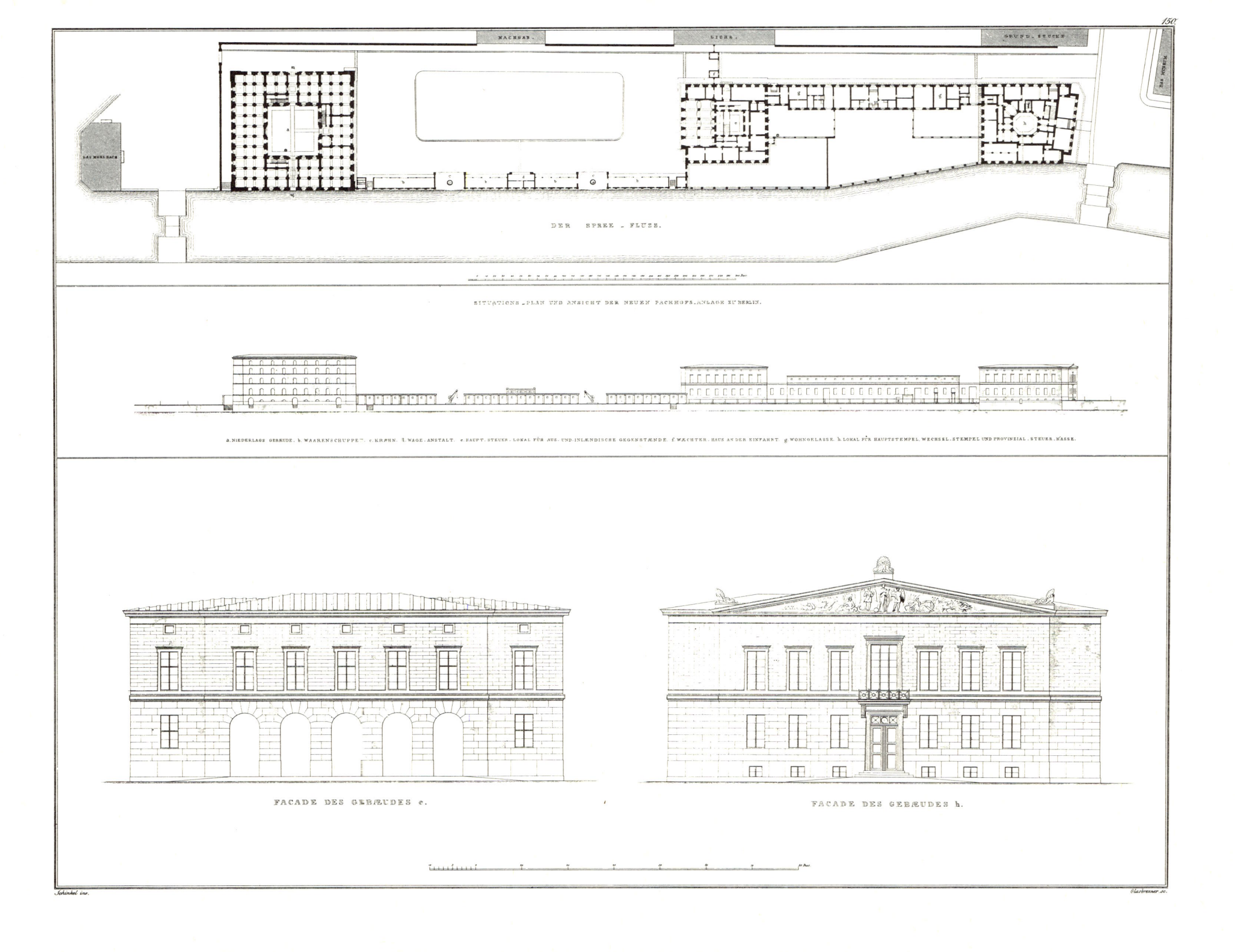

SITUATIONS-PLAN UND ANSICHT DES NEUEN PACKHOFS-ANLAGE ZU BERLIN.

a NIEDERLAGS GEBÄUDE. b WAAREN-SCHUPPE. c KRAHN. d WAGE-ANSTALT. e HAUPT-STEUER. LOKAL FÜR AUS- UND INLÄNDISCHE GEGENSTÄNDE. f WÄCHTER HAUS AN DER EINFAHRT. g WOHNGEBÄUDE. h LOKAL FÜR HAUPTSTEMPEL WECHSEL STEMPEL UND PROVINZIAL STEUER KASSE.

FACADE DES GEBÄUDES c.

FACADE DES GEBÄUDES h.

PERSPECTIVISCHE ANSICHT DER NEUEN PACKHOFS-GEBÆUDE VON DER BRÜCKE AM MEHLHAUSE.

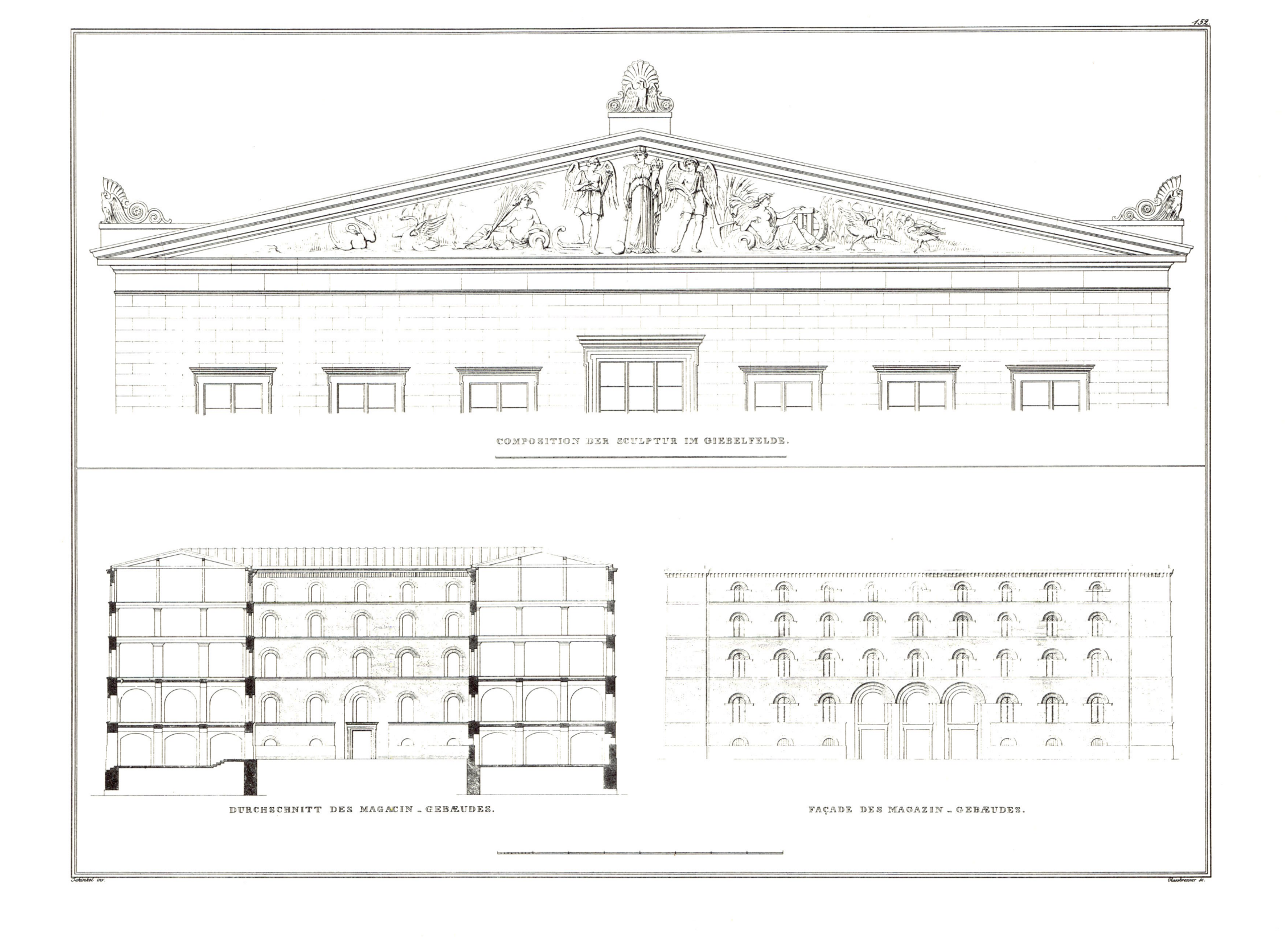

COMPOSITION DER SCULPTUR IM GIEBELFELDE.

FAÇADE DES MAGAZIN-GEBÆUDES.

DURCHSCHNITT DES MAGAZIN-GEBÆUDES.

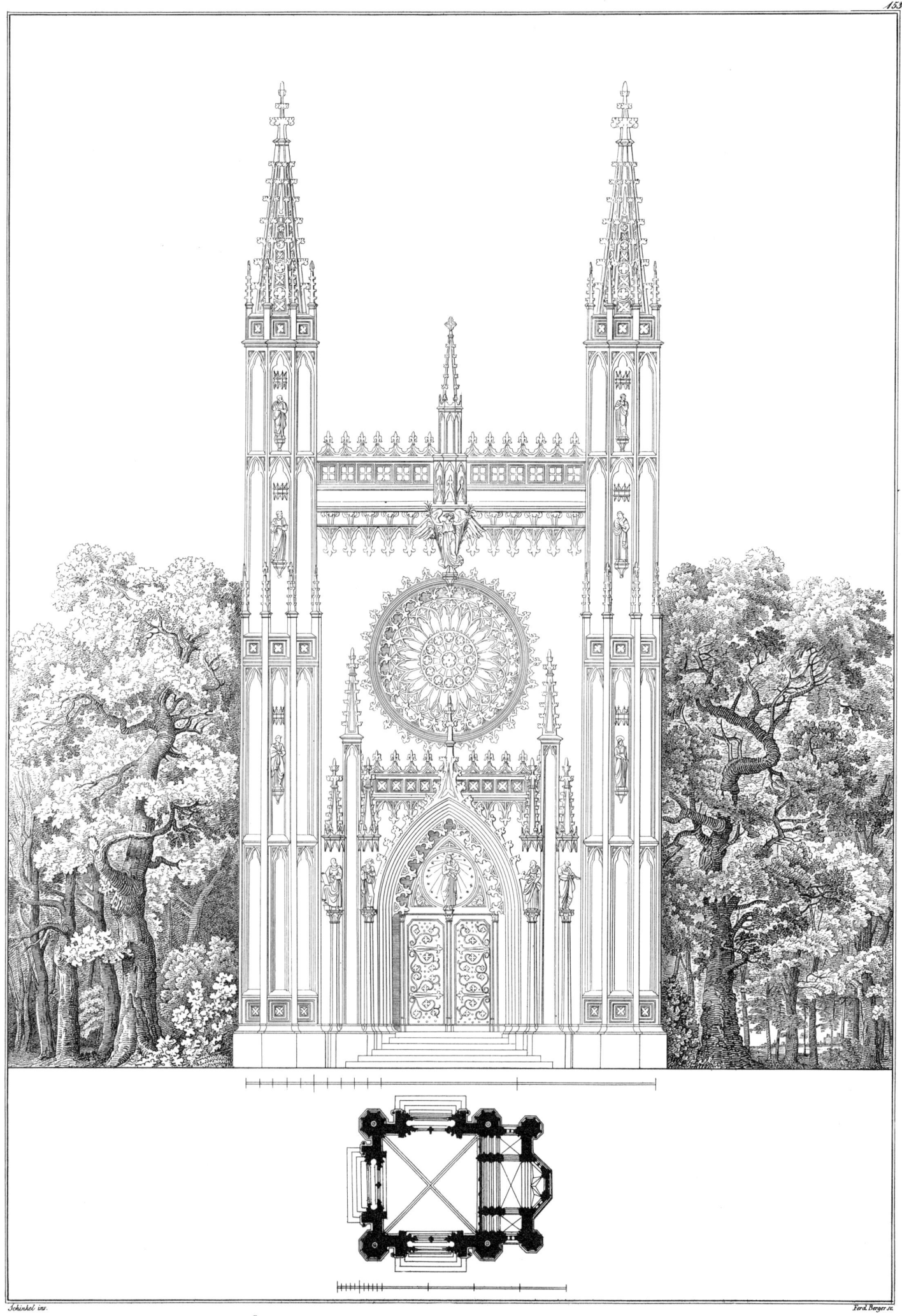

CAPELLE FÜR DEN KAISERLICHEN GARTEN ZU PETERHOF BEI PETERSBURG.

DURCHSCHNITT DER CAPELLE IM KAISERLICHEN GARTEN ZU PETERHOF BEI PETERSBURG.

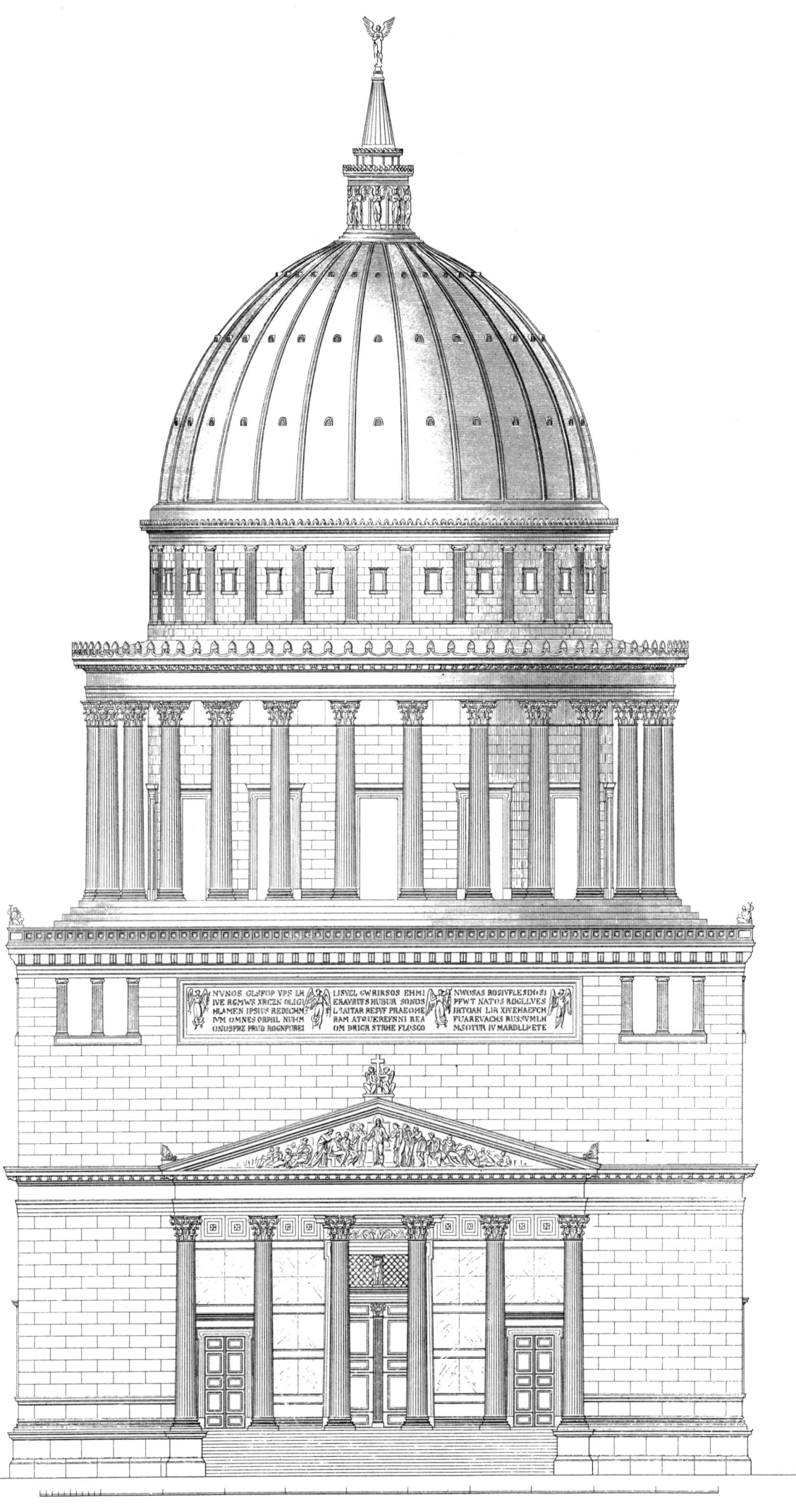

VORDER-ANSICHT DER ST NICOLAI-KIRCHE IN POTSDAM.

GRUNDRISS DER KUPPEL.

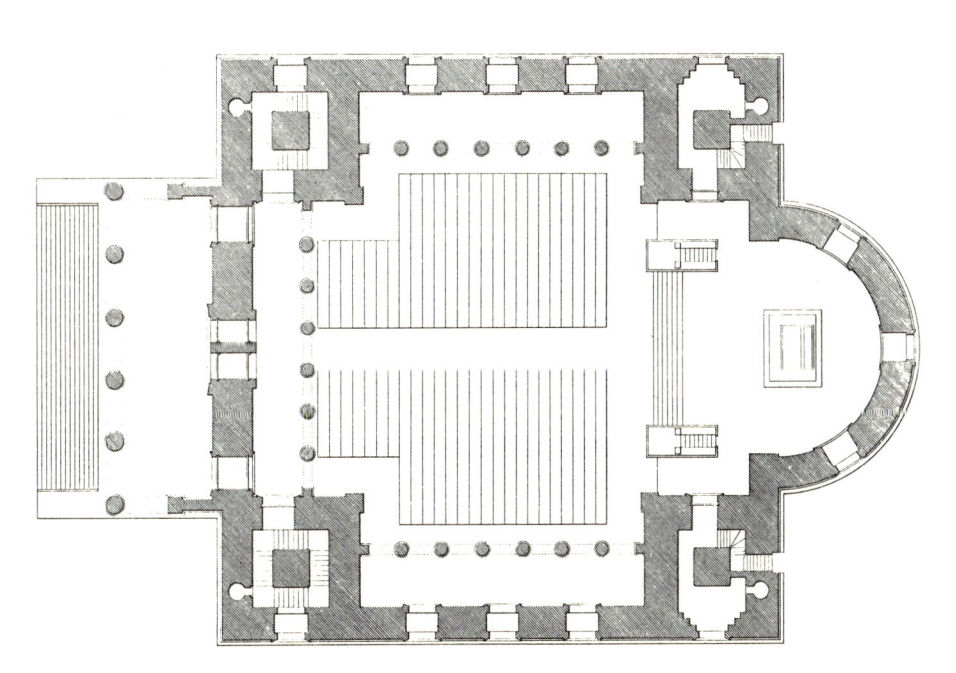

GRUNDRISS DER KIRCHE.

DURCHSCHNITT DER ST. NICOLAI-KIRCHE IN POTSDAM.

158.

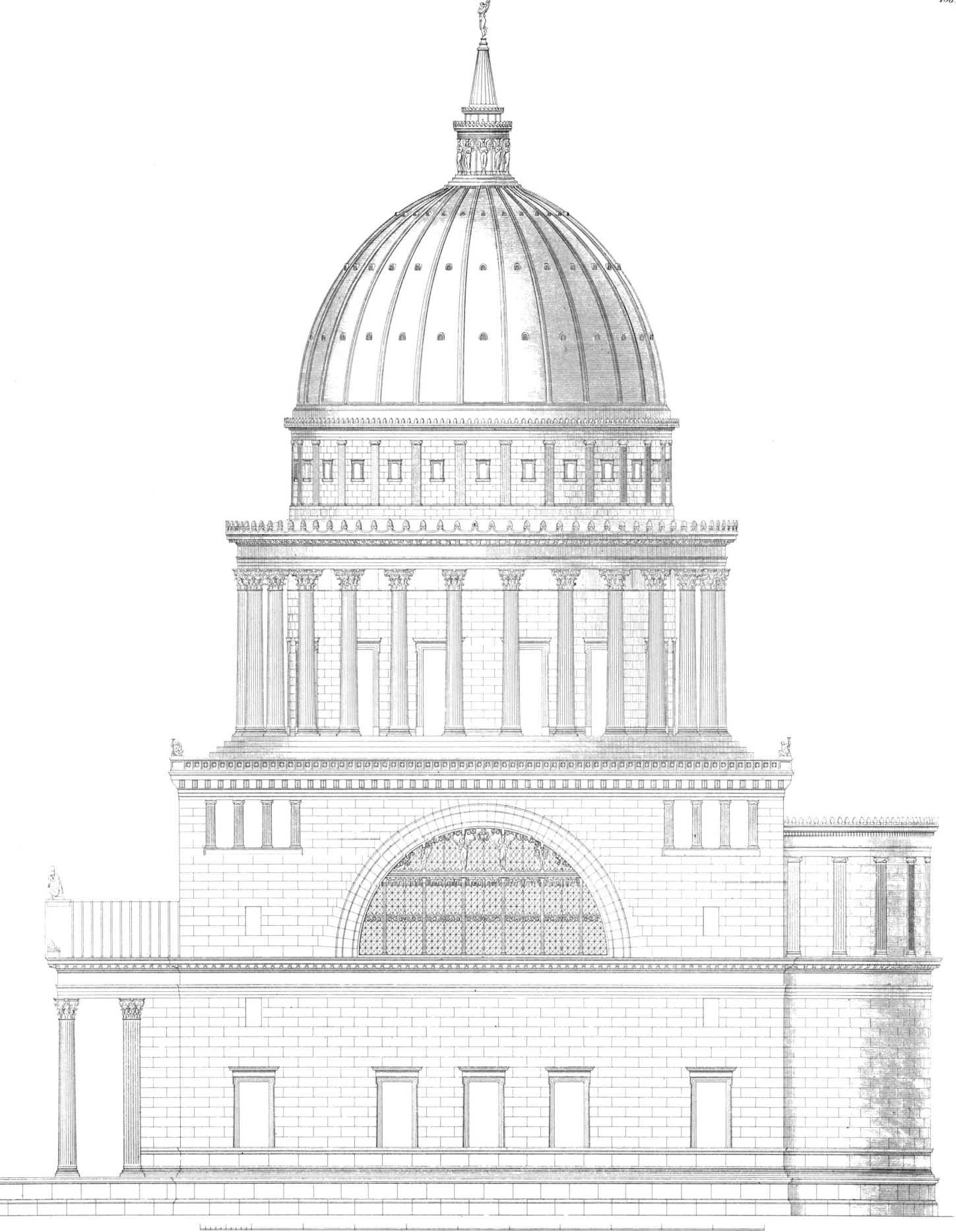

Schinkel inv. SEITEN-ANSICHT DER ST NICOLAI-KIRCHE IN POTSDAM. Schwechten sc.

KIRCHE IN MOABIT BEI BERLIN.

KIRCHE VOR DEM ROSENTHALER THORE ZU BERLIN.

PERSPECTIVISCHE ANSICHT DES INNEREN
DER KIRCHE IN MOABIT BEI BERLIN.

PERSPECTIVE DES INNEREN DER KIRCHE VOR DEM ROSENTHALER THORE BEI BERLIN.

KIRCHE AUF DEM GESUNDBRUNNEN BEI BERLIN.

KIRCHE AUF DEM WEDDING BEI BERLIN.

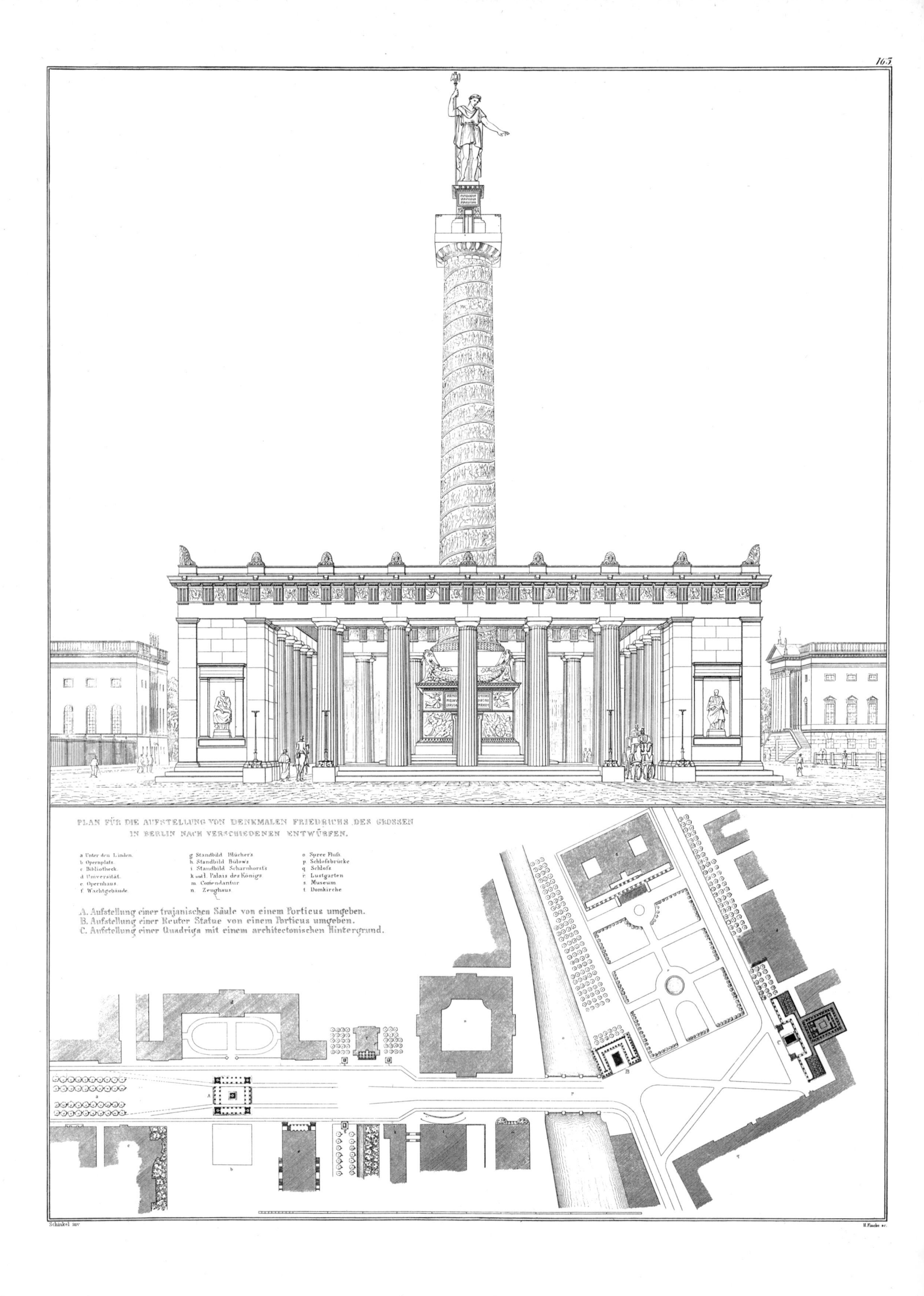

PLAN FÜR DIE AUFSTELLUNG VON DENKMALEN FRIEDRICHS DES GROSSEN
IN BERLIN NACH VERSCHIEDENEN ENTWÜRFEN.

a Unter den Linden.
b Opernplatz.
c Bibliothek.
d Universität.
e Opernhaus.
f Wachtgebäude.
g Standbild Blüchers
h Standbild Bülows
i Standbild Scharnhorsts
k und l Palais des Königs
m Commendantur
n Zeughaus
o Spree Fluß
p Schloßbrücke
q Schloß
r Lustgarten
s Museum
t Domkirche

A. Aufstellung einer trajanischen Säule von einem Porticus umgeben.
B. Aufstellung einer Reuter Statue von einem Porticus umgeben.
C. Aufstellung einer Quadriga mit einem architectonischen Hintergrund.

SEITEN ANSICHT DES DENKMALS. PROFIL DES PORTIKUS NACH A B.

GRUNDRISS DES DENKMALS.

ENTWURF ZU EINEM DENKMAL FÜR KÖNIG FRIEDRICH DEN GROSSEN.

ENTWURF FÜR EIN DENKMAL KÖNIG FRIEDRICH DES GROSSEN.

Schlofsbrücke. Spree. Lustgarten.

ENTWURF ZU EINEM DENKMAL FÜR KÖNIG FRIEDRICH DEN GROSSEN.

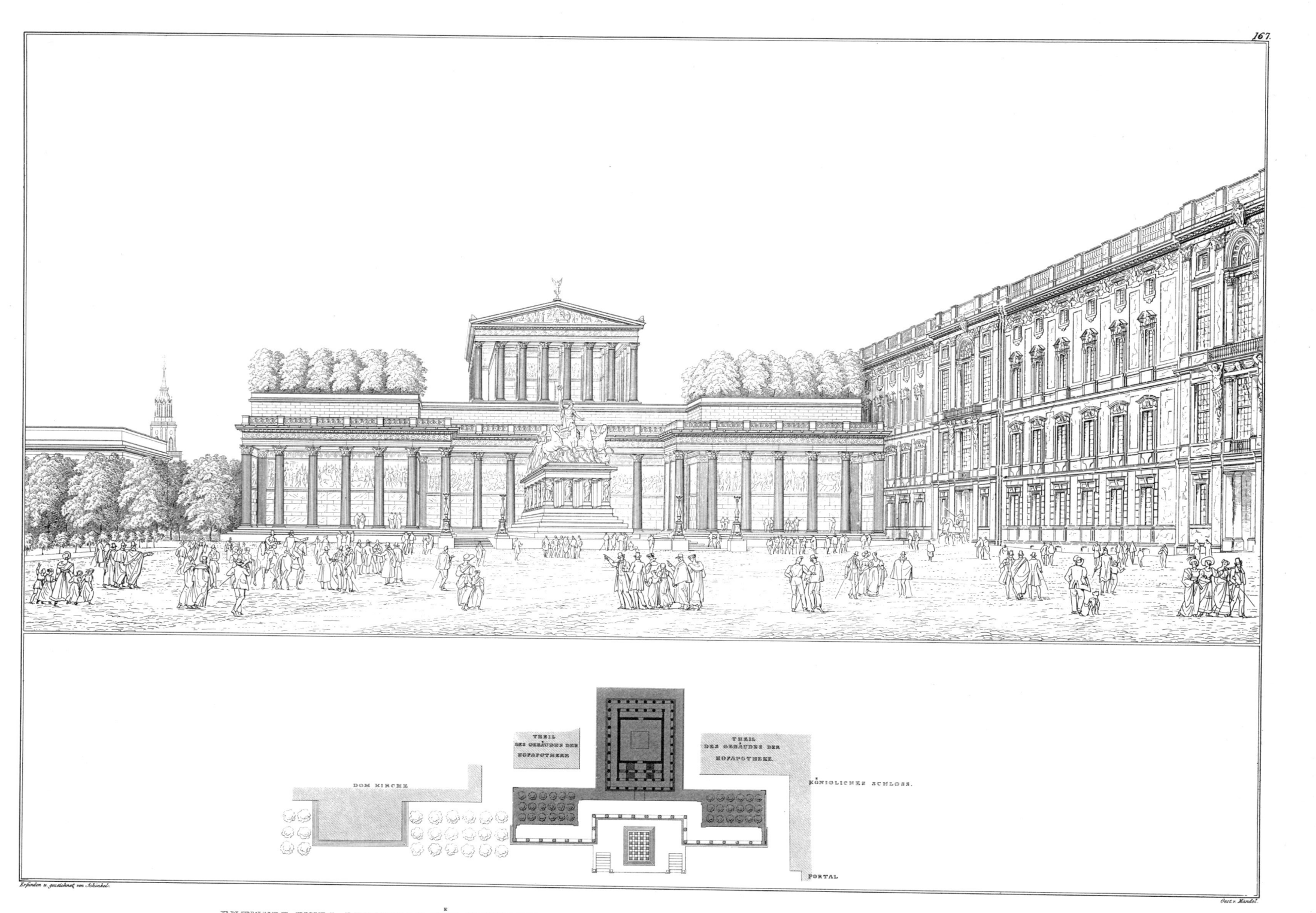

ENTWURF EINES DENKMALS FÜR FRIEDRICH DEN GROSSEN AUF DEM PLATZE DER ALTEN HOFAPOTHEKE ZU BERLIN.

DOM KIRCHE. THEIL DES GEBÄUDES DER HOFAPOTHEKE. KÖNIGLICHES SCHLOSS. THEIL DES GEBÄUDES DER HOFAPOTHEKE. PORTAL.

ENTWURF ZU EINEM DENKMAL FÜR KÖNIG FRIEDRICH DEN GROSSEN.

162.

PERSPECTIVE VON DEM GÆRTNERHAUSE IN CHARLOTTENHOF BEI POTSDAM VOM PUNCTE B. IM GRUNDRISSE AUFGENOMMEN.

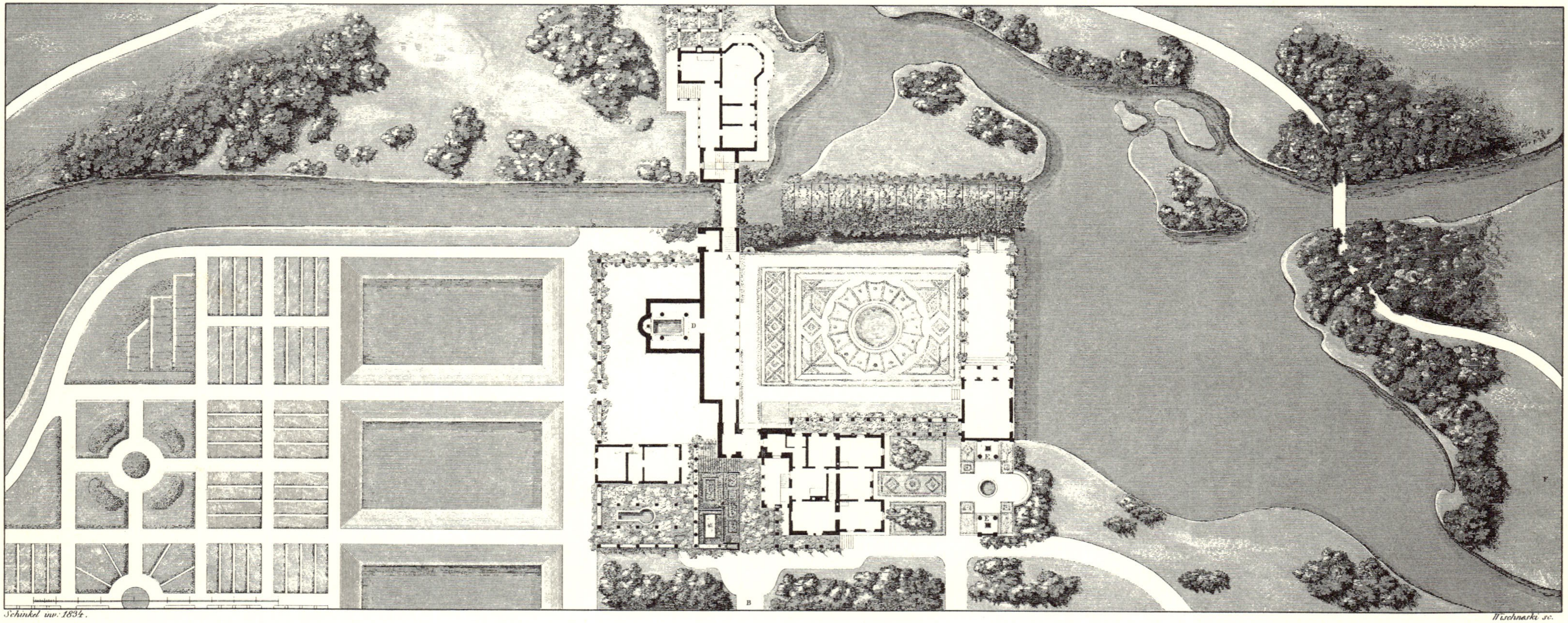

GRUNDRISS DER ANLAGE DES GÆRTNERHAUSES IN CHARLOTTENHOF BEI POTSDAM MIT SEINEN UMGEBUNGEN.

PERSPECTIVE VON DEM GÄRTNERHAUSE IN CHARLOTTENHOF BEI POTSDAM VOM PUNCTE A. IM GRUNDRISSE AUF DEM PLATTEN DACHE AUFGENOMMEN.

BALDACHIN E.E. BEIM GÆRTNERHAUSE IN CHARLOTTENHOF.

ANSICHT DES KLEINEN HOFS D. IM GRUNDRISSE BEIM GÆRTNERHAUSE IN CHARLOTTENHOF.

PERSPECTIVE VON CHARLOTTENHOF BEI POTSDAM VOM PUNCTE C. IM GRUNDRISSE AUFGENOMMEN

172.

Schinkel inv. F. Berger sc.

PERSPECTIVE VOM GARTENHAUSE IN CHARLOTTENHOF BEI POTSDAM, VOM PUNCTE E IM GRUNDRISSE AUFGENOMMEN.

Aussicht in den Garten aus dem Landhause bei Charlottenhof

Seitengarten des Landhauses.

Aussicht in den Garten aus dem Landhause bei Charlottenhof

Vordere Façade des Landhauses bei Charlottenhof im Garten unweit Sans Souci bei Potsdam.

Seiten Ansicht des Landhauses mit seinen Nebenpartieen bei Charlottenhof.

Ansicht des Hipodroms hinter dem Landhause bei Charlottenhof.

GRUNDRISS DES LANDHAUSES MIT SEINEN GARTEN-ANLAGEN.

DURCHSCHNITT DES LANDHAUSES.